AF573757

ROBSON'S GUIDE

ROBSON'S GUIDE

Stillwater Trout Flies
An Alphabetical Survey in Colour

Kenneth Robson

Beekay Publishers

Other angling titles by Beekay Publishers:

Game

The Colour Guide to Fly-tying by Kevin Hyatt

Coarse

Carp Fever by Kevin Maddocks
Success with the Pole by Dickie Carr
Pike Fishing in the 80's by Neville Fickling
Basic Carp Fishing by Peter Mohan
Modern Specimen Hunting by Jim Gibbinson
Fishing for Big Chub by Peter Stone
Top Ten — Tactics for the major species from ten leading specialist anglers.
Edited by Bruce Vaughan
Redmire Pool by Kevin Clifford & Len Arbery
Tactics for Big Pike by Bill Chillingworth

Sea

Long Range Casting and Fishing Techniques by Paul Kerry
Dinghy Fishing at Sea by Phill Williams & Brian Douglas

(All titles available direct from Beekay — send for free catalogue)

British Library Cataloguing in Publication Data
Robson, Kenneth
Robson's guide.
1. Flies, Artificial
2. Trout fishing — Great Britain
I. Title
799.1'755 SH451

First published 1985 by
BEEKAY PUBLISHERS LTD.
103 Worcesters Avenue,
Enfield EN1 4ND
England

Produced by Bow-Towning Ltd. 01-253 6934.

ISBN 0 947674 02 0

For my wife, Eileen, who has shown more patience than any fisherman

Photography by Hugh Goddard. A.M.P.A.

Flies tied by Kevin Hyatt, author of
'The Colour Guide to Fly-tying'

CONTENTS

LINE DRAWINGS

ACKNOWLEDGEMENTS

I am grateful to a number of people who have helped me in the preparation of this book, and I should like to thank specifically:

Kevin Hyatt for dressing the flies and carrying out a unique assignment with such skill, care and enthusiasm.

Hugh Goddard for his interest in the whole project and whose professional expertise is manifest in the colour photographs of the flies.

Martin Howard for his splendid line drawings of insects.

Peter Lapsley for his interest, encouragement and advice throughout.

Jessica Hollings, my secretary, for her ever-willing help with typing and duplication.

The Hertfordshire County Library for obtaining for me a number of books, and the Flyfishers' Club for the use of its magnificent fishing library.

Jack Simpson, who put the project to me, and Kevin Maddocks, head of Beekay Publishers, for enabling me to carry it out.

My wife, Eileen, who, apart from foregoing holidays and weekends so that I could either write or fish, meticulously scrutinised the book in manuscript.

My daughter, Janet, for the care and time she spent on reading the proofs.

For permission to quote from their books: Brian Clarke, *The Pursuit of Stillwater Trout*, Bob Church, *Reservoir Trout Fishing*, and Andre Deutsch for C. F. Walker's *Lake Flies and their Imitation*.

INTRODUCTION

"The fly fisherman who knows nothing of his flies is as great an anachronism as the painter who knows nothing of his paints. More, he is a bad man of business."
J. W. DUNNE *Sunshine and the Dry Fly*

It is some twenty five years since I attempted to cast out a team of flies for the first time on the Wayoh Reservoir, near Bolton. Armed only with the theory of casting from Maurice Wiggins' delightful *Teach Yourself Fly Fishing* and a meagre supply of Peter Rosses, Mallard and Clarets and Black Pennells, I soon discovered what a draughty place a reservoir could be and what incredible tangles the wind could inflict on my casts. In those early visits, my flies spent very little of their time in the water, and I had little conception of what they represented or how I should manipulate them. I had not even progressed as far as the unknown angler at Ladybower Reservoir quoted by Roger Fogg who complained that he had tried a Peter Ross, but the fish were not feeding on them!

Soon afterwards, I acquired two books, Courtney Williams' *Dictionary of Trout Flies* and John Veniard's *Fly Dressers' Guide*. I began to recognise fly patterns which is the first step for any serious fisherman. The early, monotonous and usually blank fishing days became enlivened, enriched and more profitable as I realised the variety of devices for enticing fish stretched beyond the traditional wet flies to patterns representing the creatures which lived in the water, and to lures of hair and feather which held compulsive fascination for trout. As the 60's progressed, and the new stillwaters opened, it became apparent that a whole new dimension in fly fishing was developing using the old loch traditions and methods but quickly developing its own, stimulated by the original thinking of men like Richard Walker, John Goddard and Bob Church.

Now, twenty years on, both the beginner and the more experienced angler are confronted with an immense number of flies, the majority of which have been specially devised to operate on stillwater. The moment thus seems opportune for a new alphabetical guide designed to help the keen fisherman to identify these flies, to learn something of their origins and purpose, to have ready access to their dressings and to discover how they are fished.

The photographs which accompany each entry will hopefully enable the angler to recognise the flies he already possesses. John Goddard has pointed out that it is surprising how many fly fishers of even long standing cannot always name the flies in their own boxes. Knowing what the fly looks like and the reasons why he wants it, the fisherman may make his future purchases with more confidence. For the fly-tyer, the guide is intended as a ready source of reference to be consulted for dressings. In the case of the imitative patterns a choice of dressings is offered for each natural fly. The pictures of the artificials will show what his finished product should look like. Although a number of dressings include helpful hints for tying the patterns, I have made no attempt to include specific tying instructions, firstly because of the demands of space, and secondly because there are now many excellent books on fly dressing available to the enthusiast who wishes to tie his own flies.

The guide tries to cater for the individual preferences of all stillwater trout fishermen. It includes the traditional, the imitative and the lure. The collection of imitative patterns is comprehensive so that the angler not only has those he may commonly meet, but others which he may encounter infrequently or in places far removed from his usual fishing haunts. My hope is that he will derive much pleasure from trying them out, especially if he has tied them himself, and maybe produce that occasional triumph with his imitation of a lesser known creature. There is a bewildering array of lures, so that by the time this appears in print a fresh swarm of infallible 'killers' will have appeared. I have tried to include the best, the most popular and, more importantly, those designed for a particular purpose. In a guide primarily of native flies it has been difficult to resist including the many excellent overseas patterns. I have confined them to those strongly recommended by eminent anglers, to those in common use and, finally, to patterns for which there seems to be no better native equivalent.

The compilation of this guide has been an absorbing exercise which has made me more aware of the range of opportunities afforded by a wider knowledge of stillwater flies and their usage. I hope that the reader will feel similarly enlightened so that his or her enjoyment of the sport is enhanced. The guide is an anthology of the work of all those who have thought deeply about fly fishing and the dressings they have devised. For this, I am profoundly grateful and if I have at all misrepresented their views or their flies I ask their indulgence.

TRADITIONAL LAKE FLIES

"I do not suggest that the standard lake flies should be abandoned entirely. They have caught many thousands of fish in the past and will catch many thousands more in the future, so it would obviously be absurd to aver that they are of no use. They have, however, one outstanding drawback: no one really knows what they represent in the eyes of the trout."
C. F. WALKER *Lake Flies and their Imitation*

Now that there have been so many advances in recent years in the design of flies intended to represent the insects to be found in stillwater, and many effective lures have been devised and proved to be so killing, the popularity of traditional lake flies has declined.

The case against them is summarised by the above quotation from Commander C. F. Walker. Now, with twenty years hindsight, we can see that it was somewhat overstated. It rested — and still does rest — on the objection that no one knows what these flies represent. The same can be said of the lure and the rejoinder applies equally to both: experience and knowledge tell us when to use them.

A closer look at the traditional flies reveals that they have affinities with both lures and imitative patterns. There are those flies like the Butcher, Dunkeld, Peter Ross and Alexandra fished on the point and lure-like in their qualities as flasher or attractor. Many of the others have a resemblance to forms of aquatic life: Black Pennell, Williams' Favourite and Blae and Black to chironomid pupae; Grouse and Orange and Woodcock and Orange to sedges; Woodcock and Green to lake and pond olives; March Brown to a shrimp. There are many more which can be taken for underwater creatures and with which the angler can become familiar.

A number of traditional flies have moved effortlessly into the modern stillwater era. Ancient flies like the Red Palmer and the Zulu (probably descended from the Black Fly) are commonly used as bob flies. Wickham's Fancy and Fiery Brown are both in vogue as sedge imitators; the Invicta is arguably the best representation of a hatching sedge; the Hare's Ear, whether as olive or sedge imitator, is still considered a killing fly on stillwater.

Many of the traditional wet flies developed in the last century and were pre-eminent on Scottish lochs and Irish loughs. A trip to either of those two countries or a glance at the fishing reports in *Trout and Salmon* will tell you that they still take a majority of all fish in those waters. Besides, the loch style of boat fishing with which they are intimately connected remains a delightful way of fishing. In the hands of the experts who ply their teams of flies with short, delicate casts from drifting boats, as in the international fly fishing competitions, it is both rewarding and effective.

So, although the power of the modern lure and the subtlety of the natural fly imitation may now hold sway, the traditional lake fly will continue to have many devotees.

IMITATIVE PATTERNS

"The cultivation of a sufficient awareness of natural creatures, to enable us to imitate satisfactorily the foods upon which trout live and thus to exploit what we know to be a constant, motivating factor in fish behaviour, is a calculated means to a desirable and sensible end: the capture of more trout. On the way, and as a by-product, that will give us greater satisfaction, and pleasure, too."
BRIAN CLARKE *The Pursuit of Stillwater Trout*

"I have known men so busy with the mechanical art of casting as to be completely oblivious of the flies hatching all around them, and I do not think they are in the minority."
C. F. WALKER *Lake Flies and their Imitation*

It is remarkable that whilst there has been an awareness from the beginning that artificial flies dressed for river fishing should copy insects to be found there, and the first definitive work on fishermen's insects, Alfred Ronalds' *The Fly-Fisher's Entomology*, should appear as early as 1836, very little has been written about the fly life of stillwater until comparatively recently. Dr. Howard Bell of Blagdon fame studied the underwater life of that lake from 1922 onwards, devising imitative patterns which are used today, but did not commit himself to print. R. C. Bridgett, who fished the Scottish lochs extensively, though no expert entomologist, stressed the value of imitating the forms of underwater life which trout feed on in his book, *Loch Fishing in Theory and Practice*, 1924. In another work written in 1937, *The Art and Craft of Loch Fishing*, H. P. Henzell emphasised that the stillwater fisherman would derive greater pleasure from his sport and catch more fish if he paid more attention to imitating the larvae and nymphs to be found in the water.

Professor J. R. Harris's great work published in 1952, *An Angler's Entomology*, placed for the first time in the hands of the serious fisherman a scientific and modern account of his flies. Two years later, Joscelyn Lane's *Lake and Loch Fishing* gave a number of original dressings representing stillwater flies, and made out a strong and interesting case for the angler to imitate the natural fly and thereby derive the maximum satisfaction from his fishing. Then came in 1960 C. F. Walker's *Trout Flies and their Imitation*, to be followed nine years later by John Goddard's *Trout Flies of Stillwater*, two marvellous books which no thoughtful stillwater angler can afford to be without. I urge him to acquire them so that he can acquaint himself with a knowledge of fly life either rudimentary or in depth, according to his inclinations.

An angler who fishes patterns which represent the insects living in the water will do so more successfully and enjoyably if he knows something of the stages in their growth, what they look like, where they live and how they move. I have attempted to supply this information under each individual fly, and this will be of more value to the angler if he knows something of the key points in their existence. For full details he can go to Walker or Goddard, or consult Taff Price's three splendid books, *Stillwater Flies*. Here, I intend to simplify things as much as possible by bringing together those insects with common stages of development. All creatures which live in water hatch from eggs. After that their paths diverge.

Flies which Develop from Larva to Pupa to Adult

Larva

A large number of insects hatch into young which do not initially resemble their parents. At this point in their existence they are known as larvae. They have short stumpy legs or none at all and no wings or wing buds. Most sedge larvae (caddis) live in cases made of various materials.

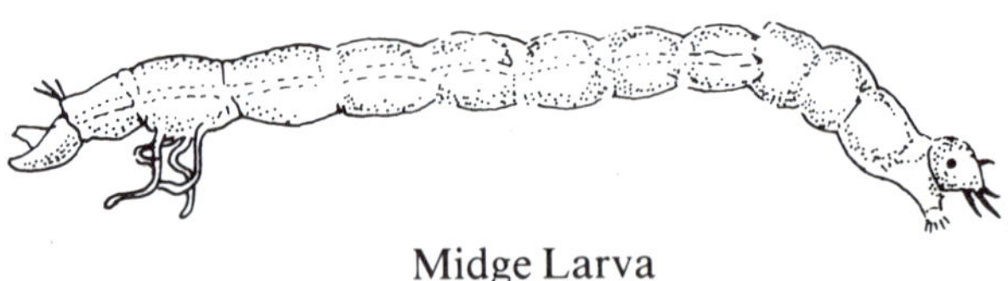

Midge Larva

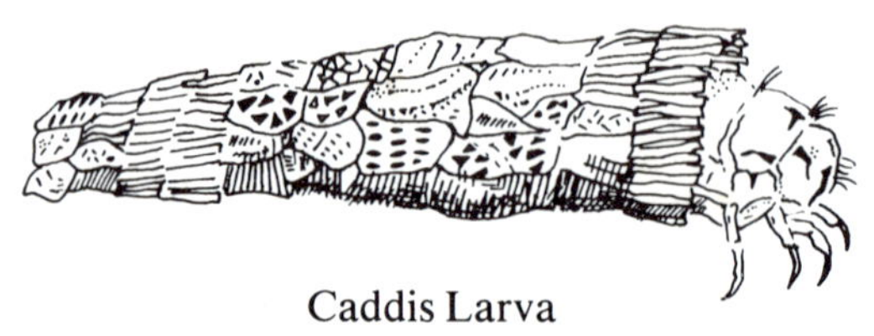

Caddis Larva

Pupa

As the larvae develop, they cast off their skins each time they outgrow them and, when fully mature, stop eating and change into a pupa.

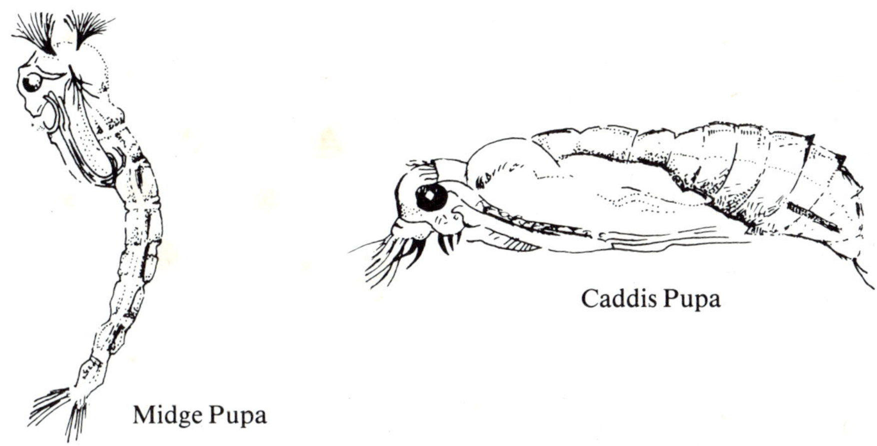

Caddis Pupa

Midge Pupa

Adult

Within the pupa the adult develops and ultimately the skin splits open and the adult emerges. This transformation occurs at the water surface for the midge and phantom fly, at the surface or on vegetation for the sedge, and pupation for the crane fly, aquatic beetle and alder takes place in damp soil near the water.

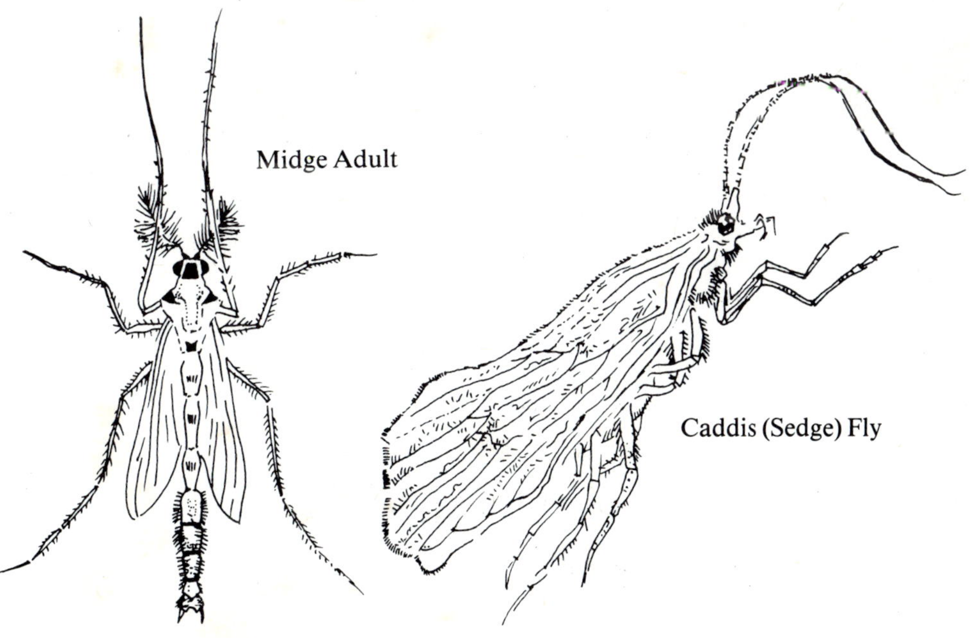

Midge Adult

Caddis (Sedge) Fly

Flies which Develop from Nymph to Dun (Sub-Imago) to Spinner (Imago)

Nymph

The eggs of the up-winged flies or ephemeroptera hatch into young which look like the adults but without wings, and are called nymphs. They have six jointed legs and wing buds. They moult at intervals, casting an outer skin each time, and their wing cases become progressively larger.

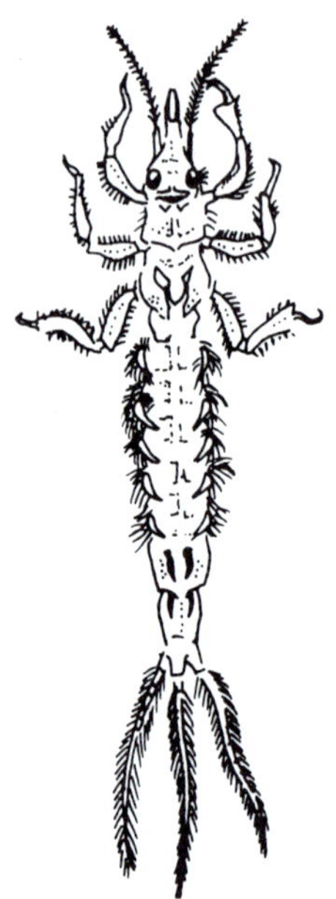

Mayfly Nymph

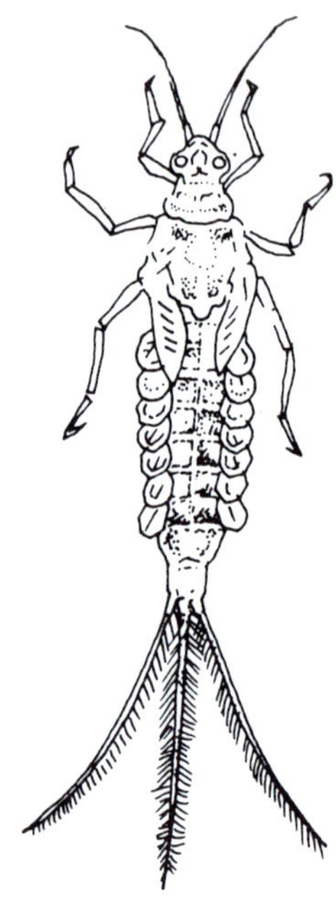

Lake or Pond Olive Nymph

Dun (Sub-Imago)

The mature nymph ascends to the surface to hatch, a process known as ecdysis. The nymphal shuck opens and the winged fly emerges on the surface. When its wings are dry it flies off.

Mayfly Dun

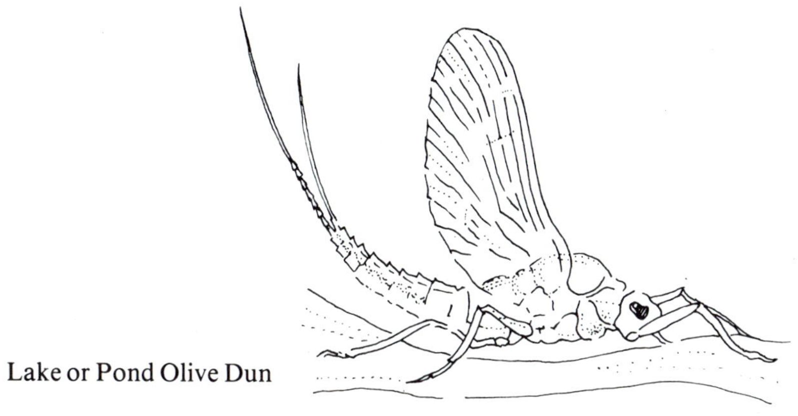

Lake or Pond Olive Dun

Spinner (Imago)

The up-winged flies are unique in that the dun or sub-imago is not the final stage of the insect. It makes its way to bankside foliage or grasses, and after a variable period of time splits its skin once more. There emerges the spinner or imago in all its beauty ready for the climax of its short life, to mate and, for the female, to drop or lay her eggs on the water surface, and then to die with her fragile wings outstretched.

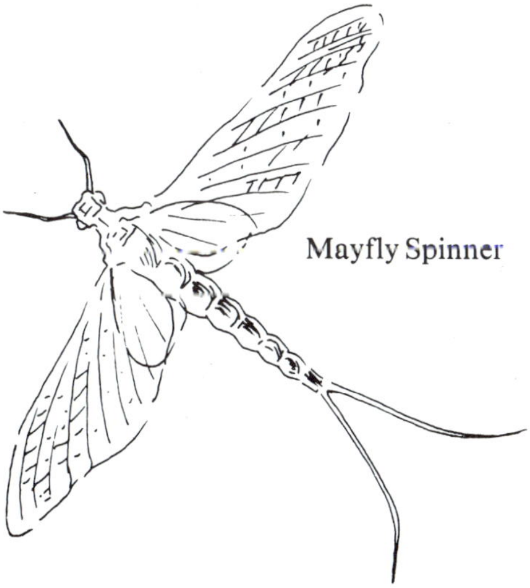

Mayfly Spinner

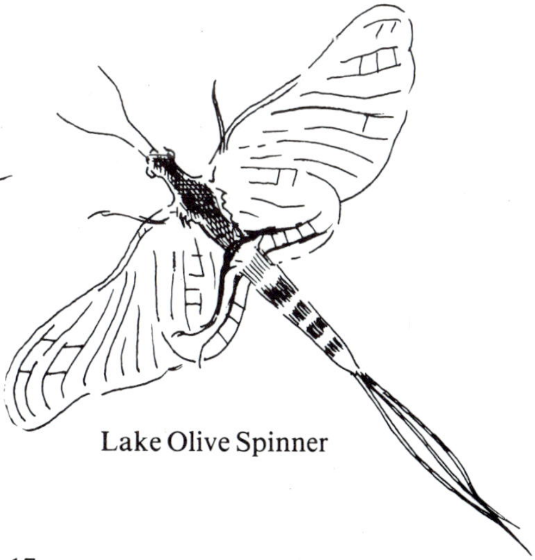

Lake Olive Spinner

Flies whose Development is Nymph to Adult

Nymph

Some insects have only two stages in their existence. The nymph develops as it feeds, casting a succession of skins until it reaches maturity. The damsel and dragon nymphs swim to the shore or to vegetation above the water level, and the stonefly nymphs crawl along the lake bottom to the bank.

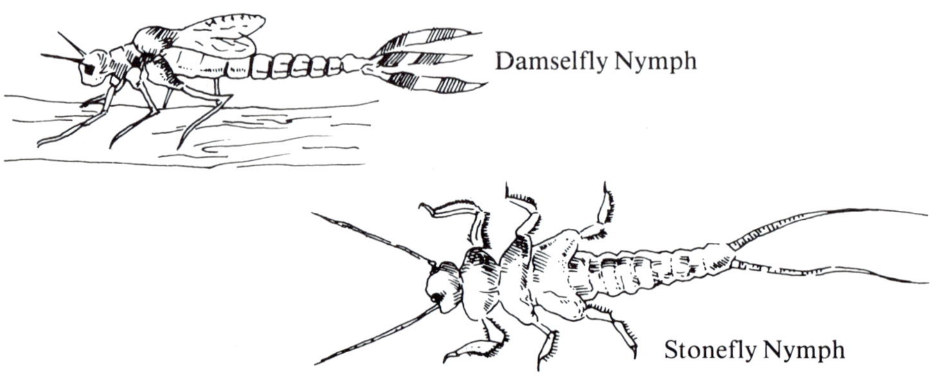

Adult

The skin of the fully grown nymph slowly splits and the adult fly comes out.

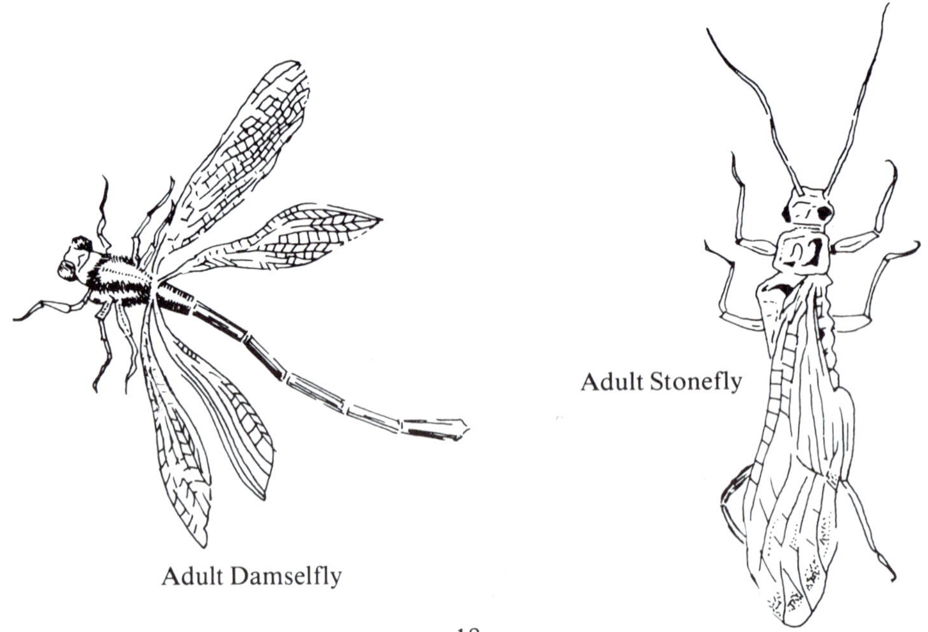

Other Creatures

Of the other water creatures which most concern the fisherman, the corixa or lesser water boatman develops from the young nymph to the adult in the water, and the freshwater louse and the freshwater shrimp simply have young which resemble and grow into adults.

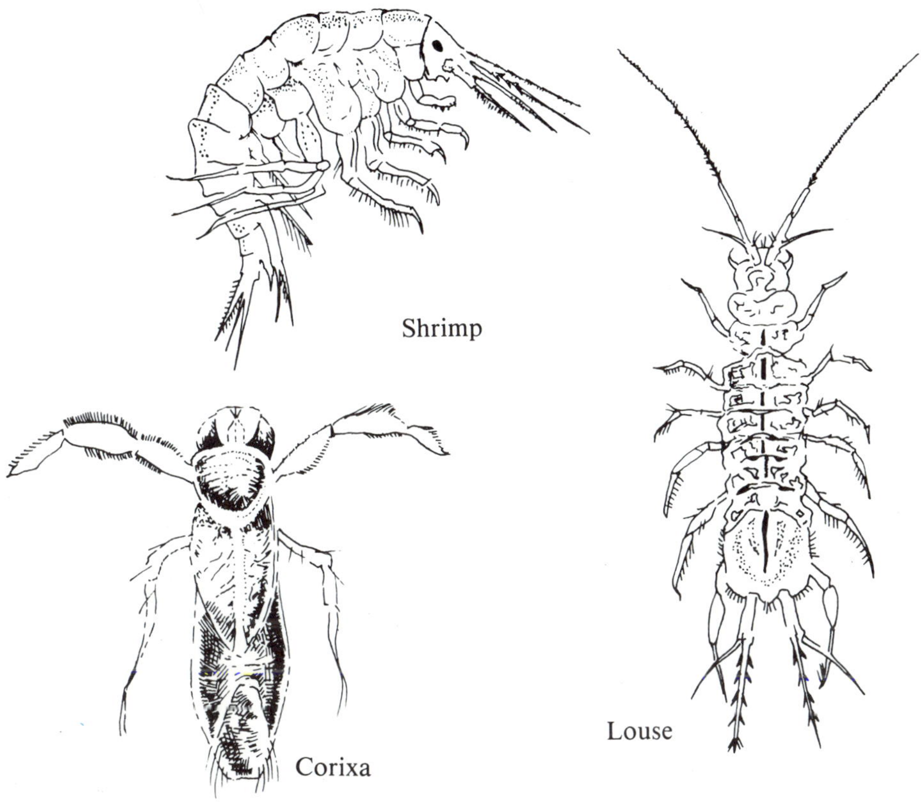

When we have a fair grasp of what the creatures of stillwater look like, when and where they appear, how they live and, very importantly, how they move, we are in a position to choose our imitations, and, even better, to dress our own. Of course, nothing with a solid hook in it can look exactly like the real living thing, but we know that if the artificial has enough features which resemble the natural even a fish feeding selectively will take it. There are grounds also for thinking that a fly which has features which are somewhat exaggerated is often attractive to trout. What those features are is for the angler to decide for himself. Richard Walker believes that colour is very important. He quotes the example of C. F. Walker's Claret Nymph where the claret tying silk showing through the body dubbing when the fly is wet is more claret colour than the natural. Skues thought that colour together with size were more crucial than shape. Mottram, on the other hand, placed shape or silhouette before colour. Dunne placed emphasis on translucence. He would have admired John Goddard's PVC Nymph. In the guide, I have endeavoured to point out some of these particular aspects of dressings and the appropriate circumstances which make them so effective, so that the angler can choose for himself which ones are suitable for his purposes.

So the angler with some knowledge of entomology and of the artificials available to him can base his strategy on observing the fly on the water or making an intelligent guess as to what the fish are feeding on at that particular time of the day and season. If he then captures a trout he will also be able to see what it has eaten if he spoons it out. He can then present his chosen fly so that both the speed and pattern of its movement resemble that of the natural he is imitating.

The pleasure to be derived from this form of fishing is twofold. Firstly it is based on one irrefutable fact: fish must eat. It thus enables the angler to bring a logical and positive approach to his fishing. Secondly, it contains the elements of intellectual challenge. The fisherman is seeking to find out what the trout is feeding on, then to imitate it and, hopefully, to outwit the trout into taking that imitation. For some, this is the height of satisfaction to be derived from fly fishing.

LURES

"Lure fishing is a highly skilled business and not a haphazard, chuck-and-chance-it exercise."
BOB CHURCH *Reservoir Trout Fishing*

Though lure fishing may well be frowned upon by a proportion of anglers, it is the most common and popular form of fly fishing on stillwater from boat or bank. David Collyer believes that eighty per cent of all trout caught in the United Kingdom are taken on lures, and in the competitions for the biggest fish caught on the top waters run by the angling magazine, *Trout Fisherman*, at least half are regularly recorded as caught on lures. A walk along any lake bank and a cursory glance at the many open fly boxes — some of gargantuan proportions — will reveal a bewildering multitude of gaudy offerings enshrined in feather, hair, marabou, fur, tinsel and chenille.

The modern lure is an adroit combination of these and other materials dressed on a long shank or tandem hook. Some of the traditional lake flies have lure-like qualities and flies uncommonly like lures were used at Blagdon before the First World War. However, the accelerated and sophisticated development of this form of fishing is a product of the last thirty years stimulated by the opening of public reservoirs and private stillwater fisheries, and influenced by American models.

Lures can be broadly divided into two types, streamers and bucktails. In the former, one or more pairs of feathers are bound by the butts near the hook eye and low over the shank, thus providing an attractive and sinuous silhouette. An occasional disadvantage is the catching of the feather under the hook point during casting. The matuka style of tying avoids this by securing the feather on top of the hook shank by taking the ribbing through the fibres and around the body. Bucktail lures have wings made of hair such as squirrel, goat, skunk, bear and bucktail. They are durable and filter light attractively. Marabou, a soft, delicate feather, which responds to the slightest movement of the fly, is now a common wing material. Some lures like the Appetiser with its marabou and squirrel tail and the Hanningfield Lure utilising goat hair and turkey feather combine the virtues of more than one material. The latter is a tandem or multi-hook pattern of which the Black and White Lures are the most common examples. Flies more difficult to classify include the Baby Doll, Polystickle, Mylar Minnow and Jersey Herd which have few or no 'moving parts' yet are good fish catchers.

Why do trout take lures? The prime motive for fish taking any bait is that of hunger. This applies equally to those lures commonly described as deceivers which are a likeness of a small coarse fish or a minnow or stickleback. Their presentation, involving considerations of weather, water conditions and geography, observation, colour, shape, depth, simulation of the natural's movement, calls for a high degree of experience and skill. This is a logical extension of the art of imitative fishing.

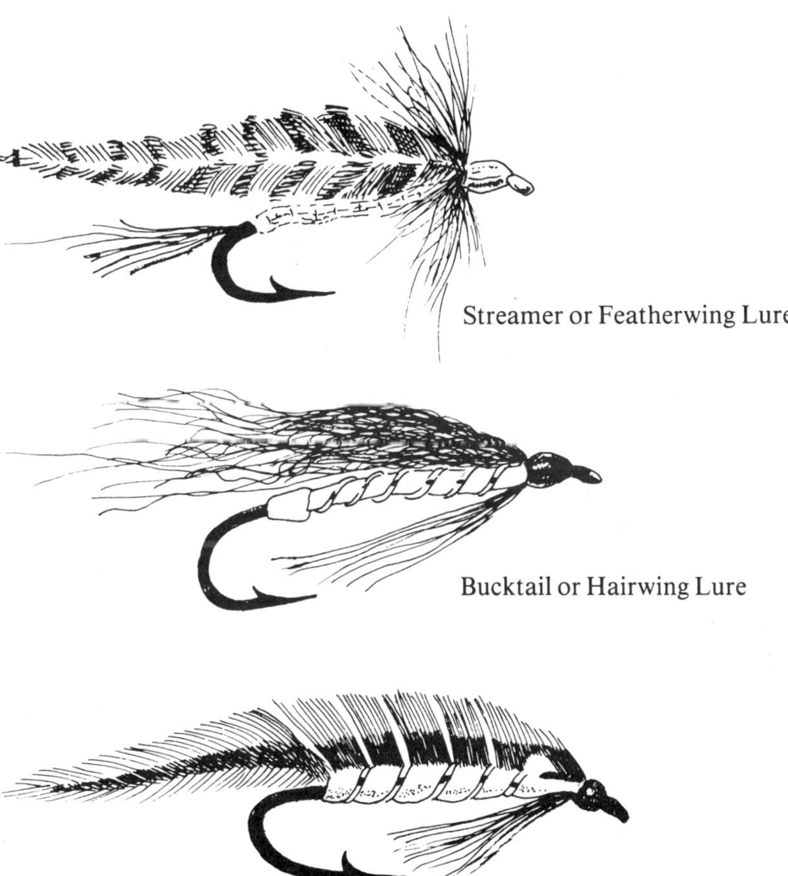

Streamer or Featherwing Lure

Bucktail or Hairwing Lure

Matuka Lure

Why, however, do trout take vivid creations of hair and feather known as attractors which have no resemblance to anything with which they are familiar in their habitat? Many reasons have been advanced including a combination of irritation, anger and aggression occasioned by an invasion of their territory by a strange and garish creature, or a desire to pursue it in keeping with their predatory natures. I agree with Brian Clarke that curiosity may well be a major factor. How often does one see a trout tracking a lure and seemingly scrutinising it? Sometimes this is followed by a pluck and then the fish loses interest. Continued use of the pattern seems quickly to exhaust the inquisition of all the trout in the neighbourhood as if it has now become an accepted part of that water scene. The introduction of another pattern of differing size, colour or action often renews the interest. At times fish appear to be in a very lively and playful mood, responsive and alert to the appearance of anything new in their environment, and in this case may take the angler's lure from what Taff Price describes as sheer devilment or joie de vivre.

The imitative fisherman can base his strategy soundly on the feeding instinct of the trout and a simulation in appearance and movement of the creatures they eat. The reasons a trout takes the lure may not be as conclusive or as visible, but the fisherman knows that they are no less valid. The skill lies in creating the situations in which those responses will operate. Too often the accusation of 'lure stripping' or 'chuck-and-chance-it' are only too true as any angler can see for himself by taking a stroll around the piece of water he is fishing. He will come upon practitioners who rarely progress beyond what I deem a conception of the water they are fishing as a flat area where length and speedy retrieval are the sole dominating dimensions. They catch fish, but the whole process seems mindless and monotonous.

Hopefully they will progress to regarding the water as the volume it is with length, breadth and depth to be exploited by methods which activate the trout's food-seeking, belligerent or inquisitive instincts. This will involve thought and imagination as to the appropriate category of lure to use, the kind of line relative to the depth required, and a capacity to vary the speed and retrieval pattern of the fly. The fisherman generally brings his fly back in a straight line, but sideways action can be imparted to some extent by the rod tip. The experienced angler is also aware of the vertical dimension by fishing, for instance, a buoyant lure on a sinking line. The advent of lures like the Leadhead, Beastie and Dog Nobbler with their weighted heads has revealed dramatically how attractive up and down motion is to trout. This action can be reversed with a sinking line and fly with a buoyant head thus producing a down and up movement. The deer hair head of the Muddler Minnow, the cork body of the Popping Bug and the replacement of the split shot by polystyrene balls on the Dog Nobbler all lend themselves to this strategy.

In acquiring and putting into practice such a variety of skills and approaches in his use of the lure, the fisherman will enhance both his enjoyment and his catch rate, and may become encouraged to diversify his methods so that he deploys lures, traditional flies and imitative patterns as and when appropriate. A wide selection of these is placed at his disposal in this guide. Truly then will he find, to quote out of context William Lunn's famous dictum, that "The proper fly, properly presented at the proper time, generally brings forth the proper result."

THE DRESSINGS

Ace of Spades

Ace of Spades

This is a black ace that I do not mind playing any time that I want a lure of that colour. David Collyer, its inventor, was seeking to avoid the chief drawback of the very successful Black Lure, namely the feather wing twisting round under the hook points during casting and making the fly swim in a lop-sided way. He experimented initially with a hair wing but, requiring a more solid silhouette, decided on a black hen hackle wing using the matuka style of dressing. He gave it a roof wing of dark bronze mallard feather. He first tried it out at Weir Wood with great success, and also found it effective in dark churned-up water, possibly because of its dense silhouette. David found it also worked with trout rising to minute smut by casting the fly in front of rising fish.

Hook:	L/S 6-12
Silk:	Black
Rib:	Oval silver tinsel
Body:	Black chenille
Wing:	Two dyed black hen hackles tied matuka style as a crest
Overwing:	Dark bronze mallard
Hackle:	Guinea fowl tied as a false beard

I regard it as a great standby in early season fished slowly and deeply. One early day in April with some breeze from left to right I cast out and put the rod down a moment to take a biscuit from my pocket. As I took off the wrapping I glanced down at my rod to see the line snaking through the rings. A quick pick-up found a good rainbow on the end.

See also under Matukas.

The Adult Midge or Buzzer

The chironomids or buzzers or midges which constitute a larger part of the stillwater trout's diet than any other insect vary in colour, size and number of species. It is generally agreed that the imitation of the adult fly is nowhere nearly as effective as that of the pupa or even the larva in terms of attractiveness to fish. However, angler/naturalist John Goddard believes that trout do feed on the adult, sometimes to the exclusion of anything else. The accepted view is that the adults spend little time on or near the surface before taking off, but he has observed them after hatching or at a later stage flying slowly over the surface for long periods. They leave a noticeable furrow on the water as their legs hang in the surface film and trout are liable to take them as they pass above.

The difficulty with the artificial is that rising trout will ignore it if it is motionless and be scared off if it is moving too fast. John Goddard therefore recommends that the fly be fished on the point with a long rod, light line and very long leader. Even dapping can be tried if it is breezy. His dressings accommodate the variations in size and colour of the different species.

Adult Midge

His earlier dressing given in his *Trout Flies of Stillwater* represents the newly hatched insect as it rests on the water and is to be fished dry. The winging is similar to that used by Bob Carnill in his Adult Buzzers.

Hook:	U/E 10-14
Silk:	Brown
Body:	Marabou silk in red, brown or green wound thickly to give the body a cylindrical appearance
Rib:	Silver lurex covered with opaque PVC
Wings:	Pale blue cock hackle tips tied in spent fashion but at an angle towards the tail
Hackle:	Dark honey or rusty dun cock

A more recent dressing given in *The Super Flies of Still Water* uses white bucktail or polywing yarn tied across the body for wings and imitates the newly hatched fly as it becomes active in the surface film:

Hook:	D/E L/S 12-14
Silk:	Yellow
Body:	Olive-green, orange or black seal's fur, full and teased out to simulate legs
Rib:	Fine silver tinsel
Wings:	White bucktail — about twelve strands tied across the body with a figure-of-eight finish. Polywing yarn can be used instead of the white bucktail.

A feature of Bob Carnill's patterns known collectively as Adult Buzzers is the use of cock hackle points tied back over the body in a V shape. He has produced dressings for the five most common plumosus varieties. The two early season ones are:

Grey Boy

Hook:	10-12 (standard shank or Yorkshire Sedge hook)
Silk:	Grey gossamer
Abdomen:	Grey heron or grey goose herl, ribbed closely with a natural, stripped peacock quill
Wing:	Cock hackle points, dyed light iron-blue dun
Thorax cover:	A web of herl, as for the abdomen
Thorax:	Dubbed natural mole fur
Hackle:	Iron-blue dun hen

This species was originally called by John Goddard the orange and silver midge.

Medium Olive (golden dun midge)

Hook:	10-12 (standard shank or Yorkshire Sedge hook)
Silk:	Light or medium olive gossamer
Abdomen:	Medium olive herl, swan or goose, dyed. No ribbing
Wing:	Cock hackle points, dyed light iron-blue dun
Thorax cover:	A web of herl, the same as for the abdomen
Thorax:	Medium olive under fur or man-made fibre, dubbed
Hackle:	Medium to light olive hen

For June and July:

Large Ginger (large red or ginger)

Hook:	10 (standard shank or Yorkshire Sedge hook)
Silk:	Orange or golden olive
Abdomen:	Underbody hot-orange swan herl, ribbed closely with stripped peacock eye quill, dyed ginger
Wings:	Cock hackle points, dyed light blue dun
Thorax cover:	Web of hen secondary feather, dyed gingery-orange
Thorax:	Beige/brown fur
Hackle:	Pale ginger or honey hen

Large Ginger Adult Midge

The dressing of the Ginger and Beige Adult which simulates the olive midge prevalent in August is similar to the Large Ginger except that the underbody for the abdomen is beige instead of hot-orange.

For September, Bob Carnill has devised a dressing to represent dullish, olive-coloured midges which are often a feature of that month:

Large Dark Olive Adult (large green midge)

Hook:	10 (standard shank or Yorkshire Sedge hook)
Silk:	Dark olive gossamer
Abdomen:	Dark olive swan or goose herl, ribbed closely with a stripped peacock eye quill, dyed medium olive
Wing:	Cock hackle points, dyed iron-blue dun
Thorax cover:	A web of herl, the same as for the abdomen
Thorax:	Dark olive under fur or man-made fibre, dubbed
Hackle:	Dark olive hen

These patterns can be fished singly or in a team of three from boat or bank whenever fish are rising for the adult buzzers or for the spent adults as they lie with their outstretched wings in the surface film.

See also under Black Duck Fly and Chironomid Adult.

Alder Larva *(Sialis lutaria)*

Alder Larva (Stewart Canham)

Whether fish take the adult alder is a subject of debate, but there is no such doubt concerning the alder larva. The eggs are laid on bankside vegetation by the adult fly and hatch out, and the emerging larvae crawl or fall into the water where they live in the mud and detritus, sallying forth after dusk in their first few months on the lake bed looking for victims. Later in their lives they become active in daylight also. They are vicious and voracious by nature and have been described graphically by Brian Clarke as the Genghis Khan of their element.

They are dark brown in colour with six stout legs, seven prominent tracheal gills down either side, a single tail and a strong pair of mandibles. They are capable crawlers but poor swimmers. Larvae remain in the water up to two years and grow up to an inch in length. They then crawl ashore from late March to late May to pupate and hatch out into the adult flies.

C. F. Walker was one of the first to devise an imitation of the larva, and I still use it with good effect. With its single ginger hackle point for tail, sandy hen ribbing hackle to simulate gills and brown partridge hackle for legs, it set the style for most future dressings.

Hook:	Long mayfly 10-12, wire loaded
Silk:	Black or brown
Abdomen:	Brown and ginger seal's fur mixed, the former predominating, tapered steeply from head to tail
Tail:	Ginger hackle point or none
Rib:	Gold oval tinsel
Ribbing hackle:	Sandy hen (to simulate gills)
Thorax & head:	Hare's ear dubbing
Hackle:	Brown partridge

Stuart Crooks' dressing lays emphasis on the rather flat appearance of the alder larva.

Hook:	L/S 10-12
Silk:	Buff or fawn
Tail:	Light honey cock hackle point
Underbody:	Fine lead wire flattened horizontally with pliers
Abdomen:	Chestnut seal's fur, ribbed with gold wire, trimmed short above and below (but not at the sides) and re-flattened
Thorax:	Buff seal's fur (untrimmed) with buff raffia or raffene over the top

C. F. Walker described the alder larva as resembling an earwig back-to-front and clad in a hula skirt. It is this skirt or the tracheal gills which Stewart Canham cleverly imitates with marabou tied alongside the body which produces most lifelike movement.

Hook:	8-10 Partridge lurehook
Silk:	Olive or brown Danville's pre-waxed
Rib:	Gold wire
Body:	Ginger seal's fur
Wing case & back:	Brown raffene
Thorax:	Medium olive or dark brown seal's fur
Underbody:	Lead wire
Tail & gills:	White marabou
Hackle:	Brown partridge

Bob Carnill's dressing is a modification of Stewart Canham's produced after a good deal of experimentation, and I saw it catch a number of fish last year.

Hook:	Mustad extra L/S No. 79590 size 10
Silk:	Brown gossamer waxed
Underbody:	Lead wire
Rib:	No. 14 gold oval tinsel
Body & thorax:	Either a 50/50 mix of rich chestnut and dark chestnut dyed mole, or seal's fur of a similar colour
Back & thorax covers:	A web of plain or mottled brown fibres
Gills:	A pale ginger hen hackle
Tail:	Either a single brown goose biot quill dyed medium brown, or a bunch of cock hackle fibres of a similar colour

All patterns are usually fished slowly along the bottom on a floating line and long leader, but I have had a number of fish when I have speeded the retrieve briefly.

Alder *(Sialis lutaria)*

Alder (Traditional)

The metamorphosis of the alder from larva to adult embraces both character and habitat. The ferocious larva now becomes a friendly and harmless adult, often alighting on the hands and neck of the fisherman. Unlike its larva, the adult is a terrestrial, and even when the female lays her eggs she does so on the leaves of plants or on reeds overlooking the water, and does not come into contact with the water itself.

The adult, which hatches in May and June, somewhat resembles a sedge fly with its dark roof-like wings and dark head and legs. It has been imitated since earliest times, an artificial pattern being given in Dame Juliana Berners' *Treatyse of Fysshynge with an Angle*. Since then there have been countless dressings, and yet there are wide differences of opinion as to whether either the natural or the artificial is taken by trout.

Halford said it was valueless. C. F. Walker states that the winged alder never visited the water except by accident and was never eaten by trout. More recently Taff Price mentions that he has tended to consider an artificial of the adult fly useless, and Stewart Canham told me that he rates the adult alder pattern as a non-fish catcher, never having seen a natural taken by a trout.

However, here is the traditional pattern:

Hook: 12-14
Silk: Dark claret
Body: Dark claret floss silk with bronze peacock herl over
Wing: Mottled brown hen
Hackle: Black or very dark claret

Charles Kingsley, the novelist, regarded the Alder as one of his favourite patterns though we must remember that this related to running water. Skues caught many trout in this country and elsewhere on the Kingsley dressing but fished sunk. Kingsley's pattern is as follows:

Hook: 12-14
Silk: Crimson
Body: Peacock herl dyed magenta
Wings: Two pairs from the secondary feathers of a dark, freckled game hen, dull side innermost, and sloping well over the body, with the hackle in front of them. The wings should lie nearly flat
Hackle: Black or dusky hen wound in front of wings

Joscelyn Lane's pattern which I give next was devised because he thought the traditional pattern bore little resemblance to the natural and that the trout probably had the same view. He observed that in his experience they took the natural freely. Tom Stewart in his *Two Hundred Popular Flies and how to tie them* said that he was never without an alder pattern on his cast when the natural was about.

Hook: 10
Silk: Black
Body & thorax: Very long Rhode Island Red cock hackles wound coils touching from bend to eye. Fibres trimmed cigar-shaped, one eighth of an inch thick in the middle. Those above the shank clipped flush with the quill to accommodate the wing
Wing: Good bunch of fibres from a large rusty dun cock hackle, tied in by the butts on top of the thorax and trimmed to an oval shape just beyond the bend of the hook
Hackle: Three or four turns of black cock hackle

Writers like John Waller Hills and Roger Woolley have been critical of the big peacock herl body of many of the dressings, and this one by David Jacques omits it. He is convinced that the alder adult is a desirable titbit for the trout during its season and only then. He has had some of his best fish on this pattern including one of 8lb 3ozs.

Hook: D/E 10-12
Silk: Crimson
Wings: Two pairs from the wings of a brown game hen, spotted side outside, sloping over the body
Hackle: Black cock in front of the wings

The general technique is to fish the artificial on the surface if you see trout taking naturals that may have been blown onto the water.

Alexandra

Alexandra

This is a pattern about which there are very mixed opinions. It is around 120 years old and was originally known as The Lady of the Lake and then renamed in honour of Queen Alexandra. Courtney Williams said that none of the great fly fishers of the time appeared to have any great enthusiasm for it, and he could not remember anyone who had anything to say in praise of it.

However, it has always retained a certain popularity as a loch fly and, since the expansion of stillwater fishing, has made something of a comeback. One of the enthusiastic advocates of the Alexandra as a traditional loch fly was Tom Stewart who found it deadly as a tail fly provided that it was fished with a varied retrieve. He believed it was taken for a minnow or a beetle. In its new role as a lure attractive particularly to rainbows it was described by Brian Clarke as having "clip-joint spivishness".

Hook:	D/E 10-12
Tail:	Red ibis or substitute, to which is sometimes added a strand or two of green peacock herl
Rib:	Fine oval silver
Body:	Flat silver tinsel
Wings:	Strands of green herl from the 'sword' tail of the peacock, usually with a thin strip of ibis each side
Hackle:	Black hen

David Collyer has used it on reservoirs with a fairly fast retrieve and a sink-tip allowing the fly to sink about three or four feet. Joe Brooks, the American angler and author, considers the Alexandra one of the all-time greats in producing strikes.

The Allrounder

This fly has been devised by John Ketley to serve more than one purpose as its name suggests. John, one of the outstanding exponents of the traditional 'loch' style of fishing, wrote the section on traditional flies for boat fishing in John Goddard's *Stillwater Flies How and When to Fish Them*. In this he explains that the Allrounder acts nicely on the top dropper as a sedge pattern in a good wave whilst it is equally effective when shoals of tiny fish fry are about. In this situation the fly is fished on the point with short sharp pulls. The hackle tends to bring it almost to the surface, and the gold mylar glints through the palmered hackle. If pale-coloured sedges appear, John substitutes a hen pheasant tail wing for the teal, and if it is cloudy he uses a silver body.

Hook: D/E10
Silk: Black
Tail: Four fibres of honey hackle
Rib: Flat mylar (gold side)
Body Hackle: Honey cock
Wing: Rolled, teal, strongly barred
Hackle: Honey (dry fly)

The Allrounder

Amber Nymph

Created by Dr. Howard Bell who practised in Wrington and Blagdon from 1922 onwards. He fished Blagdon every Friday and Sunday for over forty years, studying the underwater life and producing a number of highly effective imitations of which the Amber Nymph is probably the most famous. It was designed to imitate the sedge pupa, more than anything else by its general silhouette and body shade. He used the larger one in May and June and the smaller in July.

Its fish-catching properties are enthusiastically endorsed by numerous writers. Brian Clarke in his *The Pursuit of Stillwater Trout* says that the Amber Nymph has given him some of the most exciting evenings he has experienced during hatches of sedge. He recommends that it be fished smoothly and steadily beneath the surface film when medium sized pale-bodied sedges are beginning to hatch. Geoffrey Bucknall is also an ardent disciple of the fly. John Goddard says it is hard to find a more rewarding nymph pattern and includes it in his list of the élite, *The Superflies of Still Water*. He feels it is intended to represent many of the species of sedge pupae that are predominantly of an orange-brown colouring.

Amber Nymph (Howard Bell)

Hook: D/E 10-11 large; D/E 12-13 small
Silk: Black (large); yellow (small)
Body: Amber-yellow floss silk or seal's fur tied rather thickly
Thorax: Brown or black floss silk or seal's fur (large); Hot-orange (small), approximately one third the length of the body

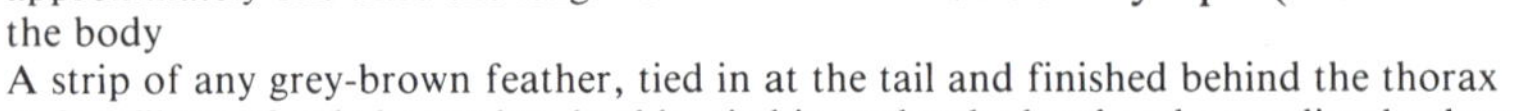

Wing case: A strip of any grey-brown feather, tied in at the tail and finished behind the thorax
Legs: A few fibres of pale honey hen hackle, tied in under the head and extending backwards

It can be fished in a variety of ways, but by its very nature it demands generally to be just below the surface and rising. Long, regular, smooth pulls using a floating line and long leader create this effect. Sometimes sink and draw from just below the surface produces takes. It can be used as a dropper fly in which case it should not be retrieved too fast. I took a trout at Lapsley's Fishery on this pattern in very early May casting direct to a fish when a few sedges were about.

Another Amber Nymph was devised by Lionel Sweet, the famous fisherman and fly caster of the Usk, to fish waters like Blagdon and Chew. The black thread is intended to emphasise the gold rib.

Hook: 10-12 weighted
Silk: Black or brown
Tail: A wisp or two of red (natural) hen
Rib: Gold oval followed by black thread tight up against the gold
Body: Amber floss
Thorax: Amber floss
Hackle: Soft natural red hen

Finally, an Amber Nymph originated by Derek Bradbury for fishing Grafham, and said by Donald Overfield in his additional section to Courtney Williams' *Dictionary of Trout Flies* to be an imitation of the sedge larva.

Hook: D/E wide gape 10
Silk: Black
Body: Rear two thirds, amber seal's fur ribbed with narrow orange lurex; front third, dyed dark brown ostrich herl
Back: Fibres from a dark brown speckled turkey tail feather, tied in from bend to eye like a shrimp dressing
Hackle: One turn only of brown partridge
Swimming legs: Two fibres, one each side tied in at the head, from the centre tail feather of a golden pheasant. The fibres twice as long as the body and pointing rearwards

Ants *(Hymenoptera)*

This is one of those patterns you may need once in a lifetime, but if you have not got it you may spend the rest of your life regretting it!

Ants are terrestrial creatures of great order and relative brain power. The workers do not fly, but once a year the winged females and winged males follow the queen and leave their nest on their first and only flight. This is pre-eminently a nuptial flight after which the males die. It is at this time that the ants may fly over or be blown onto water. All authorities are agreed that if this happens the fish receive

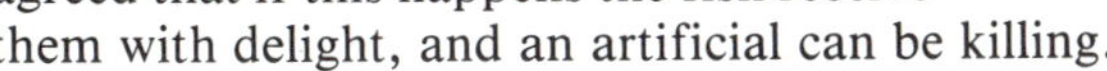
them with delight, and an artificial can be killing.

Black Ant (Taff Price)

Skues was of the opinion that trout are inordinately fond of ants and devised this dressing to represent the big dusky-winged wood ant:

Red Ant

Hook:	R/B 14
Silk:	Red ant colour
Body:	Chestnut-coloured pig's wool, fine, tied on in two blobs, the larger at the tail, and trimmed to shape with scissors (Taff Price suggests seal's fur as substitute)
Legs:	Two turns of deep blood-red cock hackle behind the smaller blob

Arthur Ransome said that, though the Winged Ant was not a general utility fly, when it was good it was very good. He devised an impressionist pattern in which the shape was more important than the colour:

Winged Ant

Hook:	14
Silk:	Orange
Body:	Pear-shaped of orange floss silk
Thorax:	Ordinary orange tying silk also pear-shaped
Wings:	Two hackle points of palest honey tied in flat and constructed to project a little beyond the body
Hackle:	Red cock

For a modern dressing, Taff Price has devised a pattern in four colours:

Black Ant

Hook:	14-18
Silk:	Black
Body:	The tying silk built up for abdomen and thorax with a waist between and varnished
Wings:	Two blue dun hackle tips of a light shade
Hackle:	Black

Brown Ant
Browny-orange tying silk and dark natural red hackle

Yellow Ant
Yellow-orange silk and light ginger hackle

Red Ant
Blood-red silk and natural red hackle

Joe Brooks, the American angling authority, says that the Black Flying Ant has proved one of his greatest fish-takers throughout all his fishing life.

Appetiser

This lure was introduced by Bob Church in 1973, and uses marabou feather which he was the first to publicise in this country. A substitute from the legs of turkeys is now commonly used. Appetiser was designed to tempt the larger trout when they were feeding on fry during the latter part of the season on the big reservoirs.

Hook:	L/S D/E 6-8
Silk:	Black
Tail:	Mixed orange and dark green hackle fibres, and just a few fibres of silver mallard feather
Rib:	Silver tinsel
Body:	White chenille
Wing:	White marabou, large spray
Overwing:	Natural grey squirrel tail
Throat hackle:	As for tail

Appetiser

One technique that Bob Church uses is highly specialised involving size 6 ordinary long shanked hooks or, if the fry are particularly big, special extra long shanked hooks up to $3\frac{1}{2}$ inches in length. Fishing deep water hot spots from a boat, he uses a lead-impregnated line and an eighteen feet untapered leader of 8lb breaking strain. The Appetiser fished in this way has taken more specimen fish for him than any other fly except the White Marabou Muddler.

In shallower water, the fishing of the pattern on a 6 or 8 in the vicinity of weed beds on a slow sink or floating shooting head at medium pace as trout surge after fry is another of his successful methods. It can also work very well retrieved just below the surface.

A variation of the Appetiser used by Steve Parton is as follows:

Hook:	L/S 6-8
Tail:	White and scarlet cock hackle fibres mixed
Rib:	Fine silver oval
Body:	White fluorescent chenille
Wing:	White marabou
Overwing:	Grey squirrel
Hackle:	Short scarlet cock, long white cock in front, raked back

He sometimes substitutes peacock herl for the grey squirrel.

Apricot Spinner *(Cleon dipterum)*

This is the common name given to the spinner of an important stillwater fly, the pond olive. It is distinctive from other spinners because of its brilliant apricot body colour.

The females fall on the water in late evening after dropping their eggs. Oliver Kite, whose dressing this is, pointed out that much of this ovipositing probably occurred after dark and hence smaller lakes can have their surface covered with these fragile dead creatures very early in the morning before the fisherman arrives.

Skues found plain hackled patterns, provided that the hackles were sharp and bright, made as good spinner patterns as necessary, and this is just such a one.

Hook:	14
Silk:	Golden-olive
Tails:	Pale yellow cock fibres
Body:	Swan primary herls dyed apricot
Thorax:	Same herls doubled and redoubled
Hackle:	Pale honey dun

Apricot Spinner

August Dun Nymph
(Ecdyonurus dispar)

August Dun Nymph
(Thomas Clegg)

The large nymphs of the august dun are very wide across the thorax and with a flattened body belong to the stone clinger group, spending most of their time on stones or boulders on the bed of the lake. Although they prefer to cling to stones, J. R. Harris says that they are agile and can swim fairly well.

Roger Woolley devised a wet fly dressing as follows:

Hook:	13
Tail:	Brown hen
Rib:	Yellow tying silk
Body:	Brown floss silk
Wing:	Pale mottled hen pheasant
Hackle:	Brown hen

The best modern dressing is that of Thomas Clegg whose expertise in the use of fluorescent materials is well known. It is given in Donald Overfield's book, *Fifty Favourite Nymphs.*

Hook:	12-14
Silk:	Light green
Tail:	Three short strands of guinea fowl fibres dyed yellow
Rib:	Copper wire and signal-green Depth Ray Fire fluorescent floss
Thorax:	Grass monkey fur of a blue dun/yellow olive hue
Wing case:	A bunch of red squirrel tail hairs
Legs:	Grass monkey fur picked out with a dubbing needle

The pattern should be fished slowly on the bottom with a long leader and occasional twitch.

August Dun *(Ecdyonurus dispar)*

August Dun (Roger Woolley)

The nymph of the august dun hatches out into quite a big fly with marked olive-fawn wings, pale greenish-brown body and two tails. As its name implies it is most common in August. It can easily be taken for a march brown. J. R. Harris in his *An Angler's Entomology* was the first writer to recognise that the fly could be found on stillwater as well as the rivers. However, it tends to be confined to the stony shores of large lakes and is more common to Wales and the West Country. Tom Stewart mentioned that he had seen hatches of the fly on Scottish lochs in Renfrewshire and Sutherland.

One of the earliest dressings of the artificial is by Alfred Ronalds, the first great angler/naturalist, who added that the fly could be made buzz by the addition of a grouse feather wound down the body.

Hook:	13
Tail:	Two rabbit's whiskers
Body:	Brown floss silk
Rib:	Yellow silk thread
Wings:	Feather of a brown hen's wing
Legs:	Plain red hackle stained brown

Roger Woolley, whose pattern I give next, commented that the august dun was the biggest of the ephemera family to appear in the autumn.

Hook:	12-14
Tail:	Fibres of dark ginger cock hackle
Rib:	Yellow silk or horsehair dyed yellow
Body:	Brown floss silk or brown quill
Wings:	Pale mottled hen pheasant
Hackle:	Brown-ginger cock hackle

Finally, a dressing from those experts in Yorkshire patterns, H. H. Edmonds and N. N. Lee, from their book, *Brook and River Trouting*.

Hook:	13
Body:	Yellow silk dubbed with yellow-olive wool and then ribbed with orange silk very lightly dubbed with fur from a rabbit's nape which has been lightly dyed red
Wings:	Mallard's breast feather, lightly tinged brown
Legs:	Medium olive hen hackle

If fish are taking the duns then cast the dry fly to individual trout.

August Dun Spinner
(Ecdyonurus dispar)

August Dun Spinner
(G. E. M. Skues)

Eric Taverner says that in August and early September, in the appropriate parts of the country, you may see with the setting sun small, fiery points dancing over the water. These are the male spinners of the august or autumn dun. Their female counterparts are distinguished by dark red bodies and long tails. The beauty of their nuptial carnival evoked from Skues; "These flies will be seen in flocks at sunset, dancing in the sun's rays, looking like so many red-hot needles."

He said that he had seen them taken very much in the same way as the sherry spinner, and that the spinner pattern was more effective than that of the dun. His dressing is that of the male spinner.

Hook:	U/E 13-14
Silk:	Hot-orange
Tail:	Honey dun cock
Body:	Flat tawsy gut ends, dyed red-orange, tied in at the shoulder and whipped over the bare hook to the tail and then back to the shoulder. Or orange seal's fur
Wing:	The freckled part (from near the root) of the red feather from a partridge's tail tied spent
Hackle:	Red cock

A rather simpler dressing by Roger Woolley is as follows:

Hook:	14
Tail:	Bright red cock
Rib:	Gold wire
Body:	Brownish-red quill
Wings:	Two small pale blue cock hackles tied spent
Hackle:	Bright red cock

J. R. Harris says that trout will rise freely to the spinners in late afternoon or evening, and the fishing technique, as with all spinners, is to cast to rising fish and allow the fly to lie motionless.

See also an imitation recommended by John Goddard under Great Red Spinner.

Autumn Dun

See under August Dun

Aylott's Orange

Aylott's Orange

Designed by Richard Aylott in the late 1970's, John Goddard placed it in his list of lures in his book, *Superflies of Still Water*. He did so because of its bright body colouration. However, both he and Richard Walker consider it resembles a sedge pupa rising to hatch, and it is often more effective in the latter half of the season.

Hook:	D/E 12-14
Silk:	Black
Body:	Arc chrome DF wool to form a fat, juicy-looking body
Hackle:	Light red cock tied sparsely
Head:	Two or three strands of peacock herl

This is a pattern which is highly visible and very useful when water is coloured or with heavy algae bloom in hot weather. It is usually best fished slowly in the sink and draw style in conjunction with a floating line.

An alternative version has signal-green DF wool for the body to simulate hatching pupae with bodies of a more greenish hue.

Baby Doll

Baby Doll

A fly created by Brian Kench in 1971 and publicised by Bob Church which has had astonishing and persistent success. This is almost certainly due to the high visibility of its brilliant white nylon wool body as it has no 'moving parts'. For this reason, Bob Church replaces his patterns after one day's use.

Hook:	L/S 6-10
Silk:	Black
Body:	Brilliant white nylon wool or daylight fluorescent white wool. Sirdar brand suggested
Back & tail:	As body. A half-inch tail with the wool shredded to produce a bushy and fish-like shape

An incredibly versatile lure, it will take fish on every type of stillwater and under all conditions. It is effective at any depth, but early in the season works best being allowed to sink to the bottom and then given a slow pull. Bob Church uses a three-inch version when simulating large fry at Grafham in late August. I have often had it taken on the drop whilst, ripped through the water in those last few desperate minutes near closing time, fish rising to minute and inscrutable flies will sometimes grab it to complete one's bag limit.

There are now numerous versions of the Baby Doll tied in green, orange, scarlet, yellow and lime, generally using fluorescent wools. The lime green can be especially profitable. Richard Walker has introduced two modifications, the Leaded DF Doll and Nell Gwynne, which are listed separately.

Another development by lure expert Syd Brock is worth trying:

Special Baby Doll

Hook: L/S 6-10
Silk: Black
Body: Rear two thirds stretched black plastic tape; front third bright red wool
Back & tail: Fluorescent green wool

Baddow Special

A pattern devised by John Poole to give a general impression of a damselfly nymph, and used with a good deal of success, I believe, at Hanningfield Reservoir.

Hook: L/S 8-10
Silk: Black
Tail: Fluorescent lime wool
Rib: Gold or silver
Body: Peacock herl
Hackle: A sparse long-fibred white cock hackle

As with most damselfly nymph imitations, it should be fished just below the surface on a floating line with a series of long steady pulls.

Baddow Special

Badger Lure and the Badger Matuka

This is a pattern which ranks alongside the Black Lure as one of the early and popular lures devised to meet the demands of the big reservoirs. Brian Clarke in his *The Pursuit of Stillwater Trout* which records his progression from lure fishing to the logic of fishing the imitation of the fly on the water admitted that he still carried a Badger Lure even if only to be used in a desperate attempt to shock trout totally preoccupied by hatching caenis! Here is Richard Walker's dressing:

Hooks: Two size 10 in tandem
Bodies: Fluorescent orange wool
Ribs: Fine oval tinsel
Throat: Hot-orange cock hackle fibres
Wings: Two large badger hackles back to back and as long as the hooks
Eyes: Two jungle cock (or substitute) feathers tied in short

Like the Black Lure, its basic disadvantage is the tendency of the wing feathers to become tangled in the bend of the hooks and around the barbs. A way of tackling this problem has been to use a single hook and the matuka style of winging. This adaptation of the Badger Lure by David Collyer is as follows:

Badger Lure

Matuka Badger Lure

Hook:	L/S 6-10
Silk:	Orange
Body:	Fluorescent orange wool
Wings:	Two badger cock hackles tied matuka style
Sides:	Jungle cock (or substitute) tied short
Hackle:	Hot-orange cock

A different version introduced by Steve Stephens in 1972 and considered to be a fry imitator moves cleanly and straight through the water. Bob Church says it often works when fished deep for brownies.

Badger Matuka

Hook:	L/S 6-10
Silk:	Black
Body:	White chenille
Rib:	Silver wire
Thorax:	Orange wool or chenille
Wing:	Two or three pairs of well-marked badger hen hackles
Throat hackle:	Hot-orange cock

Banded Squirrel Bucktail

This is a bucktail lure devised by Taff Price, and the first time he tried it out it took fourteen brown trout for him. He has fished it successfully since on such reservoirs as Hanningfield where it took fish on an otherwise blank day.

Banded Squirrel Bucktail

Hook:	L/S 6-10
Silk:	Black
Tail:	Red and white hackle fibres
Rib:	Silver oval
Body:	Mauve wool
Wing:	Grey squirrel
Hackle:	False hackle of red and white cock hackle fibres

Like most lures, it should be fished with a variable retrieve and at differing depths according to conditions and time of year.

Bare Hook Nymph

Bare Hook Nymph

Donald Overfield tells us that Oliver Kite's idea for this austere fly which has only a body came to him when fishing a battered and badly worn Pheasant Tail which was still being taken although most of the herl had disappeared.

Hook:	D/E 14-16
Body:	A thorax only of built-up turns of fine copper wire

The method of fishing was all-important in Major Kite's view, and the nymph was presented so that when it was almost before the fish's nose it was lifted to imitate an ascending nymph, a method named the 'induced take'.

It can be used on translucent stillwaters on the same principle for stalking individual fish though I have not tried it. It has, however, worked for me using a Sawyer Pheasant Tail Nymph at Damerham. The technique is commonly used by specimen hunters on the clear smaller lakes.

Barney Google

Barney Google

The lovely name given to this fly by its inventor, Richard Walker, immediately conjures up a vision of the two red beads which are its outstanding feature. The fly was designed to simulate the phantom larva which is virtually translucent. Richard Walker has pointed out that though the imitation with its beads looks flashy in the fly box they appear as a dark sepia colour once well down in the water.

Hook:	12-14
Body:	Clear polythene
Hackle:	Grey speckled mallard, partridge or widgeon feather tied beard-fashion
Heads:	Two small transparent red beads tied with either silk or fine copper wire

Fish the fly on a floating line and long leader, allowing it time to sink before retrieving with short sharp pulls. The beads help the fly to sink quickly.

Taff Price cannot see the likeness of this pattern to the phantom larva but fishes it as a beetle larva.

Barrie Welham Nymph

This is a general-purpose nymph particularly useful for casting to individual fish, originated by Barrie Welham, who has taken many specimen trout and is also a notable caster.

Hook:	Varying sizes of normal shanked hooks, often weighted
Silk:	Black
Tail:	A dual-coloured tuft of yellow and red DFM floss
Rib:	Gold oval tinsel
Body:	Brown wool tapered at each end
Breathers:	A short tuft of white hackle fibres tied back over the body

Barrie Welham Nymph

Beacon Beige

Based on a pattern originated during the First World War and called the Beige, it was developed further after the Second World War by Peter Deane, the well-known professional fly dresser, and re-christened the Beacon Beige. He added a long dark red Indian game cock hackle to the Plymouth Rock hackle. Although primarily a chalk stream fly, because it represents the olive dun it can be used to simulate the lake and pond olives.

Hook:	U/E 12-16
Silk:	Brown (sherry spinner) or black
Tail:	Four fibres from a Plymouth Rock cock hackle
Body:	Well-marked stripped peacock eye quill
Hackle:	Plymouth Rock cock, with a dark red Indian game cock wound through it

Beacon Beige

David Collyer suggests that if a rare Plymouth Rock cock hackle cannot be obtained then bars can be marked on a plain white hackle with a black marker pen like a Pantone. It is better to dab rather than try to draw it across the hackle.

Beastie Lure

Undoubtedly one of the predecessors of the Dog Nobbler. The idea came to Geoffrey Bucknall after watching his friend, Dr. Tony Richards, clip on a swan shot to the head of a normal marabou lure whilst fishing at Hanningfield.

Geoffrey Bucknall's development of this involved the use of a wing at least twice as long as the hook shank. The weighted head made the tail vibrate, and the fly dipped and rose according to the way the fly was retrieved. In his book, *Modern Techniques of Still Water Fishing*, the author places a good deal of emphasis on the killing properties of the lure's diving action. There is thus a difference of emphasis compared with the up and down motion of the Dog Nobbler produced by the snatching high-speed retrieve. Though, as Geoffrey Bucknall says, it may look like a veritable haystack out of water, once wet the Beastie slims down considerably.

Beastie Lure

For Grafham, the originator devised a Beastie with a fluorescent pink floss body ribbed with silver, a strip of magenta marabou as false hackle and underwing, and white marabou plume wings with cheeks as previously. He particularly had in mind the imitation of bream fry. At a time when fish were coming short to the Beastie, he tied it down to a size 12 hook with success.

The phenomenal success of the Dog Nobbler has tended to overshadow the earlier Beastie and Richard Walker's Leadheads with which it has much in common.

Hook:	L/S Streamer 6
Rib:	Silver tinsel
Body:	Black floss silk
False hackle:	Small bouquet of orange marabou
Underwing:	Longer strip of orange marabou feather
Wing:	Two black marabou plumes tied in back to back so that they extend well beyond the hook bend, about as long again as the hook shank
Cheek:	Black and white barred silver pheasant flank feathers tied on either side of the hook, the central stalk level with the shank. Jungle cock or substitute overlaid onto the cheek
Head:	Two layers of lead wire

Beetles *(Coleoptera)*

Over no insect is there a wider divergence of opinion as to the value of its imitation to the angler than the beetle, yet it has been imitated since the days of Charles Cotton. David Jacques tells us that beetles are the third largest order of insect in Britain, and that there are 3,690 different species in this country of which 220 are aquatic and the remainder terrestrial.

Advocates of beetle imitation include Leonard West, Roger Woolley, Courtney Williams, John Henderson and Taff Price. More doubtful of their value are C. F. Walker, David Jacques and John Goddard. Taff Price tells us that he has lost count of the number of times he has found beetles in the autopsies of trout, even from waters containing a rich diet of other creatures. He concludes that trout always seem to be tempted by a beetle. C. F. Walker, on the contrary, said that he spent much time in evolving new patterns of beetles before finding out that they did not figure in the trout's diet. He produced what he considered were some most lifelike artificials only to find that the trout avoided them like the plague! I tend to be one of the doubters, but I keep on trying!

Roger Woolley had no such doubts, stating that beetles are a very useful aid and frequently kill well. He was, of course, referring to running water.

Black Beetle (Taff Price)

Brown Beetle

Hook:	14-16
Body:	Bronze peacock herl
Wing cases:	Bronze hen wing feather
Legs:	Brown hen hackle

Red Beetle

Hook:	12-15
Body:	Bright red wool
Wing cases:	Purple feather from the outside of a mallard wing
Hackle:	Speckled cock, tied outside wing cases

Here is a dressing by John Henderson of a comparatively small beetle of the *Staphylinidae* family often called Staphs. They tend to be long and slim with abbreviated wing cases, and many are of a glossy black hue.

Black Staph

Hook:	13-15
Silk:	Nylusta (gunmetal shade)
Rib:	Thin gold wire or nylusta (gunmetal)
Body:	Peacock herl, black ostrich herl or three fibres from a magpie's tail
Body hackle:	Black cock trimmed from one eighth to one sixteenth of an inch
Shoulder hackle:	Black or dark rusty dun cock, untrimmed

A modern dressing by Taff Price is as follows:

Black Beetle

Hook:	Varying sizes
Silk:	Black
Body:	Black seal or polypropylene
Hackle:	Black palmered and clipped top and sides
Back:	Black raffene varnished

When fishing beetle patterns one should always bear in mind whether an aquatic species is being imitated or a terrestrial. The former have to ascend to the surface for air whilst the latter are usually blown onto the water. Sink and draw methods will apply to the aquatics and dry fly tactics to the terrestrials.

Other dressings for beetles may be found under Blue Leaf Beetle, Coch-y-Bonddu Beetle, Cockchafer Beetle, Dytiscus Beetle, Eric's Beetle, The Governor, Green Beast, Rove Beetle, Soldier Beetle.

Bi-Visibles

Bi-Visible (Black)

It is always worthwhile having a couple of these flies in your box because they have two very useful qualities: firstly they are excellent floaters and secondly they are easily seen in dark conditions because of the front white hackle. Their best use is as general sedge patterns in late evening.

The flies were invented by the American, Edward Hewitt, just before the end of the last century, and they remain very popular on the other side of the Atlantic where dressings are tied in black, brown, badger, blue dun, furnace, ginger, grizzly olive and pink lady. The latter uses Lady Amherst pheasant tippet fibres for the tail and pink floss for the body. The American flies are often tied with silver or gold tinsel bodies to give extra flash, but this may well detract from their floating qualities.

Black

Hook: U/E 10-12
Silk: Black or white
Tail: Tips of hackles
Body: Two black cock hackles wound palmer-wise from the bend with the tip tied in first and forming the tail. One or two turns of white cock hackle tied in by the stalk in front of the double hackle

Brown

Hook: U/E 10-12
Silk: Brown (sherry spinner) or white
Tail: Tips of hackles
Body: Two brown cock hackles wound palmer-wise from the bend with the tip tied in first and forming the tail. One or two turns of white cock hackle tied in by the stalk in front of the double hackle

There are other ways to make the fly more visible to the angler. Al Troth, the well-known American fly tyer and angler from Pennsylvania, uses a bit of orange fluorescent yarn on top of some of his flies. The trout cannot see it because it is on top, but the angler can.

Fish Bi-Visibles as you would a dry sedge pattern.

Black and Orange Marabou

See under Marabou Flies

Black and Peacock Spider

Black and Peacock Spider

Tom Ivens' most famous pattern must now be regarded as one of the classic stillwater flies and few fishermen are without it. It is notably successful when small black snails are about, and also very good for a silverhorns' rise. John Goddard considers it effective as a representation of both aquatic and terrestrial beetles. I had a particularly fine rainbow on this fly at Croxley Hall Waters where snails are common.

Hook:	6-12
Silk:	Black
Rib:	Dark silk floss
Body:	Any dark silk floss, slender at the tail and thicker at the thorax. Three or four strands of bronze peacock herl twisted together and wound over the underbody
Hackle:	Relatively large, soft-fibred black hen, two turns only

Tom Ivens places the greatest importance on how a fly is fished, and in this case insists that it should be fished very slowly at all times. During the evening rise he advises greasing the cast down to the last eighteen inches with very slow line retrieval.

The Black Bear's Hair Lure

The Black Bear's Hair Lure

Another variation on the black lure theme to keep company with the Ace of Spades, Black Chenille, Sweeny Todd etc. This one is a matuka utilising soft bear's hair which imparts to it a lifelike and animated movement in the water. The pattern was devised by Cliff Henry, and John Goddard recommends it as particularly attractive to brown trout.

Hook:	D/E L/S 8-10
Silk:	Black
Rib:	Oval silver tinsel
Body:	Black seal's fur
Wing:	A one eighth of an inch wide strip of black bear's hair with the skin cut a little longer than the hook shank

John Goddard advises that it can be fished on either a floating or sinking line with variable retrieves but with pauses to activate the bear's hair. It will take trout early on fished near the bottom, and later in summer can be tried fairly fast just below the surface.

Black Beetle

See under Beetles

Black Chenille

Black Chenille

Bob Church first tied this fly in 1970 since when it has become one of the outstanding and most versatile of all stillwater lures. The use of chenille in its dressing was novel for British fly patterns at the time though now very common. A year later, Bob Church produced a series of heavy-weight bag limits at Draycote Reservoir. He was using a size 6 Black Chenille in conjunction with a lead core line for fishing very deep from a boat. This has remained a very killing technique on all the big reservoirs. Another of his methods was to use a size 6 or 8 Black Chenille as a single fly with a small shot pinched on the line just in front of the fly, and with a floating shooting head in windy rough conditions, so that the fly was worked by the waves. This brought him incredible catches early in the season.

Hook:	L/S 6-10
Silk:	Black
Rib:	Silver tinsel
Body:	Black chenille
Tail:	Black hackle fibres
Wing:	Four matching black cock hackle feathers
Throat hackle:	Black hackle fibres

Anglers have found many other ways of using the Black Chenille. As an early season lure fished slowly from the bank on a sinking line or with rather longer steady pulls, I have found it most successful, especially at Ardleigh Reservoir.

Time and again, on small waters and big, the Black Chenille whipped back through the water fast or with a series of short, fast pulls on a floating line shortly before dusk has completed my bag limit. Trout will often grab it with gusto even though seemingly preoccupied with midges.

Black Duck Fly

See under Duck Fly

Black Ghost

This is a streamer pattern of American origin which is used by fishermen virtually world-wide. Basically a fry imitation. I have found it works well fished slowly with pauses rather like fishing a Jack Frost at the back end of the season.

Hook:	L/S 6-10
Tail:	Golden pheasant crest
Rib:	Flat silver tinsel
Body:	Black wool or floss
Wings:	Four white cock hackles
Throat hackle:	Golden pheasant crest
Shoulders:	Jungle cock or substitute
Head:	Black varnish

Black Ghost (Original version)

Another version which still retains the white cock feathers for the wing is a favourite pattern of Syd Brock, a confirmed lure specialist and Farmoor specimen hunter, who contributes to John Goddard's month by month reference work, *Stillwater Flies How and When to Fish Them*, on the subject of fishing lures from the bank.

Hook:	L/S 6-8
Silk:	Black
Tail:	Yellow cock hackle fibres
Rib:	One sixteenth of an inch wide strip of white stiff plastic tape
Body:	Black stretch PVC or black wool
Wing:	Four matched white cock feathers
Throat hackle:	Yellow cock hackle fibres

It can be used at any time of the season at any depth, and whether you use a fast sink or slow line will depend on the configuration of the bed of the lake you are fishing. Generally speaking, Syd Brock finds a fast retrieve the most effective.

Black Gnat *(Bibionidae)*

This is a fly which has had countless dressings from the time of Charles Cotton onwards. It is most commonly identified as Bibio johannis. It is commonly referred to as Bibio on the Irish loughs where its imitation is widely used. There are not only many members of the Bibio family but countless other small black flies, especially those of the Empid family, which fishermen call black gnats. Most of them look like small house flies with their wings held flat on their backs. They are not really black, but rather a dark olive brown for the female and darker for the male.

There is not a lot to choose between the dressings, but I will start with two classic patterns, the first of the male by Roger Woolley.

Black Gnat Male (Roger Wooley)

Hook:	15-17
Body:	Black quill, horsehair or tying silk
Wings:	Pale starling or two small pale blue dun hackle tips tied flat on the back
Hackle:	Black cock or starling neck feather

For the female I give Halford's dressing:

Hook:	16
Body:	Stripped peacock quill dyed jet black
Wings:	Pale starling wing quill, tied sloping back over the body
Hackle:	Glossy black starling body feather

A more modern pattern by Cliff Henry uses trimmed black cock hackle for the body like a lot of Joscelyn Lane's flies.

Hook:	16
Silk:	Black
Body:	Black cock hackle, flue trimmed to one thirty-second of an inch
Wings:	Pale starling, tied sloping back
Hackle:	Black cock short in the fibre

David Collyer uses a small wing of pale ginger hackle fibres tied to point almost upright but over the eye of the hook like the Wulff patterns.

Hook:	U/E 16-18
Silk:	Black
Body:	Dyed-black swan or goose
Wing:	Very pale ginger cock hackle fibres
Hackle:	Dyed or natural black cock, very small

Small black flies are on the water throughout the season and when they appear in large numbers trout can become preoccupied in feeding on them. At this time cast your fly to a rising fish. Taff Price suggests fishing an artificial just under the surface if the dry fly fails.

See also the dressing of the Knotted Midge.

Black Hackled Dry Fly

Versions of this fly go back to Charles Cotton who used peacock herl for the body, and Francis Francis who offered ostrich. John Henderson's pattern, which he also refers to as a Black Palmer, adds a body hackle but this is trimmed short and a shoulder hackle added. It also has a gold wire rib.

Black Hackled Dry Fly

Hook:	15
Silk:	Dark claret or black
Rib:	Thin gold wire or nylusta (dark grey)
Body:	Black ostrich or three fibres from a magpie's tail

Body hackle:	Black cock trimmed to taper from one quarter to one eighth of an inch
Shoulder hackle:	Untrimmed black cock

The trimmed hackle body over the ostrich makes it an excellent floater, and John Henderson considered it one of the most useful all-round dry flies for reservoir use as it could be taken for not only the black midge but also for other insects such as beetles and black silverhorn sedges.

Black Lure

Black Lure

From the time of the great expansion of stillwater trout fishing facilities and the opening of large waters like Grafham, the Black Lure probably made as big an impact as any other fly on the lure scene. It was the prototype for many other black lure type flies to follow. Despite its sometimes annoying habit of tangling its wing feathers in the bend of the hook, it remains a very popular and killing streamer pattern.

It is sometimes referred to as the Black Leech but, as David Collyer points out, few people can have seen a leech travelling at the speed most fishermen move a Black Lure. This method produces results when, no doubt, it arouses the aggressive tendencies of fish, but it is also highly effective fished in other ways. It will take big trout early in the season fished slowly along the bottom. Bob Church uses it in big sizes fishing very deep from a boat with the aid of a lead-impregnated line when he takes large and heavy bag limits.

Hooks:	6-12, tied in tandem, two or more
Silk:	Black
Ribs:	Oval or fine flat silver tinsel
Bodies:	Black floss
Wings:	Two black hen hackles tied back to back
Hackle:	Black cock or hen or none

There are many variations aimed at 'improving' the fly including the use of four black saddle hackles for the wing, the addition of bronze peacock herl as an overwing, the embellishment of jungle cock cheeks and even a red fluorescent tail.

The Black Midge

John Henderson wrote a series of articles for the *Journal of the Flyfishers' Club* which were collected in the form of a booklet for members. His dressings based on observation of the natural have been widely respected and recommended by modern-day advocates such as John Goddard.

Henderson devised dressings for the adult and pupal form of four different coloured chironomids, commenting that the main hatching time of the black midge was throughout April and again towards the end of July and beginning of August. He found that such hatches took place commonly at dusk and, although he observed that the adult fly was often ignored by the trout in favour of the pupa, he nevertheless gave this dressing for it.

Black Midge

Hook:	13-14
Silk:	Dark claret or black
Tail:	Point of the hackle used for the body
Rib:	Thin gold wire or nylex (gunmetal shade)
Body:	Two sooty-black fibres from a turkey's tail feather
Body hackle:	Black cock trimmed from one quarter to one eighth of an inch
Wings:	Two light grey cock hackle points at about 90 degrees to each other
Leg hackle:	Black hackle, untrimmed

Many dressings have been devised for the chironomids including the adult flies as they are one of the most popular food forms for trout in stillwaters, and these will be found under that title.

Black Nymph

This is a historical pattern because it was a very early attempt to imitate a natural insect. It was devised by R. C. Bridgett and given in his book, *Loch Fishing in Theory and Practice*, 1924, which as late as 1960 was regarded by C. F. Walker as the best work to appear on fishing in stillwater. Bridgett originally devised a pattern which he called the Green Spider, and decided that its success on the Scottish lochs, which he habitually fished, was due to its resemblance to the larva of the green midge. He renamed it the Green Nymph and proceeded to develop two further patterns on similar lines which he called the Black Nymph and the Olive Nymph.

Black Nymph

Logically, one would assume that they represented black and olive chironomids but Bridgett never specifically says so, and by their very name he may have considered them to be imitations of ephemerid nymphs. What he does say is that they should be fished on the point. His original dressing was:

Hook:	Not given but suggest 12-16
Silk:	Not given but suggest black
Tail:	Soft dark speckled guinea hen
Rib:	Fine silver
Body:	Black ostrich herl
Hackle:	Soft dark speckled guinea hen

Donald Overfield confesses that he is not sure what natural it is intended to represent, but has taken many fish with it from Scottish stillwaters and from southern trout streams. In his version a very short-fibred guinea fowl feather is used for the hackle.

Black Palmer

A very ancient fly recommended as an early season pattern for which three dressings were given by Thomas Barker in his book, *The Art of Angling*, in 1651. "Tied Palmer" refers to the hackle being wound the length of the body.

I give a dressing by Alfred Ronalds from his pioneer work, *The Fly-Fisher's Entomology*, which he said represented a hairy caterpillar and was claimed to be particularly attractive to Thames trout.

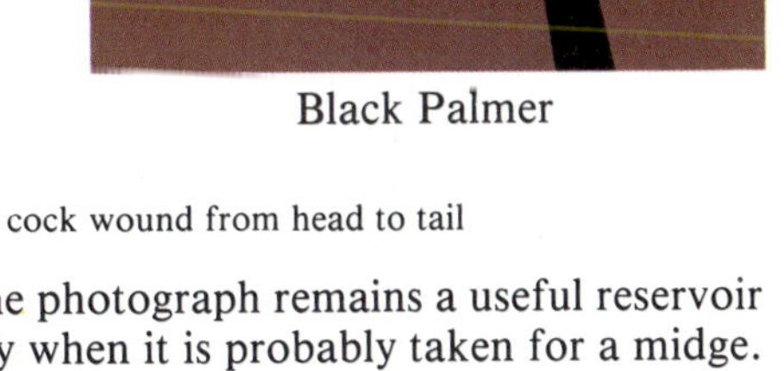

Black Palmer

Hook:	8
Rib:	Gold tinsel
Body:	Black ostrich herl wound thicker at the shoulder
Hackle:	Large furnace from the rump of a game cock wound from head to tail

The traditional Black Palmer shown in the photograph remains a useful reservoir fly. It is often used early season as a bob fly when it is probably taken for a midge. Such is its versatility, it can be taken as a general representation of a sedge or a moth or even a black beetle.

See also under Black Hackled Dry Fly, Bumbles and Red Palmer.

Black Pennell

This fly and its variations were devised by H. Cholmondeley-Pennell who introduced the turned-down eyed fly hook in 1886. Brown, yellow and green were other colours used by the inventor, but it is the black version which is probably the most popular of all flies used on the Scottish lochs. It is also used extensively on the Irish loughs. It has taken fish for me as far north as Loch Naver and as far south as Siblyback in Cornwall. I use it as a single fly, but it is commonly used when boat fishing as a top dropper or bob fly.

Hook:	10-13
Tail:	Tippet fibres. Sometimes a small golden pheasant crest feather is added
Tag:	Fine silver tinsel
Rib:	Fine oval silver
Body:	Black floss silk, very thin
Hackle:	Black cock, long in fibre and dressed sparsely

Black Pennell

What trout take the Black Pennell for is not certain, but early in the season it is probably a midge. Brian Peterson, the former Scottish champion of champions and an international fly fisher, for whom it is a favourite fly, believes it comes closest to imitating the heather fly, whilst the silver tag gives it a semblance of the hatching midge. Certainly, tied to size 16 and 18 hooks, it can be very effective in hatches of tiny black midges.

David Collyer says he has always had more success with the Claret Pennell which uses claret tying silk, gold ribbing, claret seal's fur for body and a furnace cock hackle.

Surprisingly enough this fly is not mentioned in Courtney Williams' classic *Dictionary of Trout Flies*. Is it too irreverent to think that its dressing was too close to his father's invention, Williams's Favourite, to be included?

Black Sedge
(Athripsodes nigronervosus)

The black sedge is nearly half an inch (11 to 13mm) in length with long all-black antennae which distinguish it from the black silverhorns because they have no white annulations. Another similar but slightly smaller species of black sedge is *Silo nigricornis*. These are day flying sedges often found in small swarms near the bankside.

Terry Thomas's Dark Sedge, one of his series of three representational artificials of different hues, will imitate both the black sedge and the black silverhorns.

Dark Sedge (Terry Thomas)

The deer hair gives it a natural shape and good aerodynamic and floating qualities.

Hook:	4-14 as required
Body:	Black wool or chenille
Body hackle:	Black cock tied in reverse so that it slopes forward
Wing:	Black deer hair tied on flat with cut ends to the rear and splayed out triangular fashion
Front hackle:	Black cock

It is best fished with a floating line and greased leader and cast to a rising fish or allowed to lie still with the occasional twitch. The design of the fly lends itself well to retrieving quickly so that it skitters over the water surface. This can produce exciting slashes from interested fish late in the day.

Another dressing of a Dark Sedge given by F. M. Halford in *Dry Fly Entomology* is as follows:

Hook:	10-14
Rib:	Fine gold wire
Body:	Dubbing of cream-coloured crewel (thin worsted)
Ribbing hackle:	A rusty coch-y-bonddu cock hackle
Wings:	Speckled cock pheasant wing
Hackles:	Two rusty coch-y-bonddu cock hackles at the shoulder

Black Silverhorns *(Mystacides azurea or M. nigra or Athripsodes atterimus)*

There are a number of dressings of this common sedge found in most areas between June and August even though trout do not appear keen to take them. There are three species which are black and have two long horns annulated black and white. They are often found over lakes in the daytime, but most authorities seem to think that they are more attractive to the anglers than they are to the trout.

Black Silverhorns (Alfred Ronalds)

Alfred Ronalds said they were abundant on some waters and were well taken by trout until the end of August especially in showery weather. His dressing could be made buzz by adding a silver rib and a nearly-black palmered hackle.

Hook:	13 ordinary shank
Silk:	Black
Body:	Black ostrich herl
Wings:	Feather from the wing of the cock blackbird
Hackle:	Small black cock hackle
Horns:	Grey feather from a mallard

Roger Woolley described his imitation as "worth a trial" stipulating more hackle for the lake version.

Hook: 14
Body: Very dark olive-green tying silk or black quill
Wings: Waterhen wing, rolled and tied low over body
Hackle: Black cock
Horns: Fibres from a speckled teal feather

A more modern version is by John Henderson who observed that the silverhorns do not come out in any numbers until the late afternoon.

Hook: 15
Silk: Nylusta (gunmetal)
Rib: Pale green gossamer thread
Body: Black polymer dubbing or three fibres from a magpie's tail
Body hackle: Black cock trimmed to taper from one quarter of an inch to one sixteenth
Shoulder hackle: Black hen or a small feather from a black hen's breast

Blae and Black
(Chironomus anthracinus)

This is the name given in Scotland to an early season midge of medium size with grey-black segmented body. In Ireland, this dark species appearing in the spring is referred to as the duck fly or black fly. There have been many developments of the midge pupa in recent years, some quite sophisticated, but the Blae and Black is still worth retaining as a general representation in the early season. It is commonly used on the dropper when fishing a team of flies from a boat, and works best just in or below the surface film.

Blae and Black

Hook: D/E 12-16
Silk: Black
Tail: A few fibres of golden pheasant tippet or red-dyed hackle fibres
Rib: Flat or oval silver tinsel
Body: Black floss, wool or seal's fur
Wings: Silvery-grey wild duck wing feather or medium starling
Hackle: Black hen

There is a modified version devised by Thomas Clegg who is considered by Donald Overfield and others to be one of our most thoughtful professional dressers and an expert in the use of fluorescent materials. Apart from the omission of the tail, the key difference is the replacement of the traditional wild duck wing by fluorescent floss tied spent.

Hook:	12-18, singles and doubles
Silk:	Black gossamer well waxed
Rib:	Five turns of silver wire
Body:	Black gossamer
Wings:	Six lengths of electron-white DRF floss, tied spent
Hackle:	Small black cock, one turn behind the wings and two turns in front

Other members of the Blae family include the Blae and Silver which has a flat silver tinsel body and pale badger hackle, Blae and Blue, and Blae and Gold.

Blagdon Green Midge
(Endochironomus albipennis)

Blagdon Green Midge
(Hackled version)

This chironomid found at Blagdon from which it takes its name has usually been considered to be *chironomus viridis* but John Goddard finds that *albipennis* is more common. It has a bright emerald-green body with a brownish thorax and faintly white wings. The fly hatches out over most of the summer months often across the middle of the day though never in large numbers. Fish are often difficult to tempt on the artificial like the imitations of most adult chironomids.

Hook:	14-16
Body:	Emerald-green wool
Wings:	Stiff white cock hackle wound at shoulder only

or:

Hook:	13-14
Body:	A strand from a swan's feather dyed emerald-green
Wings:	Two light grey cock hackle points
Hackle:	A Plymouth Rock (grizzle) cock's hackle wound from tail to shoulder, cut to shorten the fibres
Rib:	Thin gold wire

The latter is a dressing by John Henderson, and as trout are much more likely to feed voraciously on the pupa, I give this pattern which he called the Green Midge Nymph.

Hook:	14
Silk:	Light olive green
Whisk:	Tag of medium green floss silk or polymer dubbing cut short
Rib:	Flat silver tinsel wound on so as to show the green dubbing between turns
Body:	Medium green polymer dubbing
Thorax:	Medium olive polymer dubbing
Hackle:	Light dun hen, two turns only

This pattern should be fished like all midge pupae imitations.

Blagdon Olive Midge
(Chironomus tentans)

Blagdon Olive Midge

Whilst *chironomus tentans* is known as the Blagdon Olive Midge, Harris points out that there are several other species which could equally be called olive midges, and so the artificial can be taken to represent all of them. Most are large — over half an inch — and in Ireland, because of their habit of flying along the water surface, are also called Racehorses. They are of a pale olive-yellow hue and often hatch in the late evening in August and September.

Hook: 14-16
Body: Natural heron's herl
Wings: Two blue dun cock hackle points
Hackle: Stiff olive cock's hackle at shoulder only

J. R. Harris gives a dressing for what he calls the Large Olive Midge or Buzzer as follows:

Hook: 12-14
Rib: Gold wire
Body: Hare's ear and pale olive seal's fur mixed
Shoulder hackle: Cream badger cock tied spent fashion
Rib hackle: Cream or pale badger cock

He also points out that on the limestone lakes and ponds where the large olive midges are found the flies often hatch so prolifically that they tend to form into small swarms or clumps which trout will take in preference to single flies. He offers a special dressing for this.

Midge Clump or Swarm

Hook: 6-7
Rib: Gold wire
Body: Pale olive swan herl or seal's fur
Hackles: Three or four stiff cuckoo cock saddle or neck hackles dyed pale olive, wound from head to tail

Bloodworm

See under Chironomid Larva

Bluebottle *(Calliphora vomitoria or C. erythrocephala)*

Bluebottle (Taff Price)

Its larva — the maggot — is one of the best fish catchers ever, but I know no-one who has actually taken a fish on its terrestrial adult, the bluebottle, though Courtney Williams says that it is a good dapping fly. Yet there have been many patterns for the bluebottle since the days of Alfred Ronalds, and conceivably the natural can be blown onto the water. Ronalds' pattern is:

Hook: 12
Body: Bright blue floss silk tied with light brown silk thread, showing the brown at the head
Wings: Starling's wing feather
Legs: Black hackle from a cock wrapped down the principal part of the body

Roger Woolley also devised a dressing for the bluebottle:

Hook: 12
Body: A dyed-blue hackle with the fibre cut short
Wings: Dun cock hackle points
Hackle: Black cock
Head: Rich brown wool

Taff Price, to whom I am indebted for the Latin name of the bluebottle, has given us a most lifelike imitation:

Hook: 12
Silk: Black
Rib: Black ostrich herl
Body: Blue lurex
Wings: Grey hackle points tied over the back
Hackle: Black

Blue Leaf Beetle
(Chrysomela donacia)

Blue Leaf Beetle

This is a dressing given by Taff Price for beetles of the chrysomelidae group which live on water plants. They are numerous on his lake, and are found on the surface of the water and in trout's stomachs. David Jacques quotes authorities on the water beetle *(Donacia crassipes)* who state that the female, having bitten holes in the leaves of water plants, lays her eggs around them and the larvae consequently drop through the cavity onto the bed of the lake and feed on the roots of the plant.

Hook:	14-16
Silk:	Black
Body:	Black polypropylene tied fat
Back:	Blue raffene varnished (or blue lurex)
Hackle:	Black (optional)

Taff Price tells us that imitations of this group of beetles are worth trying on breezy days as trout take this insect more than is commonly realised.

The imitation is intended to be fished dry.

Blue Upright

Blue Upright

A well-known West Country general pattern which may suggest the dark olive or iron-blue. Here, the traditional dressing is tied on a small hook, and recommended by Peter Lapsley as an imitation of the adult midge when trout seem to be feeding on the winged insects. Peter has had some considerable success with it.

Hook:	U/E 14-16
Silk:	Purple
Whisks:	A small bunch of medium blue dun cock hackle fibres
Body:	Stripped natural peacock herl
Hackle:	Two medium blue dun cock hackles, very short in the fibre

Tied on a size 11 or 12 hook and with a big hackle which is a bright glassy dark blue, Skues considered it was suggestive of a stone fly and a willow fly in particular.

Bow-Tie Buzzer

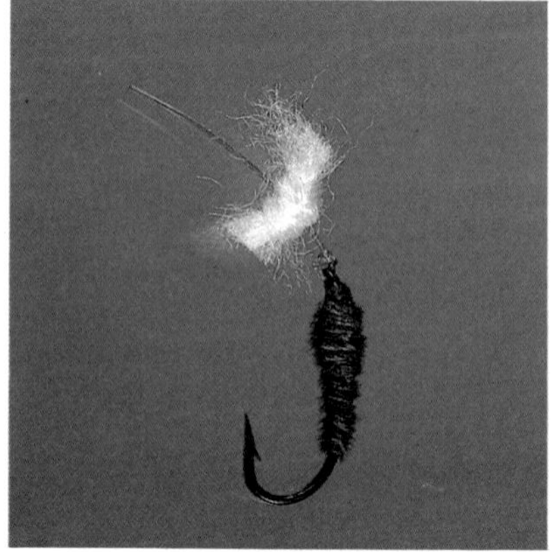

Bow-Tie Buzzer

This pattern was devised by Frank Sawyer whose book, *Nymphs and the Trout*, explained his theory and practice of nymph fishing based on over thirty years' experience as a keeper on the Wiltshire Avon. The unusual feature of his dressing is the tying of the white fringe or cilia on the leader rather than on the hook. Sawyer contended that at the point of hatching, the pupa, which is generally vertical, is in continuous movement. The piece of white nylon wool simulating the cilia moves freely on the leader to achieve this effect.

Hook:	D/E 12
Body:	Gold-coloured copper wire over silver foil
Rib:	Four or five fibres of red cock pheasant tail fibres wound together with the copper wire
Thorax:	Extra windings of the above

The white fringe or cilia is carried on the end of the leader by threading the nylon point through the eye of the hook, making a slip knot in it, and then attaching a tiny piece of white nylon wool.

Breatherlizer

This is an early British streamer type fly based on Canadian models and devised by Alec Iles for fishing Chew Valley Lake. It is meant to imitate a stickleback and was fished by its inventor with a fast retrieve which brought him good bags of trout at Chew Magna in the 1960's.

Hook:	D/E 6-8
Tail:	Fibres from a soft black cock or hen hackle
Body:	Flat silver tinsel
Wings:	Two hot-orange cock hackles, with two Green Highlander hackles outside, streamer fashion
Eyes:	Jungle cock or substitute
Hackle:	Badger wound as a collar
Head:	Black varnish

Breatherlizer

It also works well later on in the season as a fry imitator fished more slowly.

Brer Rabbit Nymph

A pattern of unknown origin given by Peter Lapsley in his excellent book, *Trout from Stillwaters*, as an effective imitation of a dragonfly nymph.

Hook:	L/S 8-12 (4-8 in high summer)
Silk:	Brown
Tail:	Three or four pheasant tail fibres
Rib:	Fine gold wire
Underbody:	6-10 turns of fine lead wire under thorax (optional)
Abdomen:	Brown wool
Thorax:	Rabbit's guard hairs
Wing case:	Pheasant tail fibres
Legs:	One turn of grey partridge hackle trimmed off above and below

Brer Rabbit Nymph

It is best fished on a floating line and long leader slowly on the bottom. As the natural will occasionally move fast by ejecting water from its rectum, a periodic sink and draw or twitch on the line will produce a take.

Brown and Green Nymph

Brown and Green Nymph

Probably Tom Ivens' best known pattern after the Black and Peacock Spider. It was described by its originator as of minnowish appearance, but I am inclined to agree with David Collyer that it is often taken for a hatching sedge pupa in its smaller sizes. It can be tied either leaded or unleaded.

Hook:	6-10
Silk:	Brown
Tail:	Tips of four strands of peacock herl
Rib:	Oval gold tinsel
Body:	Strands of green and brown ostrich herl wound together
Back:	Peacock herl carried directly to the head and tied down
Head:	The four strands twisted together and three or four turns wound to form a bold head

Twice in one week I took two rainbows on the same cast with this fly retrieving fairly fast and smoothly just below the surface. I had never done it before nor have since. In a poll of sixty anglers at Two Lakes in 1974 by David Jacques the Brown and Green Nymph was the first choice every time it was mentioned.

Brown and Green Sedge

Brown and Green Sedge

Richard Walker has devised a number of sedge patterns which utilise bunches of hackle fibres or feather fibres for wings in a similar manner to those of Joscelyn Lane, and I have found them all to be most effective. Tied in at the head and splayed out in a narrowish V they give a much more lifelike imitation of a sedge outline than palmered versions. Richard Walker recommends that immediately after tying the fly it be treated with Permaflote and again prior to use.

Hook:	L/S 10
Silk:	Hot-orange varnished to receive the twisted ostrich herl
Body:	Light green ostrich herl clipped close
Wing:	Cree (ginger grizzle) cock hackle fibres
Hackle:	Natural light red cock hackle

Fished on a floating line and fully greased leader, and either left stationary and tweaked occasionally or skimmed across the surface quickly, the fly can be most attractive to trout when brown sedges are on the water.

Brown Moth

Brown Moth

Moths are mostly beautiful nocturnal creatures chiefly of use to the angler as dusk approaches. The markings and textures of their wings are virtually impossible to imitate, and John Goddard's suggestion that the fisherman should carry patterns in shades of brown, pale brown, ginger and white is a rational and sensible one.

Courtney Williams gives the following dressing which is a general pattern designed to represent any brownish and fairly large moth.

Hook:	10-12
Silk:	Orange
Body:	Brown floss silk, rather thick
Wings:	Dark owl
Hackle:	Dark red cock from head to tail

Moths of one kind or another emerge from their chrysalises from June onwards and may fall on the water. Artificials are best fished on floating lines and greased leaders, and either pulled steadily across the surface to cause a wake or cast onto the water and allowed to lie with an occasional twitch to simulate the struggles of the natural.

Brown Nymph

Tom Ivens has a significant place in the development of stillwater angling. His book, *Still-Water Fly Fishing*, based on his early experiences on Northampton reservoirs, became standard reading for the hordes of new fly fishermen attracted by the opening up of new waters, and most of them had several of his fly dressings in their boxes including the Brown Nymph given here.

Hook:	7-12
Silk:	Brown
Rib:	Oval gold tinsel
Body:	One strand of brown-dyed ostrich herl
Back:	From bend to head stripped flue from two strands of green-dyed ostrich herl
Head:	Two strands of peacock herl twisted together. Two strands separated and carried backwards to form horns

Brown Nymph

Ivens recommends that it be fished in the middle or upper part of the water. He stated that it was excellent when fish were taking nymphs as they came to the surface and should be fished slowly. He did not claim that it represented any specific insect.

In the small sizes he said a brown wool dubbed body, well teased out, was as effective as ostrich herl. He added the cryptic comment that it seemed to be getting closer to the maggot profile!

See also under Collyer Brown Nymph.

Brown Sedge

The natural brown sedge *(Anabolia nervosa)* is an autumnal species varying in size from three to five eighths of an inch (11 to 16mm), and dark brown in colour. It is very common, emerging in some quantity often in the neighbourhood of weed beds during the evening.

Brown Sedge (Terry Thomas)

The patterns given here adequately imitate it, but are intended as general representations of brown sedges. David Jacques was one of our foremost authorities on sedge flies, and therefore his impressionistic pattern of a brown sedge is bound to be effective although he modestly says that brown-coloured flies of his colleagues' tying do equally well.

Hook:	14
Silk:	Chocolate-brown
Rib:	Fine gold twist
Body:	Any chocolate-brown silk, wool, herl or dubbing ribbed with similar colour hackle
Wings:	Game cock or hen, plain side outside, bunched and rolled, sloping back to the bend
Hackle:	Cock feather dyed chocolate-brown

This general impression of a sedge fly by Terry Thomas which is called the Standard or Brown Standard Sedge is one that I frequently use. The deer hair acts almost as a parachute thus ensuring that the fly almost always alights on the water the right way up. It also contributes to its excellent floating propensity.

Hook:	10-12
Body:	Dark pheasant tail fibres wound on thick with a body hackle of ginger cock, tied in reverse so that it slopes forward
Wing:	Grey deer hair tied on flat with the cut end to the rear
Hackle:	Ginger cock

Richard Walker's dressing which he calls the Large Brown Sedge uses a bunch of hackle or feather fibres to lie close to the body to form the wing.

Hook:	L/S 10
Silk:	Orange
Tag:	Yellow fluorescent wool or floss
Body:	Mahogany-brown ostrich herl, very fine
Wing:	Light brown cock hackle fibres
Hackle:	Light brown

The patterns can be cast to individual risers and left motionless with the occasional twitch, or skimmed back over the surface.

Brown Silverhorns
(Athripsodes cinereus)

Brown Silverhorns
(John Henderson)

The brown silverhorns, like the silver, are very common sedge flies, and are over the water on most days in summer often close to the bank. The colour of their roof-like wings tends to be brown with some mottling, and they are chiefly conspicuous for their very long antennae sometimes nearly three times as long as the flies themselves and ringed clearly with white.

Opinions as to whether they attract trout are sharply divided. Eric Taverner said that he had not met anyone who had been successful with an imitation, and John Goddard states that the naturals are only occasionally found in trout autopsies largely because they rarely descend to the water surface. C. F. Walker said that they were of little more account than the alder.

J. R. Harris informs us that fish in some of the large limestone lakes in Ireland on warm calm evenings in July and August feed keenly on the various silverhorns, and gives us a dressing which he considers one of the most useful dry flies for evenings on any small stillwater on which the naturals occur.

Hook:	13-15
Body:	Grey or green seal's fur
Rib hackle:	Brown cuckoo or grizzled cock
Rib:	Gold wire
Wing:	Speckled partridge tail tied to lie along the hook and protrude beyond the bend
Shoulder hackle:	Brown cuckoo or grizzled cock

John Henderson points out that there are not many day-flying sedges like the silverhorns to give the dry fly man a chance, and gives a dressing.

Hook:	14
Silk:	Nylusta (medium brown)
Rib:	Nylusta (gunmetal shade)
Body:	Dark green polymer or seal's fur dubbing mixed with hare's ear
Body hackle:	Rusty dun cock trimmed from one quarter of an inch to one sixteenth of an inch
Shoulder hackle:	Woodcock's neck or landrail's feather from the wing

David Collyer says that he has seen the naturals frequently taken by fish and has found them in trout stomach contents. He gives a dressing which he fishes at a rather slower speed than is usual for sedge patterns.

Hook:	L/S 12-14
Silk:	Brown (sherry spinner)
Rib:	End of tying silk
Body:	Dark speckled turkey tail
Body hackle:	Two red cock hackles palmered and clipped top and bottom
Wings:	Stub ends of body material bent back over the body and tied down with two turns of silk
Horns:	Two strands of teal breast or two hackle stalks from a Plymouth Rock cape sloping back and outwards over the body
Front hackle:	Two ginger or red cock hackles clipped bottom only

Bumbles

Golden Olive Bumble

The word 'bumble' is virtually another name for a fly tied in the palmer fashion and dates back at least to Charles Cotton, that famous fisherman of the Dove and friend and collaborator of Izaak Walton. The traditional Derbyshire patterns use floss silk ribbed with a strand of peacock's sword feather and are hackled the length of the hook. They are usually fished wet and are renowned as takers of grayling. Halford found them interesting, and devised some to use as dry flies. The Derbyshire patterns include the Orange, Yellow, Honey Dun and Steel-Blue, but possibly the best is the Claret Bumble, the dressing of which is as follows:

Hook:	12-14
Body:	Claret floss silk ribbed with a strand of peacock's sword feather
Hackle:	Medium blue dun cock wound up the body

A more modern development of the Bumble to fish stillwater, and especially the larger Irish lakes like Lough Conn, was devised by the Irish fisherman and author, T. C. Kingsmill Moore. He aimed to combine the Irish fly-dressers' flair for colour combination and translucency with the English Bumble type of construction. He wanted a general purpose fly which was opalescent, with gleam but not dazzle, with gentle but not gaudy contrasts, and would suggest the movement of insects caught in the surface film or blown along by the wind.

He found the gleam and sparkle by tying in two different-coloured cock hackles at the same point and winding them along the body together so that the fibres were completely commingled. The winding has to be done very carefully. If too close, the fly loses transparency. If too wide, the life and brilliance are lost. A long, sparse, soft hackle from a game bird is tied in at the head with longer fibres than the two stiff cock hackles. Though supported by these hackles, its longer tips are free to wave and struggle as if the creature had a movement of its own.

The Golden Olive was Kingsmill Moore's first choice, and it is based on the colouring of the Invicta.

Golden Olive Bumble

Hook:	Wide gape 8-12
Tail:	Golden pheasant topping
Rib:	Oval gold tinsel
Body:	Golden-olive seal's fur
Body hackles:	Cock dyed golden-olive, and medium red natural cock
Shoulder hackle:	Blue jay or gallina dyed blue longer in the fibre than the cock hackles

Kingsmill Moore's next most rated pattern was the

Claret Bumble

Hook:	8-12
Tail:	Four strands of golden pheasant tippet
Rib:	Oval gold
Body:	Medium claret seal's fur
Body hackles:	Cock dyed medium claret, and natural black cock
Shoulder hackle:	Blue jay or gallina dyed blue

His artificial for a dark day with low clouds and showers has its hackles wound rather more closely than the others so that its bulk may show against a dark sky. Because of its colour — like a bruise — and partly for its powers of execution it was named

The Bruiser

Hook:	8-12
Tail:	A bunch of flax-blue wool
Rib:	Silver wire
Body:	Rich gentian-blue wool
Body hackles:	Cock dyed gentian-blue, and natural black cock. These are taken the whole way to the head
Shoulder hackle:	None

Other patterns for the Bumble are Fiery Brown, Grey Ghost, Silver Blue and Magenta and Gold.

In his book, *A Man May Fish*, Kingsmill Moore does not describe how he fished his Bumbles, but a slow to steady retrieve is almost certainly the best. I intend to give them a trial on one or two of the big waters like Grafham and Rutland.

Conrad Voss Bark has extended the principle of the use of mixed palmered hackles to his nymphs. See under Conrad Voss Bark Nymph.

Butcher

Butcher

A traditional pattern of tremendous popularity virtually world-wide on both stillwater and rivers. Invented in 1836 by a Mr. Jewhurst of Tunbridge Wells together with a butcher named Moon, it was originally known as Moon's Fly. It has held sway on Scottish lochs for many years, usually on the top dropper when boat fishing.

It works particularly well early in the season, when John Goddard considers it could be taken for a midge pupa, especially that of the grey boy, formerly known as the orange and silver midge. This midge often has bright red segments on the body. Generally, however, it is regarded as an imitation of a small fish or a pure attractor. Fished on the tail in September and October, its sparkling body, dark blue back and flash of red give it a fry-like appearance.

Hook:	D/E 10-16
Silk:	Black
Tail:	Red ibis or substitute
Body:	Flat silver tinsel or lurex
Wing:	Blue mallard wing feather
Hackle:	Black cock or hen hackle

The Bloody Butcher tied with a red hackle is almost as popular as the Butcher itself. The Gold Butcher uses a gold tinsel body.

David Collyer ties a Butcher with a teal wing which he calls the Teal-Winged Butcher. Over a three-day period at Chew it accounted for a considerable number of brown trout that were attacking shoals of roach fry.

Bob Church has devised a modern version of a Bloody Butcher which he calls the Poly-Butcher.

Hook:	As required
Silk:	Black
Tail:	Red cock hackle fibres
Underbody:	Red tinsel or red silk — one layer
Overbody:	Clear stretched polythene
Wing:	Black squirrel hair and spray of black marabou
Throat hackle:	Red cock hackle fibres
Eye:	Jungle cock or substitute

He says that the polythene body makes it extremely hard-wearing, and that it has the potential to take trout when other lures are drawing a blank.

See also under Kingfisher Butcher.

Buzzer Nymph

Buzzer Nymph

This is another creation of Dr. Howard Bell who was the first person to study fly life seriously at Blagdon. Such observation produced his early and effective midge pupa imitation. The 'wings' probably mark a pioneer attempt to imitate the breathing filaments, and the 'legs' the moment of hatching.

Hook:	10-12
Silk:	Black
Rib:	Flat gold tinsel
Body:	Black floss silk taken partly round the bend of the hook
Wings:	A short tuft of white floss silk tied in just behind the head, about one eighth of an inch long
Legs:	A few fibres of brown mallard shoulder feather tied in under the head and sloping backwards

The Buzzer Nymph works best in June and from mid-August to the end of September. It can be fished extremely slowly in the surface film with a floating line and greased leader or moved more quickly with a floating line and sunk leader.

Caddis *(Trichoptera)*

Caddis

The word 'caddis' or 'cadaz' goes back to 1400, and was used at various times to describe cotton or silk used as padding for worsted yarn and, later, for tape or ribbon. Travelling purveyors of such materials, pinning their wares on their coats, were known as 'caddis men'. Richard and Charles Bowlker refer in their *Art of Angling*, 1747, to the Cadis Fly. "While in the state of a grub, he is greatly to be admired, the outside husk he lives in being curiously wrought with gravel or sand." Richard Walker's dressing of the larva of the sedge fly conforms neatly with this description.

Hook:	L/S 10
Body:	Cream or white floss silk built fat. Soaked in vycoat and while still wet shaken in a tin full of dry clean fine sand. Left overnight to set
Head end:	A few turns of amber or light green wool
Hackle:	Two turns of any soft, short-fibred black hackle
Head:	Fat and black, well varnished

The originator advises that the fly be trundled along the bottom. One of its advantages is that when a trout takes it, there is plenty of time to tighten as it feels like a real caddis which fish are in the habit of swallowing whole. Richard Walker warns anglers not to fish a point finer than 6lb as the fly is heavy and soon weakens anything less strong.

See also under Caddis Larva, Cased Caddis, Gravel or Pebble Caddis, Twig or Debris Caddis, Stick Fly.

Caddis Larva *(Trichoptera)*

Caddis Larva (Raleigh Boaze Jnr)

Some types of caddis do not live in cases but in silken tunnels in the lake bed which they may have to leave periodically to obtain food. C. F. Walker considered that these non-case-making larvae were sufficiently numerous in stillwater to devise a dressing.

Hook:	Long mayfly 11-13 weighted
Rib:	Gold tinsel, tightly wound to mark the segments
Body:	Three quarters yellow and one quarter green seal's fur only slightly tapered and fairly smooth, with a few strands left projecting at the tail end
Hackle:	A woodcock's under-covert feather
Head:	A few turns of pheasant tail herl

A version of the caddis out of its case using more modern materials is that of Raleigh Boaze, Jnr., an American. One day in the research laboratory where he worked he inadvertently wrapped a strip of latex around a pencil, and it struck him that it looked very much like a caddis larva. His Ral's Caddis Larva has each spiral of latex overlapping the other to create a segmented effect.

Hook:	8 Mustad beak 9620
Silk:	Dark brown or black
Underbody:	Light yellow nylon yarn
Outer body:	Latex strip cut from a sheet used for dental dam. Cream or light tan
Thorax:	Dubbed muskrat fur
Head:	Dark brown or black according to tying silk

Latex is available as a fly-dressing material but is, of course, inanimate without the aid of fur or feather. On the other hand, Boaze contents that the latex larva has a look and feel that is intriguing to both fish and fisherman.

Caenis Nymph
(Caenis horaria and robusta)

Caenis Nymph (John Henderson)

Every fisherman is familiar with the 'White Curse' or 'Angler's Curse' and, though there are six species, only the above two are of concern to the stillwater angler. The tiny brown nymphs have a second pair of gills large and plate-like on top of the abdomen, and C. F. Walker says that the effect divides the body of the nymph into three distinct parts, namely thorax, gills and abdomen, which give it the appearance of wearing a long-skirted coat. The nymphs creep slowly along the silt and debris of the bottom and are very difficult to see. The adults emerge from the end of May to the end of August, and this is the best time to fish nymph imitations when the naturals are rising to the surface. They may make a number of trial ascents before finally hatching, and so sink and draw a foot or so below the surface can be effective. C. F. Walker's dressing is as follows:

Hook:	16 for robusta (dusky broadwing)
	17 for horaria (yellow broadwing)
Tail:	Fibres from a speckled partridge feather, very short
Rib & tag:	Silver tinsel
Abdomen:	A few turns of medium brown condor herl
Gills, thorax & wing pads:	Dark hare's ear or brown seal's fur in two sections
Leg hackle:	Medium grizzled honey hen

John Henderson considered the nymph more effective than the dry fly as a trout catcher because caenis usually hatch massively at dusk when it becomes impossible to differentiate one's artificial from the myriad naturals on the water. He devised the following dressing:

Hook:	16
Silk:	Light flesh-coloured nylusta
Tail:	Four or five short fibres from a white cock's hackle
Rib:	Thin gold wire
Body:	Natural ostrich herl (pale stone colour)
Thorax:	Several turns of bronze peacock herl or dark brown polymer dubbing

For a modern dressing I go to Bob Carnill who takes the view that the early evening caenis hatch is a prelude to the main event, the emergence of sedges. Until then he fishes a team of caenis nymphs, hardly ever employing dry or spent patterns.

Hook:	14-16
Silk:	Brown
Tail:	Three fibres from a brown partridge hackle
Rib:	Stripped peacock quill
Body:	Strip of dark brown herl (dyed swan, goose or heron)

Wing case/ thorax cover:	Quills from the narrow side of a heron primary
Thorax:	Hare's ear
Legs:	Partridge fibres

Caenis Dun
(Caenis horaria and robusta)

Caenis Dun (F. E. Sawyer)

C. F. Walker gave *caenis horaria* the name of yellow broadwing whilst he called *caenis robusta* dusky broadwing. Though these flies are no more than one quarter of an inch (4mm) and three eighths of an inch (5 to 6mm) long respectively, they are called Broadwings because their wings are very wide in relation to their bodies. Their wings are a white diaphanous grey, thoraces murky brown and abdomens a pale creamy-grey or yellow. John Goddard says that it is very difficult to imitate the duns successfully; nevertheless a number of attempts have been made.

The fly did not escape the attention of F. M. Halford who gave a dressing which he called Fisherman's Curse devised by Sir Maurice Duff-Gordon.

Hook:	17
Body:	Black tying silk with flat silver tag
Hackle:	Badger, over three turns of black ostrich worked at shoulder

J. R. Harris devised a dressing for the dun for evening fishing.

Hook:	16-17
Silk:	Brown
Tail:	Cream cock
Body:	Cream-coloured herl or floss silk
Shoulder hackle:	Pale cream cock or henny cock tied in by the butt end with some of the soft downy fibres still remaining on the stalk; this is wound slightly towards the tail so as to occupy about one third of the hook shank

Frank Sawyer's dressing is:

Hook:	20
Silk:	Black
Tail:	Three short fibres of a cream cock hackle
Body:	Mole's fur spun on the black silk
Thorax:	Centre stalk of a black ostrich herl tied in to form a hump-backed effect with the shiny side uppermost
Hackle:	Three turns of a tiny dull dark blue hackle

Trout are said to have a characteristic rise to caenis which consists of a quick head and tail rise, and often with further rises in a direct line. Consequently, the angler should cast his fly ahead in anticipation of the next rise.

For other caenis imitations see under Last Hope and Lucky Alphonse.

Caenis Spinner

(Caenis horaria and robusta)

Caenis Spinner (C. F. Walker)

The duns of the caenis cast off their imago skins within a few minutes of leaving the water. They alight on any support, including an angler's clothes or skin, in order to moult and then return to the water after mating to lay their eggs, falling spent on the water. Often such hatches and moultings are prolific, and I remember an occasion on the Elinor Trout Fishery near Thrapston when I was covered from head to foot with the tiny creatures, making it difficult to breathe, and perforce had to retire from the waterside until the hatch subsided.

Despite the recognised difficulty of catching trout preoccupied by caenis, there are a great number of imitations of the spinner. Many of C. F. Walker's patterns based on his pioneer research have hardly been bettered, and I give his spinner dressing first.

Hook:	16-18
Tail:	White cock spade or saddle hackle fibres, long in proportion to the body
Rib:	Silver tinsel
Body:	White seal's fur
Wing:	Pale blue dun hen hackle
Hackle:	Short white cock

This is for the dusky broadwing. For the yellow broadwing the body has a dubbing of yellow silkworm silk and it is dressed on a size 17 hook.

I include Frank Sawyer's pattern to illustrate how his detailed observation develops the dressing from that of his nymph.

Hook:	20
Silk:	Black
Tail:	Three blue cock hackle fibres, about twice the length of the hook
Body:	Cream-coloured dubbing
Thorax:	Centre stalk of a black ostrich herl tied in to form a hump-backed effect with the shiny side uppermost
Hackle:	A tiny bright blue cock hackle, wound three times round, finished off with black silk and a spot of varnish

Two other dressings bring a different technique to the problem of winging such a tiny pattern. The first is John Henderson's.

Hook:	16
Silk:	Light flesh-coloured nylusta
Tail:	Four or five long fibres from a white cock hackle
Rib:	Light flesh-coloured nylusta
Body:	Fibre from a white swan feather, dyed cream
Wings:	White cock hackle spread out horizontally and trimmed to shape and size
Legs:	Light stone-coloured ostrich herl, two turns behind the wings

The best of our modern patterns when tiny spinners are on the water is that of Stewart Canham.

Hook:	U/E standard 18
Silk:	Fine midge
Tails:	Three fibres from a white cock hackle spread well apart
Body:	White polythene, narrow from a white polythene bag
Thorax:	One brown condor or turkey herl
Wings:	White hen hackles, cut with wing cutter, and tied spent
Hackle:	White cock hackle, trimmed on bottom edge, and short in the fibre

Another pattern worth trying for the dun or the spinner is that splendid fly, the Grey Duster, tied in a small size. One of the most successful imitations of recent years is John Goddard's aptly-named Last Hope which is separately listed. See also Cream Spinner.

Camasunary Killer

This is a very striking lure or attractor fly mainly because it incorporates a tail and body using wool of royal blue, an uncommon colour for fly dressings. It was originally designed by Stephen Johnson of Jedburgh whose family owns the famous Camasunary Fishery in the Isle of Skye and who is the author of *Fishing from Afar*. The fly is recommended by Peter Deane, one of our foremost fly tyers, as primarily a sea trout fly, but effective in smaller sizes for trout in lakes.

Camasunary Killer

Hook:	8-10
Tail:	Royal blue wool
Rib:	Oval silver tinsel
Body:	Two equal halves of royal blue wool, followed by Firebrand DFM wool
Hackle:	Black cock, rather long in the fibre

David Jacques has noticed that when the female winged fly of the damsel descends to lay her eggs and species of predominantly bright blue colouring are abundant, sunken lures such as Camasunary Killer are at their most effective.

The Caperer
(Halesus radiatus, Halesus digitatus)

Caperer (Taff Price)

Whilst some anglers may prefer to carry in their boxes dry sedges of varying sizes and basic colours, others like imitations of particular species. Here are artificials for two of the largest members of the sedge family which are closely related. Both are over three quarters of an inch (20 to 23mm) in length with yellowy-brown wings and browny-orange bodies. They are probably called caperer because, after hatching, they scuttle across the water surface to the bank. The females dance and flit over the water in early evening as they lay their eggs. They are most commonly seen in late August, September and October.

The classic pattern is that of William Lunn.

Hook:	12-14
Silk:	Crimson
Body:	Four or five strands from a dark turkey tail feather, and two strands from a swan feather dyed yellow. The swan to make a ring of yellow in the centre of the body
Wings:	From a coot's wing quill feather which has been bleached and dyed chocolate brown
Hackles:	One medium red cock hackle and one black cock hackle wound together in front of the wings

Taff Price contends that Lunn's Caperer is not an imitation of the natural caperer and gives the following:

Hook:	L/S 8-10
Silk:	Orange
Rib:	Orange silk
Body:	Orange seal's fur or poly dubbing mixed with hare's ear
Body hackle:	Cree or light ginger
Wing:	Cree fibres clipped to shape
Hackle:	Cree (two)

The fly should be fished motionless and merely twitched, or pulled back in fits and starts or retrieved quickly to achieve a scuttling motion over the water. Use a well-greased leader.

Cardinal

In the naming of flies the imagination knows no bounds. We have the contrast of the Cardinal and the Harlot but with something in common — the colour red. If, however, the flies are placed side by side, it is not difficult to decide which is the Harlot and which the Cardinal! Shall we say that the Harlot's dressing is scarlet and gaudy whilst the Cardinal's vestments are red.

Hook:	D/E 8-12
Silk:	Scarlet or black
Tail:	Red ibis or substitute
Rib:	Fine gold wire
Body:	Scarlet floss silk
Wing:	Dyed-red swan, ibis or duck
Hackle:	Scarlet-dyed cock hackle

Cardinal

It resembles nothing living, but David Collyer recalls a red(!) letter day at Weir Wood when fish were coming short to his Royal Coachman which has mainly a scarlet body and, on changing to the Cardinal, taking five fish and being broken on the sixth. Without his sole Cardinal he took no more fish.

To bring the Cardinal down in the world, Taff Price considers that with a little stretch of the imagination it could be taken for a bloodworm. After that, I will leave you to work out for yourself how to fish this priestly fly!

Cased Caddis

Early in the year, though there may be little sign of insect activity on the surface, the larvae of a number of creatures are populating the lake bed. Among these are the various caddises of the sedge fly. Most live in cases of one sort or another, and there are several realistic imitations which depict the head of the larva protruding from the case. Bob Carnill achieves this effect by tying in a head of white swan herl and calls the dressing the

Cased Caddis (Bob Carnill)

Cased Caddis

Hook:	L/S 10-12
Silk:	Black
Underbody:	Lead wire
Body (case):	Hare's ear fur, well mixed from hook bend to three quarters way along the shank
Rib:	Silver wire
Body (larva):	White swan herl, last quarter to the eye, and ribbed
Hackle:	Small black hen

In Derek Bradbury's pattern the pheasant herls and gold twist simulate the case of the caddis made up of stones and sand whilst the turn of peacock herl can be taken for the head.

Caddis Larva

Hook:	L/S D/E 10
Rib:	Gold twist, size 15
Body:	Several fibres from a centre tail feather of a golden pheasant. Just in front of the body is dubbed a small portion of hare's ear fur
Legs:	One turn of brown partridge hackle
Head:	Peacock herl

These patterns are best fished on the bottom slowly and with a very long leader.

Caterpillar *(Lepidoptera)*

The caterpillar is the larva, of course, of the butterfly and the moth, and trout undoubtedly appreciate such delicacies if they drop into the water from overhanging bushes or trees. I must confess that I have never had the enterprise to carry an artificial in my box for that special occasion, but imitations do exist, and here is one by 'Halcyon' (Henry Wade) which is at least one hundred years old and still looks to have as much potential as any.

Hook:	Limerick 12
Body:	One or more strands of green peacock herl
Rib:	Narrow gold or silver tinsel
Hackle:	Red cock or black cock, even and palmered

Green Caterpillar
(Courtney Williams)

Courtney Williams considered that caterpillar imitations offered distinct possibilities especially if the banks were overhung by trees and bushes, and, in particular, oak trees. His dressing is as follows:

Hook:	12-14 (suggest Yorkshire Sedge hook)
Body:	Emerald-green wool
Hackle:	Stiff emerald-green cock hackle wound the length of the body and clipped short

A version of the caterpillar using more modern materials is given in the Sue Burgess Fly-Tying Library:

Hook:	L/S 8-12
Silk:	Green-olive
Rib:	Yellow rayon floss
Body:	Polybody mixed to a caterpillar-green colour according to species imitated
Back:	Thin natural latex sheet
Head:	Black varnish

Chew Nymph

Chew Nymph

This is Thomas Clegg's version of the Chew Reservoir nymph which utilises fluorescent materials. Donald Overfield, who gives the pattern in his book, *Fifty Favourite Nymphs*, thinks it is worth a trial on any stillwater fishery.

Hook:	8-10
Silk:	Red
Tail:	Neon-magenta DRF filaments or three short lengths of DRF floss of the same colour
Rib:	DRF floss
Body:	Dubbed mole's fur
Back:	Mottled turkey feather over entire body
Hackle:	Folded brown hen hackle

Chief Needabeh

Chief Needabeh

A dazzling American streamer pattern named after a real Red Indian chief. David Collyer recommends its use on those hot windless days when everything has gone completely dead. He advises a floating line but with a leader of at least fourteen feet treated to make it sink. In his book on *Lures for Game, Coarse and Sea Fishing* Taff Price admits that he has never caught a fish on Chief Needabeh, but includes it because it was the first streamer pattern he ever tied and it looks so attractive — to the angler at least!

Hook:	L/S 6-10
Silk:	Black
Tag:	Oval silver tinsel
Body:	Scarlet floss silk
Rib:	Oval silver tinsel
Wings:	Two yellow hackles back to back inside, and two orange hackles outside
Hackle:	Mixed yellow and scarlet
Shoulders:	Jungle cock or substitute
Head:	Black varnish

The fly is cast as far as possible and pulled in fast with a continuous retrieve so that it is fishing not far below the surface.

Roy Masters has taken this pattern, adapted it to his own requirements, and called it:

The Chief

Hook:	L/S 8-10
Body:	Firebrand fluorescent floss silk, scarlet, or fire-orange DRF floss
Tag:	Silver tinsel
Rib:	Oval silver tinsel
Wings:	Two yellow hackles back to back inside, with two scarlet hackles outside with a jungle cock eye or substitute each side
Hackle:	Mixed scarlet and yellow cock
Head:	Black varnish

Whilst the yellow inside hackles of the wing may be hen, the outside scarlet hackles must be cock. These must be a bright scarlet and of the slim pointed type to give a striking contrast to the fly.

Chironomid Larva *(Chironomidae)*

The larvae of the chironomid or midge often comprise fifty to seventy per cent of the total deep fauna of lakes, and often in the staggering density of more than three thousand per square yard. They are thus one of the most important sources of food for fish. Their potential for the angler is great but then so is the problem of imitating them. The four hundred species of midge larva vary in size from one eighth to three quarters of an inch (2 to 19mm), and their colour can be green, blue-green, yellowish, white and red. The red, which contains haemoglobin, is familiar to the coarse fisherman as the bloodworm. Their habitat varies too although the majority live in the surface layer of mud at the bottom in U-shaped tubes open at both ends.

The biggest problem of all for the angler is to simulate their movement. They do emerge from their domiciles from time to time and swim vigorously with what John Goddard describes as a figure-of-eight lashing movement. One of the earliest attempts at imitation was that of Joscelyn Lane in his book, *Lake and Loch Fishing for Trout*. To allow for the larva's peculiar movement he devised a detached body as follows:

Red Bloodworm

Hook:	10-12
Silk:	Blood-red
Body:	(Detached) Blood-red floss tied on top of the hook and trailing for about three quarters of an inch

John Goddard's own answer was to prescribe a piece of curled feather for the tail which will clench and unclench as the fly is manoeuvred through the water. He advises a sinking line to allow the artificial to remain on the bottom and be twitched occasionally.

Red or Green Larvae

Hook:	D/E L/S 8-12
Silk:	Brown
Tail:	Two or three very curly fibres from an ibis quill (red) or heron dyed red or green to match body-colour
Rib:	Narrow silver lurex
Body:	Three or four crimson or olive-dyed condor herls or substitute mixed with a strand of fluorescent silk floss of the same colour
Thorax:	Two or three fibres of buff condor or pale brown-dyed turkey

The supple and sinuous properties of marabou for the tail fished on a very long leader and floating line or slow sinker, using long, slow pulls with the occasional twitch represent Taff Price's solution.

Marabou Bloodworm (Taff Price)

Marabou Bloodworm

Hook:	L/S 12-14
Silk:	Crimson
Tail:	A tuft of red marabou
Rib:	Fluorescent red silk
Body:	Segmented red floss silk
Head:	Peacock herl (optional)

An interesting pattern, made to look more effective by the use of a Yorkshire Sedge hook, is that devised by John Wilshaw, the editor of *Trout and Salmon*.

Bloodworm

Hook:	Yorkshire Sedge hook 10-14
Silk:	Red
Rib:	Oval gold tinsel
Body:	Scarlet seal's fur

See also under Wobble-Worm.

Chironomid Pupa *(Chironomidae)*

Chironomid pupae imitations proliferate almost as profusely as the number of chironomid species, and that is over four hundred. This is not surprising because not only do some species or other appear from late March through to October, but they vary a great deal in size and colour.

One of the pioneer attempts at imitating the midge pupa was by J. C. Mottram in his book, *Fly Fishing: Some New Arts and Mysteries* in 1914-15. He called it a Midge Larva, but with white silk ribbed with black floss silk for a body and a thorax of black floss silk it is more likely to simulate the pupa.

Much of the early systematic investigation was carried out by J. R. Harris and C. F. Walker, and the latter's dressing provides us with a versatile model accommodating different sizes and colours.

Midge Pupa

Hook:	D/E 12-16
Body:	Gut or nylon in different thicknesses dyed in shades of green, olive and brown. A strand of horsehair may be alternated with the nylon for the 'Footballer'
Thorax:	Ostrich, condor or peacock herl
Wings & legs:	A short hen hackle with the top fibres clipped off, or none

Though he did not trouble to reproduce the breathing filaments or tail appendages he suggested the upper hackle fibres could serve for the one and the tip of a small hen hackle for the other.

This provides a basis for future dressings which have tended to become more complicated and sophisticated. One of the best is John Goddard's:

Hatching Midge Pupa
(John Goddard)

Hatching Midge Pupa

Hook:	Straight eye R/B 10-14
Silk:	As body colour
Rib:	Silver lurex
Body:	Black, brown, red or green marabou silk with a strand or two of fluorescent Firebrand wool of the same colour mixed in if desired
Tag:	Strand of white nylon filaments projecting below bend by one eighth of an inch
Body covering:	A one eighth of an inch wide strip of natural colour PVC
Thorax:	Three strands of peacock herl or dyed turkey
Head filaments:	Short strand of white fluorescent wool

Another close imitation of pupae at or close to the surface is that of Bob Carnill:

The Poly Rib Chironomid Pupa

Hook:	10-14 Standard shank wide gape or Yorkshire Sedge hook
Silk:	Gossamer well waxed — colour to match the general overall appearance of the completed pupa
Tail:	Two, three or four strands (according to hook size) of DRF electron-white floss nylon
Abdomen:	A web of good-quality herl — swan, heron, goose, etc
Abdominal segments:	A length of pre-stretched clear polythene (heavy duty) cut into narrow parallel strips and then stretched
Thorax cover:	A web of fibres as used for the abdomen — same colour or a little darker
Wing cases:	Two biot quills (found on the 'narrow' side of a swan primary flight feather)
Thorax:	Mole's fur, dubbed and wound on. Colour to match abdomen or a slightly darker shade
Head breathers:	A short length of white baby wool. Soft nylon wool with daylight-fluorescent properties is recommended

This is a representation of Halfordian proportions which might raise the question as to whether we credit the trout with too much sophistication and intelligence. This is echoed by Arthur Cove, one of Britain's leading nymph fishers, in an article in *Trout Fisherman* in April, 1983 when he questioned what he called the tying of these ever-so-clever buzzer pupa imitations, and stated that he had forsaken standard buzzer patterns for little spider flies with tiny hen hackles or sometimes cock hackles in the various colours used for buzzers. In Bob Carnill's defence his pattern has accounted for vast numbers of trout over some years.

It was inevitable that the supple qualities of marabou would be seen as enhancing a midge pupa, and this is incorporated in Taff Price's.

Marabou Midge Pupa

Hook:	10-14
Body:	Floss silk
Tail:	Marabou feather (black, orange, olive, etc)
Rib:	Fine oval silver tinsel
Thorax:	Bronze peacock herl
Breathing filaments:	Soft white feather fibres

Another interesting dressing is one sent to Richard Walker by R. J. Redrup which specifically sets out to imitate the hatching pupa at the point where some take on an orangy-red colour in the wings.

Black and Red Midge Pupa

Hook:	10-16
Rib:	White cock hackle stalk
Body:	One strand of crimson-dyed swan feather fibre, plus two strands of natural black feather fibre, twisted together
Thorax:	Natural black feather fibre or bronze peacock herl wound fat
Head filaments & tail:	Bunches of white cock hackle fibres, clipped to a short length

Both John Goddard and Taff Price observe that the wings take on a momentary orange colour at the point of ecdysis. John Goddard also points out that whilst the pupae often hang hook-like and stationary in the surface film, there are times when they swim downwards, and even occasions when they move horizontally just beneath the surface. Consequently, there is much conflicting advice as to how to fish the pupa. The most common method is to fish the artificial with a well-greased leader in the surface with barely any movement. Richard Walker and others have recommended that some movement will at times prove effective. Either way, the draw of the leader has to be watched carefully.

An American pattern called the Cooper Bug which has an underbody of peacock herl and an overbody of moose hair or elk or deer hair is dressed to conform to the theory that, just prior to hatching, midge pupae lie parallel to the surface film with air developing within the shuck thus giving a silvery appearance. The moose hair is attached to the bend leaving the points to act as a tail, and brought forward over the underbody and tied in, leaving a stubby head. The fly floats extremely well and is intended to be left motionless to trout taking the naturals. The loose hair tends to attract bubbles of air as in the shuck of the real midge.

For other chironomid pupae imitations see under Bow-Tie Buzzer, Buzzer Nymph, Footballer, Grey Midge Pupa, Orange/Silver Midge, Small Hatching Midge, Suspender Midge.

Chironomid Adult *(Chironomidae)*

I have given separately two major imitations of the adult midge by Bob Carnill and John Goddard. There are a number of others despite the oft-stated view that fish rarely seem to feed on them. Taff Price has devised three imitations to represent three possible taking times which he defines as the hatching stage, the resting stage, and the stage when the midge is in the air with its legs just touching the water.

Emergent Midge

Hook: U/E 10-14
Tail: Small grizzle hackle (imitating the pupal shuck)
Rib: Fine gold tinsel
Body: Black, grey or olive polypropylene or seal's fur
Thorax: As for body
Wing: Dyed-orange swan, tied down at head and tail over the back of the fly
Hackle: Appropriately coloured cock hackle clipped underneath

Resting Midge

Hook: U/E 10-14
Rib: Fine gold tinsel
Body: Appropriately coloured polypropylene dubbing or seal's fur
Thorax: As for body
Wing: Grey hackle fibres flat across the back
Hackle: Cock hackle of appropriate colour

The final stage is based on an American skater pattern devised by Edward Hewitt called the Skating Spider. These were tied on light-wire hooks and were big and fluffy, yet delicate, so that the angler could skitter them across the surface. Joe Brooks, the author of many American fishing books, contended that a skater could save the day when there were no signs of fish feeding and would bring them up from a considerable depth. With this technique the cast and line must float well and the fly be waterproofed.

Skating or Whirling Midge

Hook: U/E 14
Rib: Gold oval tinsel
Body: Appropriately coloured polypropylene dubbing or seal's fur
Hackle: Appropriately coloured cock hackle of good quality almost two inches in fibre length

Richard Walker has found very few small-winged flies in trout autopsies. He believes that this is because when chironomids hatch they do so very quickly. Their emergence time from pupal form is incredibly brief and they speedily leave the water. Even those sitting on the surface instinctively become aware of a trout's presence and make their escape by taking off.

For other chironomid adult dressings see under Adult Buzzer, Adult Midge, Black Midge, Blae and Black, Blagdon Green Midge, Blagdon Olive Midge, Duck Fly.

Skating or Whirling Midge
(Taff Price)

Chompers

Developed and perfected by Richard Walker in the early 1970's, this is a family of flies whose colour combinations can be varied to meet a variety of needs. They can bear a resemblance to a corixa, a freshwater shrimp, a louse or even a small sedge larva.

Hook:	D/E 10-12
Silk:	Brown, black or olive
Body:	Three or four strands of ostrich herl dyed amber or olive or natural white
Wing case:	A strip of brown raffene

Chompers

For a more durable pattern, the tying silk along the shank should be varnished before winding on the body material. Chompers can be easily weighted by using copper wire or lead underneath the dressing. The most useful colours are brown back and olive herl; brown back and amber herl; buff back and amber herl; brown back and white herl. For a corixa imitation, Richard Walker suggests a tip of silver wound at the bend before the raffene or feather fibres are tied in.

The patterns can be fished slowly on the bottom in small jerks on a sinking line or by using sink and draw on a floating line. I have found them useful in stalking individual trout when they may be taken in their weighted versions as they go down or when they come up.

Chris's Orange Sedge

Chris's Orange Sedge

This is a general representation of a sedge fly given to Taff Price by Chris Padley. It is a pattern which was very successful at Weir Wood Reservoir and, like a number of flies, acquires some mysterious attractiveness to trout by virtue of the use of bright orange in its hackle.

Hook:	U/E 12-14
Silk:	Brown
Rib:	Flat gold lurex or gold tinsel
Body:	Hare's ear
Wing:	Rolled partridge tied flat over the back
Hackle:	Hot-orange tied in front of the wing

Retrieve the fly quickly over the water surface or in a series of short, fast jerks.

Christmas Tree

Christmas Tree

This is a marabou lure generously decorated like a Christmas tree with gaudy green, red and silver. It has been a popular fly at Rutland Water ever since it opened. The original was devised by Les Lewis.

Hook:	L/S 6-10
Silk:	Black
Tail:	Fluorescent green wool or floss
Rib:	Silver oval tinsel
Body:	Black chenille
Wing:	Generous spray of black marabou
Collar:	Red fluorescent wool or floss

The fluorescent green of the body is said to be particularly effective when the water is soupy with algae.

Steve Parton has developed two tandem variations as follows:

Black Christmas Tree

Hook:	L/S 8
Tails:	Two thicknesses neon magenta wool
Rib:	Silver oval
Body:	Black chenille
Wing:	Black marabou
Cheek:	Green fluorescent wool

White Christmas Tree

Hook:	L/S 6-8
Tails:	Eight strands of arc chrome fluorescent floss
Rib:	Silver oval
Body:	White fluorescent chenille
Wing:	White marabou
Cheeks:	Green fluorescent wool

Church Fry

Devised by Bob Church in 1963 and tremendously successful by 1966 after being introduced to the angling press largely by Richard Walker, the Church Fry marked an important stage in the development of lure fishing with its hairwing after the pioneer appearance of the Jersey Herd several years previously. The Church Fry was designed to imitate perch fry at Ravensthorpe Reservoir in Northampton, and has since accounted for many thousands of trout even in waters which have no perch.

Church Fry

Hook:	D/E 6-10
Silk:	Black
Tail:	White feather or hackle fibre
Rib:	Gold tinsel or silver tinsel
Body:	Orange chenille
Wing:	Grey squirrel tail
Throat hackle:	Orange fibres or crimson-dyed hackle fibres

The lure can be very killing in July and August when temperatures are high and there is a great deal of algae in the water. In these conditions rainbows often become afflicted with what Bob Church calls "orange madness" and, retrieved very fast, either just below the surface on a floater or in the top six feet on a sink tip or slow sink line, the lure will produce dramatic interceptions by pursuing fish. It is particularly effective at Grafham where Bob Church avers that lures will take fish two thirds to three quarters of the time.

Cinnamon and Gold

A traditional lake fly which remains popular in Scotland and Ireland. David Collyer believes that this is a fly which deserves to be more popular and is one that he would not be without. He is particularly taken with the blending of the colours.

Hook:	8-12
Silk:	Brown
Tail:	A few strands of cinnamon cock hackle or golden pheasant tippet
Body:	Gold tinsel or lurex
Wing:	Cinnamon hen wing feather
Hackle:	As for tail

David suggests that it should be fished about a foot below the surface with fairly slow and long retrieves. He claims that every trout he has caught with the fly has been hooked in the scissors. The fly may well be taken as a representation of the cinnamon sedge.

Cinnamon and Gold

Cinnamon Sedge
(Limnophilus lunatus)

Although *L. lunatus* is considered to be the cinnamon sedge and was used by Halford for his model, the name is applied to many medium-sized sedge flies which have mottled or plain cinnamon-brown wings. Though the natural is cinnamon-coloured, its name is said to derive from the scent it gives off which is similar to that of cinnamon. These sedges are on the water from June through to the autumn, hatching somewhat sparingly throughout the day.

Cinnamon Sedge (C. F. Walker)

There are many dressings. I include two which are tied buzz and two which use bunches of hackle fibres for wings. Joscelyn Lane's also has a body of ginger cock's hackle clipped short and I do find that this adds to its buoyancy. It is, however, susceptible to the ravages of the trout's teeth unless the body is varnished before the hackle is wound on.

Hook:	10
Silk:	Golden olive
Tail:	Pale ginger cock hackle fibres (optional and used for balance only)
Body:	Ginger cock hackle clipped short
Wings:	Pale ginger cock hackle fibres tied in a bunch and clipped roughly triangular beyond the bend of the hook
Hackle:	Ginger cock

C. F. Walker's has the greenish body of the female.

Hook:	12
Body:	Condor quill dyed dull yellow-green
Body hackle:	Ginger cock
Wing:	Brown mottled hen
Shoulder hackle:	Two ginger cock hackles

John Henderson's dressing can be tied for either the male or the female and has no wing.

Hook:	11-12
Silk:	Nylusta, light brown
Rib:	Fine gold tinsel
Body:	Light yellowish-brown seal's fur mixture for males, green seal's fur dubbing for females of *L. lunatus*
Body hackle:	Light red or ginger cock
Shoulder hackle:	Light red cock followed by a light brown feather from a brown hen's breast

Richard Walker's patterns often seem to have something extra over other dressings which add to their attraction. In this case I think it is the yellow fluorescent tag.

Hook:	L/S 10
Silk:	Hot-orange
Tag:	Yellow fluorescent floss
Body:	Buff ostrich herl
Wing:	Buff cock hackle fibres, preferably barred
Hackle:	Ginger or red cock (natural red)

As with all dry sedges, a greased leader and variation of retrieve ranging from fast to jerky to twitchy is most effective.

Claret Nymph
(Leptophlebia vespertina)

This is the nymphal form of the claret dun fly which hatches in mid-May to mid-June in predominantly acid or peaty waters. The nymphs resemble those of the sepia dun very closely. They are almost half an inch (6 to 12mm) long, dark brownish-red with seven pointed gill filaments and three tails widespread and half as long again as the body. They tend to be slow crawlers on the bottom and among weeds, and probably rely on camouflage for self-preservation.

Claret Nymph (Peter Lapsley)

C. F. Walker gave one dressing for both the claret and the sepia nymph except that the claret was to be tied on a smaller hook.

Hook:	D/E 15
Tail:	Four or five fibres from a black hen hackle as long as the body and well splayed apart with a turn of tying silk
Rib & tag:	Silver tinsel or lurex
Abdomen:	Dark brown seal's fur mixed with a little ginger
Gills:	The body material well picked out with a dubbing needle, or a dark honey dun hen hackle (two or three turns)
Thorax & wing pads:	Black seal's fur
Leg hackle:	Dark brown hen

John Henderson's dressing is chiefly notable for its use of claret which is the characteristic of the adult spinner.

Hook:	13
Silk:	Dark claret
Tails & body:	Three fibres from a cock pheasant's tail, dyed dark claret, the points forming the tails (short), the remainder are wound up the shank to the shoulder to form the body
Rib:	Fine gold wire
Thorax:	Very dark claret seal's fur
Hackle:	Two turns of dark dun hen

Peter Lapsley's pattern incorporates a silver tinsel rib which may simulate the slightly shiny gaseous appearance of the mature nymph prior to hatching at the surface, and a thorax underbody of copper wire to help it sink.

Hook:	D/E 14
Silk:	Black
Tail:	Four to six black cock hackle fibres
Abdomen:	Dark brown seal's fur ribbed with fine silver wire
Thorax:	Dark brown seal's fur
Wing case:	Any dark brown or black quill slip
Hackle:	One turn of black hen hackle or none

Early in the season the artificial should be fished on a floating line and long leader very slowly on the bottom. Later on, when the first duns begin to appear, it can be fished just below the surface with a sink and draw action.

For another effective claret nymph imitation see Sawyer's Pheasant Tail Nymph.

Claret Dun *(Leptophlebia vespertina)*

Most authorities agree that claret is a misleading term as the dun is a dark russet-brown colour. The natural is about one quarter of an inch (7 to 8mm) long with four wings, the front pair of which are much the larger. The dark ashy-grey forewings contrast markedly with the buff-coloured back ones. The claret dun is found commonly in Ireland, but also in the West Country and peaty lakes in the North. The fly usually hatches around mid-day or early afternoon, and Peter Lapsley has found that the newly emerged adults often sit on the surface for a little time drying their wings before flying off.

J. R. Harris says that on some lakes during May when the flies are plentiful trout feed very keenly on them. A good dry fly pattern is then essential, and he gives the following:

Hook: 14
Silk: Claret
Tail: Dark blue dun cock
Rib: Fine gold wire
Body: Dark heron herl dyed dark claret, or mole's fur and dark claret mohair dubbed
Shoulder hackle: Dark blue dun cock, six or seven turns with a V clipped underneath it

Claret Dun (John Henderson)

In John Henderson's pattern, the dark claret of the body may well be an exaggeration of the natural's colour but, as Richard Walker has pointed out, this often makes an imitation more attractive to the fish.

Hook: 13
Silk: Dark claret
Tail: Rusty dun cock spade hackle fibres
Rib: Fine gold wire
Body: Dark claret seal's fur
Hackle: Rusty dun cock

A dressing by Taff Price is as follows:

Hook: 14
Silk: Claret
Tail: Bronze mallard fibres
Rib: Maroon silk
Body: Tail end brown-claret polypropylene, darker brown for the rest of the fly
Wing: Blue dun hackle points, set upright
Hackle: A black and a claret hackle

The artificial should be fished with a floating line and greased leader, often cast at a rising fish, and left to lie motionless on the water surface.

Claret Spinner *(Leptophlebia vespertina)*

The female spinner of the claret dun is one form of the fly which may fairly lay claim to claret hues in its body. The wings are almost clear and the spinner has three light brown tails. It is generally on the water in early evening for the purpose of laying its eggs.

I give four dressings, each of which deals with the problem of representing the wings in the spent position in a different way. Harris's technique is to clip a V-shaped section from the hackle on the underside.

Hook: 14
Silk: Claret
Tail: Dark blue dun cock
Body: Dark claret seal's fur
Hackle: Blue dun or rusty dun cock

In John Henderson's dressing the hackle is wound on in the normal way then divided into two equal parts separated by the tying silk in two figure-of-eight bindings.

Hook:	13
Silk:	Dark claret or dark brown nylusta
Tail:	Five fibres from a very dark dun cock spade feather
Rib:	Fine gold wire
Body:	Dark claret seal's fur
Hackle (wings):	Light dun cock, long in fibre
Hackle (legs):	Very dark dun cock

Claret Spinner (C. F. Walker)

C. F. Walker uses a similar technique with the hackle fibres divided laterally by two cross lashings of silk but without bunching them closely. He observes that the fly must lie flat in the surface film, a minimum number of turns of hackle being helpful in this respect.

Hook:	14-15
Tail:	Brown mallard fibres
Rib:	Gold tinsel
Body:	Dark brown and yellow seal's fur
Wing:	Palest blue or brassy dun cock hackle
Hackle:	Dark furnace or coch-y-bonddu cock, or none

Taff Price uses treated raffene for wings in the classic tied spent position.

Hook:	14
Silk:	Claret
Tail:	Bronze mallard or dark black-claret hackle fibres
Rib:	Yellow silk
Body:	Dark claret and brown polypropylene dubbing
Wing:	Treated raffene grey colour, tied spent
Hackle:	None

Casting to a rising fish with a longish leader and floating line, and allowing the fly to remain still on the water is the best method.

Coachman

Said to be the invention of a coachman to the British royal family, it is certainly a fly which is over one hundred and fifty years old. The traditional pattern which is fished pre-eminently as a dry fly on lakes, although it can be fished wet, is as follows:

Hook:	8-16
Body:	Copper-coloured or bronze peacock herl
Wings:	White swan or white duck wing quill
Hackle:	Natural red cock

A plain hackled pattern is:

Hook: 10-16
Body: Copper-coloured peacock herl
Hackle: White cock hackle with a shorter red one in front or the two mixed together

There are several variations of which the Royal Coachman is the best known. The modification to the original dressing is that the body has a centre section composed of red floss silk, the peacock herl forming a butt and a thorax.

David Collyer has a dressing called the Hacklepoint Coachman which he says is a dry fly which has taken more fish for him than any other:

Coachman

Hacklepoint Coachman

Hook: 10-14
Silk: Brown (sherry spinner)
Body: Bronze peacock herl
Wings: White cock hackle points
Hackle: Ginger or red cock

The wings are tied in a semi-spent position and the hackle clipped square below the hook so that it is just longer than the gape. This helps it to land on the water in the upright position most of the time.

This is an excellent general fly pattern which may be taken as a sedge. It is equally popular in the U.S.A. and Canada. Joe Brooks, the American author, considers the Coachman, fished wet, one of his favourite flies. When the fly is retrieved in short jerks he believes that its white wings resemble a very tiny minnow darting along.

Coch-Y-Bonddu *(Phyllopertha horticola)*

This is a very old fly which has a number of other names including Marlow Buzz, Brackenclock, Shorn Fly, Hazel Fly, Fern Web and June Bug. It is generally agreed that it represents a small beetle of about half an inch (13mm) in length of bluey-green colour and with reddish-brown wings. It is a terrestrial insect which breeds in very large numbers in June, particularly in Wales and Scotland, and is often blown onto the water. When this happens, especially in Wales, trout will take them with great gusto.

Hook: 12-14
Body: Two or three strands of copper-coloured peacock herl twisted together, tipped with flat gold
Hackle: Coch-y-bonddu

Joscelyn Lane thought the artificial resembled a large number of kindred species of beetle, subaqueous and otherwise. He thought beetles had an important part in the nutrition of lake trout and figured regularly in trout autopsies. Although he agreed that peacock herl could not be bettered to give the iridescent effect of the beetle's exterior, he felt the herl lacked the solidity and opacity of a beetle, so he introduced a solid core of chocolate-brown silko with a touch of varnish on which to wind the peacock herl.

Coch-Y-Bonddu (Traditional)

Obviously to be cast to rising fish if there is a fall of beetles. However, it can be used throughout the season and is effective as a top dropper on a dull, warm day or at dusk. It can also be used below the surface on a sinking line.

Cockchafer Beetle
(Melolontha melolontha)

This is one of our largest terrestrial beetles being just over one inch (27mm) long and half an inch (13mm) wide. It appears mainly from mid-May to mid-June. It is red-brown in colour and black and grey underneath. Such beetles can be blown onto the water when trout are said to take them.

John Henderson's dressings take into account that when the cockchafer, like most beetles, lands on the water its wings remain unfolded and project beyond the end of its body. Thus the wing feather tends to hold the fly up and help it to float.

Cockchafer Beetle
(Condor Herl Body)

Cork Body

Hook:	L/S 7-8
Silk:	Nylusta, brown
Tail:	Two light dun cock hackle points three quarters of an inch long
Body:	Oval-shaped cork, flat on underside, grooved down the centre with hook shank pressed into the groove and glued, painted grey
Wing cases:	Two cock pheasant feathers with black edges, one on top of the other, tied by the stems close to the hackle and extended down the body
Hackle:	Large red cock

Condor Herl Body

Hook, Silk and	
Tail:	As for Cork Body
Body:	Seven or eight dark grey condor fibres tied in at bend leaving about half an inch of the tags of the condor fibres to be tied in firmly along the top of the shank and fixed with varnish. The condor herls taken round the shank and over the tied-in tag ends, towards the head, so as to make the body as bulky as possible
Rib:	Fine gold tinsel which was tied in at the tail
Body hackle:	A large red cock, tied in at the shoulder and wound down the body through the hackle to shoulder and fixed with two half hitches
Wing cases:	Two feathers from a cock pheasant's breast and tied in as described in the first dressing

Caribou Fur Body

Hook, Silk and	
Tail:	Similar to first dressing
Body:	Caribou fur trimmed to size of body of the natural insect, that is, about one inch long and half an inch in diameter
Shoulder hackle	
& wing cases:	Similar to first dressing

Henderson considered that the Caribou Fur Body pattern, tied on a 10 or 12 wide gape hook, was the most satisfactory dressing because of its bulk and buoyancy.

Collyer's Nymphs

This series of nymph imitations resulted from David Collyer spending an afternoon towing a plankton net around Weir Wood Reservoir wherever he saw fish feeding on nymphs, and rarely can such an outing to a stillwater have had such profitable and far-reaching results. From his real-life models, David produced three differently coloured patterns intended to be general representations of nymphs, and they are used by fishermen not only throughout the United Kingdom but beyond.

Collyer's Nymph (Green)

Most anglers have found the Green Nymph the most effective, and I would agree with this, having taken a number of trout with it fished very slowly, often in the vicinity of weed beds.

Green Nymph

Hook:	D/E 10
Silk:	Olive
Tail:	Tips of body material half as long as the hook length
Rib:	Oval gold tinsel
Body:	Olive goose or swan
Thorax:	Olive-dyed ostrich herl
Back:	Butt of the body material over parted ostrich flue

The Brown Nymph is David Collyer's personal favourite.

Brown Nymph

Hook: D/E 10-12
Silk: Brown
Tail: Tips of body material half as long as the hook length
Rib: Oval gold tinsel
Body: Cock pheasant centre tail
Thorax: Chestnut-dyed ostrich herl
Back: Butt of the body material over parted ostrich flue

The original black dressing was later discarded by David Collyer and replaced by a grey which resulted in the dramatic capture of the then-record rainbow of 9lb 7oz at Nether Wallop Pool.

Grey Nymph

Hook: D/E 10
Silk: Black
Tail: Tips of body material half as long as the hook length
Rib: Oval silver tinsel
Body: Undyed heron primary feather
Thorax: Natural undyed hen ostrich herl, badger colour
Back: Butt of the body material over parted ostrich flue

I find these all-purpose nymphs not only effective fish catchers but easy to tie. When fished they often result in the gentlest of takes, and so the line or leader has to be watched with great concentration.

Concorde

An esoteric lure designed by Peter Gathercole and Bob Church with an aerodynamic specification similar to the aircraft after which it is named.

Hook: D/E L/S bronze 6-8
Silk: Black
Wing or tail: Dyed-red skunk tail hair over two small well-marked Plymouth Rock hackles
Hackle: Two Plymouth Rock hackles dyed red
Nose: Copper candle-lite or red tinsel
Head: Black varnish

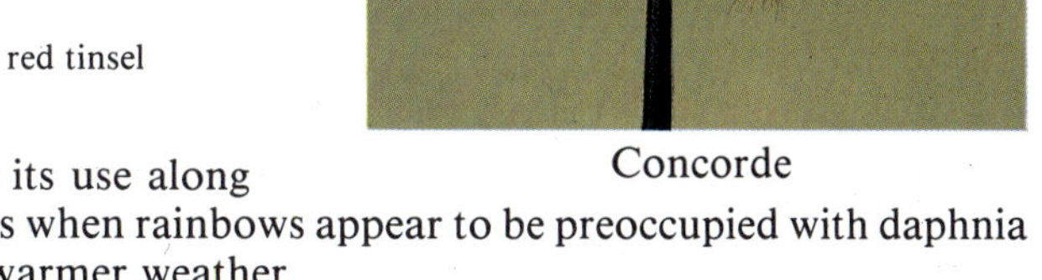

Concorde

Bob Church recommends its use along with the other big bright lures when rainbows appear to be preoccupied with daphnia on the big reservoirs in the warmer weather.

Connemara Black

Connemara Black

A traditional wet fly pattern originating in Ireland but popular everywhere for trout and sea trout.

Hook:	8-14
Silk:	Black
Tail:	Small golden pheasant crest feather
Rib:	Fine oval silver tinsel
Body:	Black wool or seal's fur
Wing:	Bronze shoulder feather of a mallard
Hackle:	Black cock with blue jay tied in front

This is a personal favourite of David Collyer for whom it has taken good trout in many different parts of the United Kingdom and many different types of water. He favours using it as the light falls and into the dark. He draws the line a foot or so at a time. Fished with a steady retrieve with pauses, it took a nice trout for me recently at Church Hill Farm in daylight and gale conditions when, for a brief period, a few fish started taking something indiscernible in the surface film.

Conrad Voss Bark's Palmer Nymph

Conrad Voss Bark's Palmer Nymph

Conrad Voss Bark, well-known journalist, broadcaster and fisherman, having rejected the techniques of both lure fishing and that of exact imitation, fishes almost exclusively a series of nymph patterns. The nymphs are palmered down the full length of the abdomen to the tail, using two different coloured hackles on the principle put forward by Kingsmill Moore for his Bumble flies. These give the nymph a mobility, life and sparkle.

Hook:	D/E 8-12
Silk:	Green
Tail:	Golden pheasant topping or tippet, short
Rib:	Fine gold or silver wire
Body:	A mixture of yellow, olive and dark olive seal's fur, darkening towards the thorax over lead or copper wire to form a pronounced thorax shape
Body hackle:	Short-fibred cock, one natural red and one white cock dyed a golden-olive, wound not too close nor too far apart
Head hackle:	Brown or red cock on the larger nymphs

The way the nymph is worked is all important. In calm weather he fishes the nymph slowly and smoothly; in water with a ripple he often uses the induced take by periodically pulling the line sharply with his left hand; for deep-lying fish he uses a larger and heavier nymph on a long leader.

Conrad Voss Bark's book, *Fishing for Lake Trout*, puts forward his own highly personal and challenging viewpoint on what constitutes true fly fishing for him without in any way seeking to impose it on anyone else. Unlike some of our latter-day pundits, he does not regale us with accounts of limit bags, but, instead, we share with him the ordinary fisherman's vicissitudes on the way to his fishing philosophy.

Corixa *(Corixidae)*

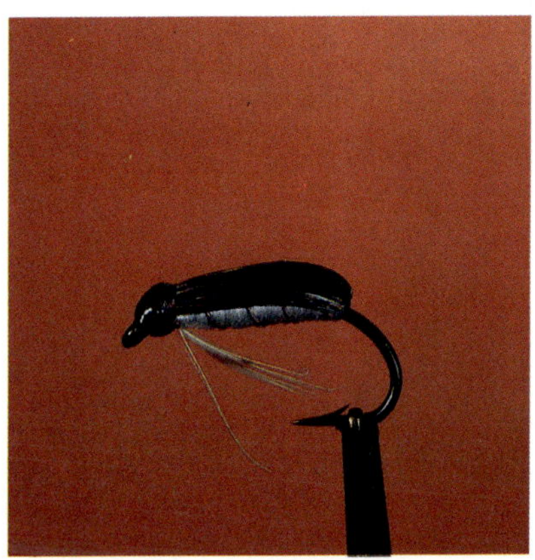

Corixa (John Goddard)

A survey made over thirty years ago of the stomach contents of thousands of fish including 2,400 brown trout from different parts of the United Kingdom showed that in every type of water approximately ten per cent of the trout population were corixid eaters. When you think of the massive invasion of our waters since then by the rainbow, the corixa imitation has much potential as a fish catcher. There are thirty to thirty-six species of this insect commonly known as the lesser water boatman. Eggs are laid after mating in January and February. The nymphs look like smaller versions of the adult which is oval-shaped with brownish-yellow, often patterned, wing cases. From the fisherman's point of view there are two salient features. Firstly, the corixa is air-breathing, holding a silvery bubble of air beneath the creamy-coloured body, and thus has to make journeys to the surface to replenish this vital supply. Secondly, of its three pairs of legs, the hind ones are feathered, spreading out on the backstroke and dragged passively through the water as they move forward, thus enabling the creature to move at great speed when required.

It is relatively easy to dress a lifelike imitation, and there are many representations, some of which I list under their specific names. A straightforward dressing which I find works very well is the one recommended by John Goddard.

Hook:	D/E 10-12
Silk:	Brown
Rib:	Fine silver wire
Body:	White silk floss
Wing cases:	Bunch of squirrel tail fibres stretched over the top of the body
Throat hackle:	Six fibres from a grouse hackle

Bearing in mind that the corixa has to commence its journeys from the bottom, a weighted pattern like Peter Lapsley's makes sense.

Hook:	D/E 10-12
Silk:	Pale primrose
Tag & rib:	Medium silver tinsel
Underbody:	Fine lead wire, flattened horizontally
Body:	White floss silk
Wing cases:	Speckled brown hen's quill slip tied over the completed body and given at least four coats of fine polyurethane varnish

Richard Walker has provided us with two dressings which simulate the paddles of the natural.

Olive-backed

Hook:	12
Silk:	Olive
Rib:	Gold wire
Body:	White or olive floss
Back:	Olive-dyed turkey tail brought to the eye and all but the two outside fibres cut off. These are bent back along the body and tied down at an angle of about thirty degrees

Brown-backed

Hook:	10
Silk:	Light brown (sherry spinner)
Rib:	Gold wire
Body:	White or olive floss
Back:	Cock pheasant centre tail bent back at the eye to create paddles as in the Olive-backed

Imitating the movement of the corixa is altogether more difficult than imitating its appearance. Its lifestyle is one of contrast. It spends some time on the bottom; on the other hand it is capable of flight and can move from one stretch of water to another. Its air bubble may be easy to imitate, but as the creature returns from the surface with it, its speedy movements become even more erratic. Weighted patterns thus are best fished sink and draw. Non-weighted ones can be drawn quite quickly just below the surface in early mornings and late evenings.

The naturals live in relatively shallow water in the vicinity of weeds, and are therefore of more significance in the smaller stillwaters. Though present throughout the year, they are most common during August and September, and may often be taken in the latter month when trout move into shallower water.

Do not confuse the lesser water boatman with the larger species, the water boatman *(Notonecta glauca)*, which swims on its back. The latter has to swim vigorously or cling to something to stay below the surface. It will feed on any living creature it can attack, including some bigger than itself.

For other corixa dressings see under Green Corixa, Large Brown Corixa, Plastazote Corixa, Silver or Streaked Corixa, Yellow Corixa.

Cove's Pheasant Tail Nymph

Few fishermen would be without this pattern evolved by one of the Midlands' most successful and skilful anglers, Arthur Cove. Although designated a nymph it has the outline of a midge pupa.

Hook:	Standard and L/S 8-10
Silk:	Black
Rib:	Copper wire to produce seven segments
Body:	Cock pheasant fibres taken around the bend
Thorax:	Rabbit fur to produce a small round ball
Wing case:	Pheasant tail feather fibres

Cove's Pheasant Tail

The one tied on the long shank hook uses a green seal fur thorax in place of the blue-grey rabbit when the water is thick with green algae. Neither nymph has a tail.

The inventor fishes the nymph very slowly indeed with a floating line and a long leader. It also catches many fish inched slowly along the bottom. Brian Clark feels that its deliberate exaggeration also probably works with fish feeding on midge pupae. It is a splendid standby when no fish are showing, and the depth at which it is to be fished can be easily adjusted until contact is made. I have taken many fish with it.

Cowdung *(Scatophaga stercoraria)*

Cowdung (Taff Price)

It is quite remarkable how some flies which are generally considered to be of little consequence to the angler have been imitated many times. Dressings for the cowdung fly are given nineteen times in W. H. Lawrie's *A Reference Book of English Trout Flies*. To be fair, most have been given for river use. The cowdung fly goes back at least to Charles Cotton in 1676 and Alfred Ronalds had a dressing for it which included the brown fur from a bear!

The larvae of the cowdung feed on the excrement of cattle and the females lay their eggs in it. The adult looks rather like a common house-fly. It has a yellow-brown body, dark thorax and two wings with veins and a small dark spot on each.

The fly has its advocates. Courtney Williams wrote at length about it and recommended T. J. Hanna's dressing.

Hook:	12
Rib:	Light green tying silk
Body:	Brownish-yellow chenille
Wings:	Tips of two darkish honey dun hackles tied on to lie flat over the body
Hackle:	Dark honey dun

Roger Woolley said that it was a land-fly which appeared early and if it was blown onto the water it was eagerly taken by the trout. His dressing was:

Hook:	12-13
Body:	A mixture of yellow and brown-orange dubbing with a few fibres of green intermixed, rather fat
Wings:	Landrail (or substitute)
Hackle:	Reddish-ginger

Taff Price gives a modern dressing:

Hook:	12-14
Silk:	Golden-olive
Rib:	Olive silk
Body:	Mustard-yellow polypropylene or seal's fur
Wings:	Cinnamon-coloured hen wing slips
Hackle:	Browny-olive

Tom Stewart said that on bright sunny days when there is a strong ripple on the water he considered the cowdung one of the best of flies.

If there are cattle in the vicinity of the water it is possible that these flies might be blown onto the lake, in which case the fish may take them if there are no other flies available. The artificial is fished dry.

Crane Fly Larva *(Tipulidae)*

Crane Fly Larva

Very few patterns have been devised in this country to imitate the larva of the crane fly. Only a few species of crane fly or daddy-longlegs have larvae which spend their time in mud or water. Those which do can be as long as one and a half inches (38mm) and would therefore be a succulent mouthful for a trout. Taff Price, who has devised this dressing, suggests that the most likely occasion when they would become available to trout would be on larger waters during rough weather when the bottom could become disturbed and various living things washed out.

Hook:	L/S 8
Silk:	Brown
Rib:	Gold oval tinsel
Body:	Yellow-coloured dental latex over wool or silk underbody
Hackle:	Small clipped white hackle

No doubt, this is best fished on a floating line and long leader slowly on the bottom.

Crane Fly *Tipulidae)*

Crane Fly (Richard Walker)

Few are unfamiliar with the daddy-longlegs or crane fly of which there are over three hundred species in the United Kingdom. One of the largest and most common is *Tipulidae maxima* which can be one and a quarter inches (32mm) in length. It has a long, slim body, sometimes dull, sometimes striped. Though it has two wings it is a weak flier, and its outstanding characteristic is its six long fragile legs. Though they are regarded by most fishermen as flies to be imitated and used from August, there are some species around from April.

There are many imitations but Richard Walker's is far and away the most popular. He uses knotted pheasant tail fibres to represent the legs, an idea probably first proposed by T. J. Hanna. Where Richard Walker's pattern is unique, however, is in his recommendation that the legs be tied on trailing and not on each side as in the natural on dry land. He states that not only is an artificial with trailing legs at least ten times more likely to catch trout than one with its legs spread out, but that the wings should slant back also.

Hook: L/S round bend 10
Silk: Light brown
Body: Swan secondary feather dyed a muddy cork colour
Legs: Eight pheasant tail fibres knotted twice and trailed backwards
Wings: Cree hackle points
Hackle: Cree or ginger, long in fibre

Geoffrey Bucknall has devised a pattern using a plastic detached mayfly body.

Hook: U/E 10-12
Silk: Brown
Body: Special plastic detached mayfly body tied in about halfway along the shank
Wings: Light ginger hackle points
Legs: Six strands of black horsehair or nylon
Hackle: Collar of light red cock hackles — six turns

In his *Fly Fishing Tactics on Stillwater* he modifies the dressing with legs of cock pheasant tail knotted in the middle and wings of brown cock hackle points tied spent. I have seen some superb detached bodies recently which use plastazote.

Taff Price, who gives us a pattern to represent the brightly coloured yellow and black species, contends that in his observation the leg configuration when floating on water is similar to when the crane fly is resting on land.

Hook: L/S mayfly 10
Silk: Black
Rib: Black silk
Body: Yellow polypropylene
Wings: Blue dun hackle tips
Legs: Pheasant tail fibres
Hackle: Ginger

All these patterns should be fished on a floating line and lightly-greased cast, and allowed to lie inert on the surface. Richard Walker is particularly adamant on this point. Many writers aver that it appeals especially to big fish.

Cream Spinner

This is a dressing of John Goddard's for imitating the male spinner of the large and small spurwing. In a small size it can be used to represent the caenis spinner.

Hook:	15-16
Silk:	Cream
Tail:	Pale blue cock fibres
Rib:	Thin gold wire
Body:	Cream baby seal's fur or substitute
Wings:	Wings of two small pale blue dun cock hackles tied spent
Hackle:	Cream cock hackle tied sparsely, two turns only

Cast in the path of a rising fish.

Cream Spinner

Cree Sedge

A pattern devised by Roy Masters, using cree feather, to imitate a sedge fly.

Hook:	W/G 13
Silk:	White
Body:	Cree hackle or hackles wound along the hook shank and trimmed very short to a cigar shape
Wings:	A bunch of natural red cock hackles, tied in to lie along the body and trimmed at the end in a sort of fan shape
Hackle:	Cree hackle of correct size from a cree cape

Cree Sedge

Daddy Long Legs

See under Crane Fly

Dambuster

Dambuster

One's first reaction on looking at this pattern is to say that it is only a Wormfly tied on a single hook. However, like all Richard Walker's creations, it is designed for a purpose, and this is to fish reservoirs from a boat within casting range of the dam walls when waves are washing over the stones. The tactic is to cast onto the stones and draw off in the backwash of a wave. The stiff cock hackle enables the fly to come quickly and unscathed from off the stones, and the DF wool tag adds to its attraction. Richard Walker explains that most of the takes come from within a few feet of the stones. The whole of the dam wall can be methodically searched.

Hook: L/S 8-12
Body: Peacock herl with a small tuft of yellow or red or arc chrome DF wool at tail
Hackles: Natural red cock hackles, one at the shoulder and the other about the middle of the body

The fly can also be fished on the bottom and left static as trout will pick up food forms there just as they will off the top. The function of the midway hackle is to lift the hook from off the lake floor so that it does not catch on vegetation or stone.

Recommended by Richard Walker for use when you want a rest or are having your lunch!

Damselfly Nymph
(Odonata zygoptera)

Damselfly Nymph (Peter Lapsley)

The sheer beauty of the adult damselfly with its brilliant body, especially the blue, and its transparent wings is the quintessence of summer as it darts and hovers over the water, holding the angler enthralled. There are conflicting views as to whether it is of similar interest to the fish.

The nymph has none of the brilliance of the adult with its dull green, yellow or brown body, but, paradoxically, it is very attractive to the trout. It is bigger than the ephemerid nymphs with no lateral gills on either side of its abdomen, but, instead, three leaf-shaped projections from its final segment which are its tracheal gills. Like the dragonfly nymph it catches its prey by means of its 'mask' or pincers.

Though the nymphs live among weed, and crawl, when the time comes for them to transform to adults they ascend to the surface and swim ashore with a wriggling motion to nearby vegetation. With the advent of many more small stillwaters, damselfly nymphs have assumed a greater importance to the angler.

One of the earliest dressings was given by Joscelyn Lane and may still be worth trying.

Hook:	10
Silk:	Golden-olive
Tail:	A big bunch of cock hackle fibres, dyed olive and cut off square to a length of one quarter of an inch
Rib:	Fine gold wire ending short of the thorax
Body & thorax:	Carrot-shaped. Of olive-green silk or 3X nylon, tapering from tail end up to a full one eighth of an inch at the thorax
Leg hackle:	A bunch of cock hackle fibres dyed olive tied under throat to lie close beneath the body

The dressing I have found most successful is that of Cliff Henry. The body seems much brighter than the natural's, but its gaudy translucence appeals strongly to the trout.

Hook:	D/E L/S 8-12
Silk:	Green
Tail:	Tips of three olive cock hackles
Rib:	Flat gold tinsel
Body:	Medium olive seal's fur
Thorax:	Dark olive brown seal's fur
Wing case:	Brown mallard shoulder feather fibres doubled and redoubled
Legs:	Bunch of six fibres from a grouse hackle

I find that there are some days when this pattern will not work but the trout will respond instead to Peter Lapsley's rather more sober version with green body and darker wing cases.

Hook:	L/S 8-10
Silk:	Yellow or green
Tail:	Three medium olive cock hackle points about one eighth of an inch long
Rib:	Fine gold oval tinsel for abdomen only
Abdomen:	Olive or green seal's fur
Thorax:	As abdomen with eight strands of cock pheasant tail fibre over the top
Wing cases:	The butts of the pheasant tail fibres turned back and divided so that they project for about one eighth of an inch on either side of the abdomen
Legs:	One turn of grey partridge tied as a beard

Weighted versions can be used to fish slowly on the bottom or to stalk big fish.

I have had much success from June onwards with a floating line and long leader, retrieving in long steady pulls. This can be very exciting as the bow wave of a following trout is seen and the fly is taken with a swirl. The trick is not to lose one's nerve, and either slow down or speed up the retrieve. The take may come very close in. Sometimes, casting the fly out, allowing it to sink briefly and then activate with sink and draw will produce confident takes.

There are times when the natural nymphs seem to be attached to patches of floating weed prior to hatching when the weed sails along in the breeze with a strong escort of adults. Casting close by with a sink and draw action can be deadly.

There are occasions when, after a period of frenzied activity, and just as the angler looks in imminent danger of acquiring his bag limit prematurely, the trout suddenly go off the artificial and completely disregard it.

For other damselfly nymph patterns see under Damsel Wiggle Nymph and Lamb's Wool Damsel Nymph.

Damselfly Adult *(Odonata zygoptera)*

Blue Damsel Adult
(Terry Hellekson)

Adult damselflies can have green, red or honey-coloured bodies but blue predominates. They are distinguished from dragonflies because they have equal wings which are held closed or nearly closed when at rest whereas the dragonflies' wings are unequal and are held open when at rest.

Opinions are divided as to whether they are taken by trout. Harris does not even mention them in his entomological work, Walker rejects the adult as impossible to imitate satisfactorily, and Goddard says they seem unattractive to trout and, on the occasions he has seen them spent on the water, he has never seen a fish take them.

Taff Price, however, gives us a dressing:

Hook: 10-12
Body: A quill from a mallard shoulder feather, painted light blue. When dry, black bands painted on
Thorax: Blue synthetic fur
Wings: Pale blue dun hackle points (four)
Hackle: Blue, palmered over the thorax fur
Wing case: Blue swan or goose feather
Eyes: The blue swan feather tied down, then furled back to form two loops

The real problem is that the naturals do not sit upon the surface. Terry Hellekson, the American, has attempted to overcome this in his dressing by having a hackle at each end of the hook to lift the body clear of the water.

Hook: L/S 10-12
Silk: Grey
Tail: Light blue elk hair
Rib: Fine silver wire
Body: Light blue floss tied thin
Rear hackle: Light blue. Hackle should only extend just past the point of the hook
Wings: Two light grizzle hackle tips tied together on edge over the body as narrow as possible
Front hackle: Light blue

This is more realistic until the angler attempts to impart movement as no natural creates wake or water disturbance.

An exciting new way of tackling the problem has been evolved by Peter Lapsley and William Sibbons. The former contends that trout do take adult damselflies and in prodigious numbers. He observes that they flit about a couple of inches above the water's surface, flying in fairly straight lines and stopping briefly when they change direction. The trout appear to 'track' them when they are moving and to take them as they change course.

Damselfly (William Sibbons)

William Sibbons, who has probably taken more specimen trout from the smaller stillwaters than any other fisherman, argues that the trout cannot differentiate between an artificial damselfly skimming along two inches above the surface and one behaving similarly two inches below it. So he ties his pattern with a very streamlined shape and retrieves it very quickly on a slow-sinking line. The evidence in support of this being an 'imitative' technique rather than mere lure stripping derives from the frequency with which he takes fish which he has seen to be feeding on adult damselflies, and the regularity with which autopsies conducted on the fish he has caught produce three or four adult damselflies. There may be some corroboration of this from David Jacques' observation that when the female winged fly of the damsel descends to lay her eggs and species of predominantly bright blue colouring are abundant, a sunken lure like the blue Camasunary Killer is at its most effective.

Here is William Sibbons' dressing to try for yourself:

Hook:	L/S nickel silvered 10
Silk:	Light blue
Tail:	Light blue wool
Body:	Light blue ostrich herl, waisted in the middle with tying silk or light blue DRF rayon floss
Hackle:	Light blue henny cock hackle, tied sparsely and swept back

Damsel Wiggle Nymph

These are much more demanding dressings of the damselfly nymph based on the principles evolved by the American fly-dressers, Swisher and Richards. John Goddard, in the following dressing, has adapted the idea in order to simulate the serpentine action of the damselfly nymph as it moves through the water. He suggests dressing the tail hook in the usual way and then clipping off the entire bend of the hook. The tail fly is then connected with the main body using fuse wire through the eye and a whipping on the main hook.

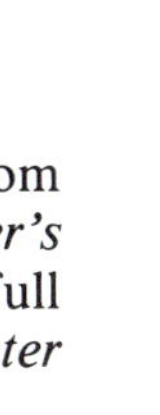

Hook: D/E 8-12
Silk: Brown
Tail: Tips of three olive cock hackles to extend three eighths of an inch
Rib: Flat silver tinsel
Body: Olive seal's fur
Thorax: Dark olive seal's fur
Wing cases: Three strands from a brown-dyed turkey tail feather, doubled and redoubled
Legs: Bunch of olive hen hackle fibres

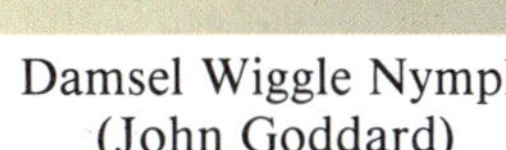

Damsel Wiggle Nymph
(John Goddard)

The second dressing is taken from Whitlock and Boyle's *The Fly Tyer's Almanac* by Taff Price who gives full details of how to tie the fly in his *Stillwater Flies Book 2*.

Hook 1: Straight-eyed L/S 8-10
Silk: Tan or olive prewaxed nylon
Tail: Marabou fibres light olive or golden-brown
Body: Mixtures of beaver belly fur and synthetic fur olive/light brown
Rib: Gold oval tinsel
Linkage: Sea trace wire (Whitlock used piano wire)
Hook 2: D/E wide gape 8-14 weighted with lead wire
Thorax: As for body
Wing case: Brown turkey dyed olive/light brown
Hackle (legs): Partridge dyed olive/light brown
Eyes: Bead chain or plastic beads painted olive/light brown

Both patterns should be retrieved with pauses to reproduce the sinuous action of the natural. I have found that the wiggle action can be achieved much more simply by adding a tail and a beard of olive-green marabou to a single hook, and have taken a number of fish this way.

Dark Spanish Needle

One of the smallest of the stoneflies is the needle fly. Two very similar species cover the months of March to June and June to November. On rivers, few fishermen can have failed to see this dark brown thin fly with glossy wings. Its appearance on still-water is probably spasmodic though I have encountered it, and the interest of the trout questionable, but I should feel well equipped to deal with any sudden outburst of enthusiasm on their part with these dressings by T. E. Pritt of these northern spider flies.

Dark Spanish Needle

Dark Spanish Needle

Hook:	14
Body:	Orange silk
Hackle:	Feather from the darkest part of a brown owl's wing tied sparse
Head:	Peacock herl

Light Spanish Needle

Hook:	14
Body:	Crimson silk
Hackle:	Feather from the inside of a jack snipe's wing or from the breast of a young starling
Head:	Peacock herl

Pritt comments that the Dark Spanish Needle is best for warm days, and that the shades of the natural flies vary considerably.

Dark Stonefly Creeper

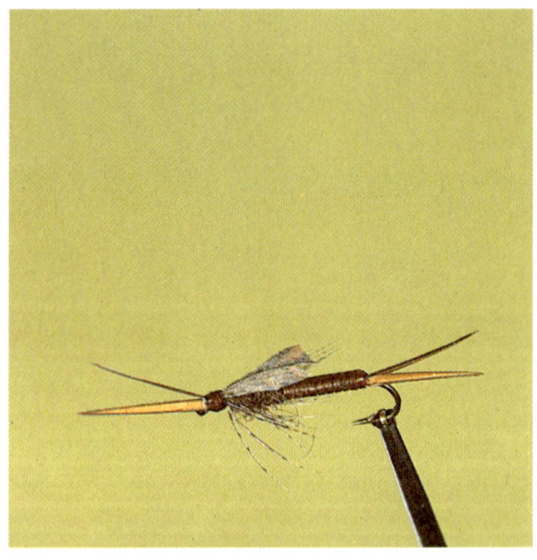
Dark Stonefly Creeper

This is a dressing designed to imitate the creepers of any of the average-size stonefly larvae which are of a darkish brown hue. Further details of this family can be found under Stonefly.

Hook:	L/S 14
Silk:	Brown
Tail:	Two brown goose or swan feather fibres
Body:	Dark brown silk, close ribbed with brown monofil nylon
Thorax:	Brown seal's fur
Wing pads:	Any small brown feather lacquered and cut to shape
Hackle:	Brown partridge
Antennae:	As for tail

As the stonefly larvae or nymphs almost universally crawl rather than swim, any imitation must be inched slowly along the bottom.

Dark Tup

David Collyer considers that this dressing, which is similar to Tup's Indispensable except for the thorax colour and general darker hue, is more successful for him than the original.

Hook:	U/E 12-16
Silk:	Olive or brown (sherry spinner)
Body:	Lemon floss silk
Tail:	Honey dun cock hackle, or very pale ginger
Thorax:	Mole's fur
Hackle:	Honey dun cock hackle, or very pale ginger

He uses it as a high floater and so utilises fairly long hackle fibres with the tail whisks sloping well down. The larger sizes are the most successful on stillwater.

Dark Tup

Dark Watchet

An old and popular northern wet fly pattern devised primarily to represent the iron blue. Pritt, in his *North Country Flies*, gave four dressings for what he called the Little Dark Watchet of which this is generally considered the best.

Hook:	15
Body:	Orange silk dubbed with mole's fur
Wings:	From the breast of a water hen
Hackle:	A dirty-whitish-brown feather from a hen's neck, or hairs from a calf's tail, dyed yellow
Head:	Orange

The expression 'watchet' is a northern one for pale blue, and Edmonds and Lee incorporate a bluey feather in the hackle of their dressing.

Hook:	14-16
Body:	Purple and orange silk twisted together, dubbed lightly with mole's fur and wound on the body so that the orange feather and purple show in alternate bands
Hackle:	A dark smoky blue feather from a jackdaw's throat
Head:	Orange silk

Dark Watchet (Edmonds and Lee)

Not only will the Dark Watchet serve as an artificial in the fairly unlikely event of your encountering iron blues on stillwater, but it will also act as a representation of the dusky yellowstreak, a dark grey fly with a yellow streak on each side of its thorax, found on upland and stony lakes.

Delta Wing Caddis

There are several views as to how best to imitate the low-lying roof-like wings of sedge flies (or caddis flies as they are known in the United States and Canada) and the triangular shape of the fly. Joscelyn Lane, who was one of the first to study natural flies from underwater by means of an observation tank, contended that sedges move along the surface by leg movements and not by fluttering their wings, and therefore the thick hackling of an artificial was unnecessary. He used bunches of fibres to simulate the wings and achieve the correct outline.

Delta Wing Caddis

This dressing imitates a particular period in the life of a sedge, and was developed by the American, Larry Soloman, who fishes the Catskill waters. It was originally called the Boeing Caddis because of its jet-like wings and is designed to imitate a sedge in the surface film that is either partly emerged or disabled. The wings have a very lifelike action when twitched to give the impression of a struggling insect. The inventor feels it is most successful during an emergence period and as a suggestive pattern in quiet periods when no hatching activity is apparent.

Hook:	8-10
Silk:	Tan
Body:	Olive-tan fur consisting of light ginger mink and medium olive rabbit fur (olive-tan seal's fur could be used as an alternative)
Wing:	Two matched ginger hackle points
Hackle:	Ginger cock

The above dressing by Poul Jorgenson, the American fly-tyer, from his book, *Modern Trout Flies and How to Tiė Them*, involves tying in two matched ginger hackle points one at a time so that they are parallel to the sides of the fly and lie perfectly flat. He emphasises that great care needs to be taken in setting the wings and that when in position they should be secured with a drop of cement or fixative.

Devon Dumpling

A general dry fly pattern originated by James Nice of Sidmouth, one of the country's leading fly-tyers. Recommended for lake fishing as an imitation of several olives.

Hook:	12
Silk:	Yellow
Tail:	Blue dun cock fibres
Rib:	Finest gold or silver wire
Body:	Orange or lime DFM or just tying silk
Body hackle:	Blue dun cock
Head hackle:	Blue dun cock

Devon Dumpling

Doctor

Doctor

Considered by many anglers to be the best of the patterns of the Reverend E. Powell, inventor of the exotically-named Baby Sun Fly. The Doctor is designed to imitate several beetles and can be used throughout the season on rivers and lakes.

Hook:	12-14
Tail whisks:	Fibres from a stiff coch-y-bonddu cock hackle
Body:	Black rabbit fur with the rear quarter white rabbit dyed yellow to bright yellow. The body should be bulky to suggest a beetle-like shape
Hackle:	One large coch-y-bonddu cock wound ten or eleven turns

Said by Courtney Williams to derive from the Devonshire Doctor which has an all-black body usually ribbed with thin flat gold tinsel.

Dog Nobbler

Dog Nobbler (Trevor Housby)

The Dog Nobbler was introduced to the angling scene by Trevor Housby in September 1980. A controversial fly, loved by some and hated by others, it has been described by Bob Carnill as the most deadly lure ever devised which remains within the accepted definition of a trout lure dressing. The principle of a weighted head used in American 'fly rod jigs' was first adapted in this country by Richard Walker in his Leadhead patterns and Geoffrey Bucknall in his Beastie lures. The Leadhead used split shot and the Beastie lead wire at the head to produce a head-down effect. However, Trevor Housby's imaginatively named pattern combining the up and down action of the lead shot with the delicate mobility of marabou tails in a variety of colours has hugely attracted both angler and trout — often big trout.

Hook:	Various sizes
Tail:	Very long, twice body length marabou of different colours
Body:	Chenille of various colours
Head:	Split shot

Though it can be fished in a variety of ways, the best results are obtained on a floating line allowing the fly to sink to an appropriate depth, and working it at high speed with six to twelve inch sharp snatches combined with a slight shake of the rod tip.

Since its introduction, more sophisticated versions have been developed. Sid Knight, the well-known professional tyer, has introduced palmered patterns with a set of whiskers three quarters of the length of the body, pointing forward and out by tying in two hackles. The quivering of the whiskers is said to add to its capacity as an out-and-out agitator.

I give two dressings by Bob Carnill who has refined the Nobbler further by painting eyed heads, using fluorescent tags, ribbing in some patterns, and adding collar hackles.

Black Nobbler

Hook:	Mustad 7780C for short shanks and Mustad 79580 for long shanks
Silk:	Black Naples (waxed)
Tail:	Black marabou
Tag:	DRF signal-green or phosphor-yellow (fuzz wool or chenille)
Body:	Black chenille
Collar hackle:	Black hen or henny cock
Head:	Split lead shot

White Nobbler

Hook:	As for Black Nobbler
Silk:	Red Naples
Tail:	White marabou
Rib:	Flat silver tinsel appropriate to hook size
Body:	DRF white chenille
Collar hackle:	White or hot-orange
Head:	Split lead shot

An Orange and White Nobbler with a palmered body hackle and collar hackle, Mini-Nobblers and Bob Church's Frog Nobblers are other developments.

An idea for using polystyrene balls instead of the lead shot on a Nobbler on the model of suspender buzzers, originally tried with nymphs by Gordon Fraser, the well-known Midlands fly dresser, and extended to the Dog Nobbler by John Pinnegar, makes it extremely buoyant, the reverse of the original, the vertical movement being obtained by the use of a sinking line. Alternatively, it can be fished on a floating line and degreased leader when a series of short pulls bulge the surface film. Having tried one, I can certainly vouch for its floatability in a heavy ripple. The two polystyrene balls encased in nylon mesh and mounted on the hook shank at the eye have led to the fly being christened by its innovators the Booby Nobbler.

Dogsbody

This is a dry fly which is a dogsbody in more senses than one. It literally has a dog's body and is also an all-purpose pattern. The body was created in a moment of inspiration by Harry Powell, the famous Usk fisherman and fly-tyer, when a farmer came into his shop in 1924 with a mongrel sheep-dog whose hair Powell adjudged was perfect for the fly he was dressing.

Hook: 14-16
Silk: Brown
Tail: Three strands from the tail of a cock pheasant
Rib: Oval gold tinsel
Body: Dubbed camel-coloured dog's hair or seal's fur dyed this colour
Hackle: Grizzle (Plymouth Rock) with a red cock hackle in front

Courtney Williams said it killed with equal facility on lakes as well as rivers, particularly if fish were preoccupied with small naturals and not taking their imitations.

Dogsbody

Don's Perch Fry

Designed by Donald Downs, fine illustrator of many fishing publications and President of The Fly Dressers Guild, this is an imitation of perch fry. It is particularly worth trying on large reservoirs like Grafham, Rutland or Kielder nearer the end of the season when perch fry can be profuse.

Hook: According to size required
Silk: White
Tail: Cream hackle fibres
Wing: Two light red hen hackles back to back, first barred with a black felt-tipped pen
Hackle: Scarlet hen hackle fibres tied beard-fashion

Don's Perch Fry

Dragonfly Larva or Nymph *(Odonata anisoptera)*

Adult dragonflies have been found in trout autopsies, but they are rarely imitated because of their size and the fact that they scarcely ever settle on the water. They have been imitated by American fly dressers but, on the whole, both they and tyers in the United Kingdom find a representation of the larva or nymph a more lucrative proposition.

The dragonfly larvae form large, juicy mouthfuls for trout with their long, plump, olive-green bodies, tracheal gills which look like tails, and nasty pincers described by Joscelyn Lane as a "gruesome weapon". The latter reaches out to secure a victim, and I watched recently a larva captured by my pupils for study purposes which grabbed a smaller damselfly nymph about the middle and defied all attempts to make it release it.

Dragonfly Larva (Taff Price)

These creatures mostly crawl on the bed of the lake but, when in danger, can move fast by jetting water from their rectums. They generally hatch into adults by crawling ashore at night, and so do not provide the same opportunities for the angler as their cousins, the damselfly nymphs, which swim ashore.

One of the earliest attempts to imitate the nymph of one of the larger dragonflies was devised by a doctor friend of Joscelyn Lane. Both he and the doctor found it killing up to the end of May and then later in September.

Hook:	9-10
Silk:	Green
Tail:	Three lengths of thick knitting wool one quarter of an inch long; one medium green and two dark brown
Rib:	Open turns of tying silk touched with varnish
Body:	Two pieces of similar wool, one medium green and one dark brown, twisted together and wound on tightly. Body cigar-shaped and a quarter inch thick in the middle
Hackle:	One turn of brown speckled partridge hackle dyed very dark green

A dressing devised by Taff Price is as follows:

Hook:	L/S 8-10
Silk:	Black or brown
Tail:	Two short olive goose fibres
Rib:	Green terylene
Body:	Fat, of olive-brown wool or seal's fur
Hackle:	Brown partridge
Head:	Peacock herl

I have found this a good pattern. I generally fish it slowly on the bottom, and most of the trout I have taken when I have given it a brisk and occasional one-foot pull.

A pattern given by John Veniard is:

Hook:	Mayfly U/E 6-10 loaded with one or two layers of thin copper wire
Silk:	Dark red
Tail:	Two hackle tips from a Rhode Island Red cock
Rib:	Gold oval tinsel
Body:	Fiery-brown seal's fur
Hackle:	Rhode Island Red hen

Another useful pattern for the dragonfly larva or nymph can be found under Brer Rabbit Nymph.

Drone Fly Larva *(Syrphidae spp)*

Drone Fly Larva (Taff Price)

The members of this family are terrestrial in habit, but one species, eristalis, has a partly aquatic life. Its larva lives in the mud of shallow water and rejoices in the malodorous name of rat-tailed maggot. It is half an inch long (13mm), grey in colour and has an ingenious breathing apparatus consisting of a tail with long tube which is telescopic. It is quite often found in still-water, is fairly active and can swim.

Peter Thomas has devised an artificial. The natural only has one tail but he ties his with three or four as they break off rather easily. The trout do not seem to notice!

Hook:	12
Tail:	Undyed swan fibres
Rib:	Buff hackle stalk
Body:	White DFM wool
Head:	Two turns of medium-brown ostrich herl

Richard Walker's model has a bleached cock pheasant tail which does not break off so easily.

Hook:	12
Tail:	Bleached cock pheasant tail
Body:	White DFM wool and hare's ear

Taff Price's version is slightly more complicated.

Hook:	8-10, weighted if required
Tail:	A long hackle stalk to simulate the breathing tube
Rib:	Black silk or oval tinsel
Body:	Grey fur mixed with a little DFM material
Back:	Grey latex. The body fur must be picked out to simulate the rudimentary legs of the natural

The artificials are best fished slowly on or near the bottom.

Drone Fly *(Syrphidae spp)*

The larva of the rat-tailed maggot hatches out into something which looks like a drone bee, hence its name of drone fly. Drone flies and hover flies are members of the same family and, although they resemble bees and wasps by virtue of the yellow and black bands on their bodies, they do not sting. Like all diptera they have only two wings. Most, being terrestrial by habit, are rarely of interest to the fisherman unless they are blown onto the water, but the eristalis females return to the water to lay their eggs when they may attract the attention of the trout.

Bob Church says that the Drone Fly artificial was invented by Cyril Inwood whose fishing prowess is mentioned with awe by those who knew him. The pattern is:

Hook:	12-14
Silk:	Red
Rib:	One strand of peacock herl
Body:	Yellow chenille
Wings:	Two white cock hackle tips
Hackle:	Full circular, medium brown
Head:	Red

Drone Fly (Grafham Drone Fly)

Although generally associated with small areas of water, the flies have been found at Hanningfield and Grafham. Indeed, one of the few patterns devised is named the Grafham Drone Fly.

Hook:	12
Rib:	Black wool
Body:	Yellow wool tied fat
Thorax:	Black wool
Wings:	Blue dun hackle tips
Hackle:	Yellow
Head:	Crimson silk or red ostrich herl

I have no experience of fishing this fly, but it is considered best cast out to rising fish and left motionless on the surface.

Duck Fly

Chironomid flies have had many names given them by anglers, the most common of which are midges and buzzers. In Ireland, the early forms appearing in the spring are called duck flies or black flies, and the dressings that follow come from an Irishman, J. R. Harris and are taken from his classic work, *An Angler's Entomology*.

Black Duck Fly Dry (J. R. Harris)

Black (Dry)

Hook:	13-14
Body:	Black floss silk thickened near the shoulder
Wings:	Two dun or cream cock hackle points tied sloping backwards along the hook
Hackle:	Rusty-black cock tied in front of the wings

Black (Wet)

Hook:	12-14
Body:	Black silk or wool wound thickest at the shoulder
Rib:	Crimson or claret silk
Wing:	Starling secondary tied short, divided and inclined towards the tail

Olive (Dry)

Hook:	12-14
Rib:	Gold wire
Body:	Olive-coloured floss silk or dyed pale green-olive swan herl
Wings:	Two blue dun or cream cock hackle points tied sloping backwards along the hook
Hackle:	Pale grizzled or rusty-dun cock tied in front of the wings

Some Irish loughs like Corrib have huge catches of duck fly in April. In 1982, the fishing correspondent of *Trout and Salmon* quoted an angler as saying that the density of rising fish to the duck fly reminded him of a fish farm at feeding time!

A more recent tying of the adult buzzer is by Bob Carnill.

Hook:	12-14
Silk:	Black, waxed
Abdomen:	Black herl, dyed swan, goose or heron
Wing:	Cock hackle points, dyed light iron-blue dun
Thorax cover:	A web of herl, as for abdomen
Thorax:	Dubbed mole's fur dyed black
Hackle:	Black hen, sparse

Dunkeld

A traditional lake fly and a flashy fly, the Dunkeld is descended from the salmon fly of that name and fished on the point. However, there are many anglers who find it more successful on the middle dropper. It is generally considered as imitating a small fish, but it might also be taken for a sedge fly.

Hook:	10-12
Silk:	Brown or orange
Tail:	Golden pheasant topping
Rib:	Fine gold wire
Body:	Gold tinsel or lurex
Body hackle:	Hot-orange cock or none
Wing:	Rolled bronze mallard finished off with a tiny jungle cock or substitute
Hackle:	Hot-orange cock tied as a beard

Dunkeld

My regard for this fly arises from the fact that it took my first-ever trout at Grafham. It works best for me fished slowly and, although effective from early season onwards, I like it best later on when orange has that special appeal to the rainbows. It is particularly good when there is a lot of daphnia present in the water.

Dytiscus Beetle Larva
(Dytiscus marginalis)

Dytiscus Beetle Larva (Taff Price)

John Goddard has concluded that the larva of water beetles may figure more largely in the trout's diet than the beetles themselves. It may be worth carrying at least one representation in the fly box, and this dressing by Taff Price of the great diving beetle larva, which can be anything up to one and a half inches (25 to 38mm) long and is a creature of great ferocity, should be tried.

Hook:	L/S 6
Tail:	Short olive or brown hackle fibres
Underbody:	Wool or silk, green or brown
Overbody:	Latex
Thorax:	Olive or brown seal's fur
Wing case:	Latex
Hackle:	Partridge. The body and wing case marked with a brown felt-tipped pen

For obvious reasons, another name for the larva of the great diving beetle is water tiger, and this is what David Collyer calls his dressing.

Hook:	L/S 8-10
Silk:	Brown (sherry spinner)
Tail:	Tip of body material
Body:	Sepia condor herl (pale)
Rib:	Copper wire over the peacock herl
Gills:	Bronze peacock herl down the body
Thorax:	Yellow-olive wool or seal's fur
Wing cases:	End of body material
Side hackles:	Brown partridge (as a beard but at the sides)

There are two particular features of the larva to bear in mind when considering how to fish it. Firstly, it is lighter than water so that it automatically floats up to the surface if it is not swimming or holding on to something. Secondly, it has swimming hairs on the side of the rear end of the abdomen which it uses in the same way as those on its legs. It can put several inches between itself and an enemy in the twinkling of an eye, so a variety of retrieves and depths can be explored often at a fair speed.

Dytiscus Beetle *(Dytiscus marginalis)*

The adult of the great diving beetle is equally as ferocious as the larva and can give you a good nip. There is little evidence that trout take it, but Joscelyn Lane tells us that in examining the stomatch contents of a 3½lb trout he found several dytiscus beetles about one inch (25mm) long and very much alive.

Taff Price has given us a dressing.

Hook:	6 weighted with lead wire and flattened
Rib:	Black silk or gold oval tinsel
Body:	Creamy-yellow wool
Back:	An olive goose or swan wing feather tip varnished
Paddles:	Goose wing fibres dyed olive
Thorax:	As body
Wing case:	As back

Like the larva, it can be fished on a floating line with a long leader and, bearing in mind that the natural can at times move speedily, worked from the bottom to the surface in sink and draw.

Dytiscus Beetle (Taff Price)

Eric's Beetle

C. F. Walker, partly on the evidence of trout autopsies, felt that Courtney Williams and other writers greatly exaggerated the importance of beetles to the angler. However, beetle patterns are surprisingly old and certainly common. This one was designed by Eric Horsfall Turner specifically for the River Derwent near Scarborough, but has become a popular and successful pattern for stillwater.

Eric's Beetle

Hook:	10-12
Silk:	Brown or black
Tag or tail:	Yellow wool
Underbody:	Yellow wool over which is wound a bunch of peacock herls
Hackle:	Small feather from the base of a starling's wing

It is best fished with a floating line and the leader greased to near the point. It will also take trout fished well down in the water.

Ermine Moth *(Spilosoma lubricipeda and urticae)*

The ermine moth, as its name implies, is white with black spots, and has a wing span of almost an inch (25mm). It is not an aquatic species but the dressing by the

Reverend Edward Powell may be taken for any number of white or pale-coloured moths.

Hook:	12-14
Rib:	One strand of unravelled three-ply black knitting wool or coarse black thread
Body:	White rabbit
Tag:	A loop of two-ply yellow-orange wool tied in flat, protruding a quarter of an inch beyond the bend of the hook and then cut off so as to make a short fork
Hackle:	Two large grey speckled partridge feathers

Ermine Moth (Rev. E. Powell)

It can be fished on a floating line and greased leader from June onwards. Here is one instance where the fly falling heavily on the water is an advantage, and the artificial should be retrieved in short, quick pulls to simulate the fluttering of the natural trapped on the surface.

Taff Price points out that the water ermine is more likely to be found near water than the ermine moth as its larvae feed on the kind of plants to be found around lakes. It is very similar to its relative but with fewer black spots. His dressing, which he calls the Water Ermine, is:

Hook:	L/S 12
Silk:	Black
Rib:	Black silk
Body:	Rear half orange poly dubbing. The rest white poly dubbing or white rabbit fur
Hackle:	White cock hackle with a grey partridge in front

Fiery Brown

An old and renowned Irish pattern both as a salmon and trout fly. It is described in an old book I have of the 1880's, *How and Where to Fish in Ireland*, as one of the best flies known. The traditional Irish dressing of the trout pattern is:

Hook:	6-10
Tail:	Tippet
Rib:	Gold wire
Body:	Fiery-brown seal's fur
Wings:	Bronze mallard feather
Hackle:	Fiery-brown or deep blood-red cock

Fiery Brown (Bob Carnill)

A modern dressing by Bob Carnill omits the tail which is probably an inheritance from the salmon fly and uses a hen hackle instead of a cock. This is because he uses it to imitate the sedge pupa as it is taken in the surface film in the act of hatching. If you see the trout's head or neb showing above the surface, it is usually taking the pupa in the surface film. The leader should be greased to within an inch or two of the fly which should be twitched back slowly so that its back imperceptibly shows above water.

Hook:	8-12
Silk:	Brown gossamer
Rib:	No. 14 oval gold tinsel
Body:	Fiery-brown seal's fur
Wing:	Dark bronze mallard (two layers, folded)
Hackle:	Rich-brown hen

The Fiery Brown can be used, too, in a team of sedge imitators, usually on the middle dropper. Bob Carnill also has a leaded version which is cast directly into the ring of a rise when trout appear to be submerging adult sedges with a tail slap.

Footballer

Footballer

One of the earliest patterns that I learned to tie at Geoffrey Bucknall's fly-tying classes in London, and still a winner to represent chironomid pupae.

The evolution of the Footballer came from his photographing the natural pupa and enlarging the results. This revealed the segmentation and the hooked abdomen. He used black and white horsehair to achieve the striped or footballer effect, and I still use the horsehair he so generously used to dole out at his classes. John Goddard points out that black and clear monofilament can be used in place of the horsehair, and colour variations can be obtained by winding clear nylon over coloured fluorescent floss.

Hook:	D/E 10-18
Silk:	White
Body:	Black and white horsehair
Thorax:	Natural mole's fur
Head:	Single strand of bronze peacock herl

Geoffrey Bucknall initially developed a technique of fishing the Footballer just through the surface film for a particular target fish with the intent of intercepting its approach by casting near to its head. The fly had to cut through the surface film cleanly and so extra appendages such as breathing tubes were omitted. The leader is greased to within six inches of the fly and when cast to a rising fish a few seconds are allowed before one steady pull. If there is no result on either the sink or the draw, the line is taken back for the next rising fish. This can be effective and thrilling fishing.

As an example of how analytical minds can work towards the same solution, C. F. Walker and Alex Behrendt identified an early season midge pupa with stripy segments at Two Lakes which was known to them as the 'Footballer'.

Freshwater Louse
(Asellus aquaticus or meridianus)

Freshwater Louse (Peter Lapsley)

The freshwater louse figures most regularly in the diet of trout but, because of its habits and movement, it is not easy to imitate or fish. It also requires considerable patience, in my experience. In appearance the adults resemble the land-based wood louse and are from half an inch to one inch (13 to 25mm) long. Colours range from dark brown to grey to almost white. Their bodies are clearly segmented and flattened from back to front. They have seven pairs of lateral legs of which the longest are at the back. *Asellus* is the only water louse where the male carries the female under him, but only in the winter.

The best artificial pattern is recognised to be Commander C. F. Walker's.

Hook: 11-14
Rib: Silver tinsel
Body: Mixed grey and brown hare's ear, flattened horizontally
Legs: A grey-brown partridge hackle halfway up the body from the tail

Peter Lapsley omits the hackle which in C. F. Walker's pattern is intended to represent the set of lateral legs.

Hook: D/E 12-14
Silk: Fawn or brown
Rib: Fine silver tinsel
Underbody: Fine lead wire flattened horizontally
Body: Mixed brown and grey hare's ear, trimmed short on top

Ann Douglas's dressing is notable for the use of the green raffene in the middle section of the body to represent the eggs carried by the female louse. As the artificial is mostly fished on the bottom, whether the trout are aware of this device is another matter.

Hook: 10-12
Silk: Brown
Body: In three sections: the first third from the tail is hare's ear and mole mixed; the second is green raffene; the third hare's ear and mole mixed
Back: Brown mallard flank
Legs: Brown partridge hackle
Feelers: Brown partridge

Convincing movement is at the root of the problem of fishing the artificial louse, as the natural clambers among the plants or scutters on tiptoe on the bottom along the detritus and debris. Peter Lapsley fishes his pattern slowly on the bottom in the shallower water and has noticed that provided the angler remains concealed a fish will follow for some distance and take under the rod tip.

This is primarily a pattern for use on the smaller stillwaters.

Freshwater Shrimp
(Gammarus pulex)

The Shrimper (John Goddard)

Considering that Courtney Williams had little success with shrimp patterns, and that John Goddard considers them of doubtful value for those fishing stillwaters largely because they tend to figure more in the trout's diet in winter, there is a remarkable number of artificial patterns.

The several species of shrimps vary in size from under half an inch to over three quarters (13 to 19mm). They are curved in appearance with many legs and two sets of antennae at the head. The body colour is predominantly greyish-olive. The shrimp only goes a yellowy-orange when it is dead. The male often carries the female underneath. One authority states that this is because there are so many more males than females. A novel way of tackling such a shortage! Occasionally the whole family swims together, the male carrying the female with her attached eggs or young.

Though they are usually found under stones or on the soft surface of mud, they also swim or scud with surprising speed, often on their sides. This is achieved by straightening out the hind part of the body and moving the legs.

C. F. Walker's dressing remains an excellent one.

Hook: D/E Limerick 10-13
Rib: Gold tinsel
Body: A mixture of watery-olive, pale brown and amber seal's fur, taken round the bend of the hook and clipped on the back and sides
Legs: A water-olive hen hackle at the shoulder and tufts of the body material picked out on the underside with the dubbing needle

Richard Walker's pattern uses a dubbing of mixed fawn, pink and green wool to give a pinkish-olive effect to the body. The artificial is also designed to fish upside-down and, as the shrimp are often to be found in the vicinity of weed beds, this is especially useful.

Hook: 10-12
Silk: Brown (sherry spinner)
Body: Wool, over five layers of lead foil bound onto the top of the hook shank by copper wire or silk
Hackle: Long cock hackle (ginger or buff) wound palmer-wise, clipped off on the back and the sides
Back: A thorough soaking in cellulose varnish to produce a smooth back

Though the shrimp tends to be a major part of the trout's diet in the colder months only, John Goddard says that it is surprising how many fish are taken on the artificial during the season. His dressing is called The Shrimper.

Hook:	D/E Limerick 10-14
Silk:	Orange
Body:	Fine copper wire wound on thickly at centre to form a hump, covered with olive-brown seal's fur
Hackle:	Honey dun or olive cock
Back:	Strip of PVC or latex rubber, length of hook, cut wide in the centre and tapering at each end

Oliver Edwards has recently given a most lifelike shrimp imitation in *Trout and Salmon* which is based on C. F. Walker's original model. His mixture of partridge fibres and hare's fur as dubbing produces a much more realistic effect than the use of cock hackles.

Shrimp (Oliver Edwards)

Hook:	Straight shank, wide-gape 10-14
Underbody:	Lead foil or lead wire to create a hump effect on top of the hook
Body:	Dubbing of light partridge fibres mixed with hare's white belly fur dyed pale olive
Tail appendages:	Seven or eight pale olive-dyed partridge hackle fibres lashed down right around the bend
Back:	Pale olive-dyed polythene cut wide in the middle and tapered at each end
Rib:	Four-pound B.S. mono over the back to create a segmented effect
Front appendages:	A clump of pale olive-dyed partridge hackle fibres tied in on the underside of the hook eye and projecting one third of the way along the shrimp's body. About four similar fibres tied in by the butts above or below the hook eye to project one third to one half in front of the eye

Fished in the shallower water on a floating line and long leader, these patterns can be allowed to sink to the bottom and be retrieved in short, sharp pulls with pauses. Sink and draw and other variations are worth trying.

The G. & H. Sedge

Much original thinking has gone into obtaining the correct outline of sedges combined with maximum buoyancy by Joscelyn Lane, Richard Walker, Terry Thomas and others. The latter created wings out of deer hair. John Goddard and Cliff Henry have used the same material in the manner devised for Muddler Minnows to form a body of deer hair which can be cut and shaped to obtain the outline of the wings of the natural. The dressing represents the mottled sedge and any of the lighter sedges according to hook size.

Hook: L/S 8-10
Silk: Green
Underbody: Dark green seal's fur dubbed on to the silk and tied in at the bend. After the body of deer hair has been tied in and shaped, the seal's fur is stretched along under the body and tied in at the eye
Body: This is formed from several bunches of deer hair trimmed to the shape and silhouette of the wings of the natural sedge fly
Hackle: Two rusty-dun cock hackles tied in together at the eye and wound slightly down the body. The top of the hackle is then trimmed off to simulate the head of the natural. The stripped butts of the two hackles can be left to form antennae if desired

The G. & H. Sedge

The finished fly has magnificent floating capability which enables it to be fished in a number of ways. When sedges are hatching it can be retrieved on a long floating leader across the top of the water when it may attract smash takes. Alternatively it can be allowed to lie motionless or given a slight tweak. Its inventors consider that its supreme use is as an attractor on the top dropper from a drifting boat from June onwards especially if there is a good breeze. They have taken many trout in this fashion.

It is not an easy pattern to dress, and this is why I have given John Goddard's instructions in some detail. Take care not to leave excessive amounts of deer hair below the hook shank in case it interferes with the fly's hooking qualities.

Geronimo

This is Brian Harris's answer to Muddler flies which he does not particularly care for. Geronimo's ruff of bright yellow and orange hackles gives it an outline and movement similar to the Muddler. In order to achieve this, as David Collyer points out, it is important that the orange hackle lies back at the correct angle by taking a turn or two of silk over the base of the fibres whilst the bright yellow hackle is more at a dry fly angle but just very slightly sloping backwards. Four furnace greenwell hackles can be used instead of the cree.

Geronimo

Hook:	L/S 8-12
Silk:	Yellow
Tail:	Mixed, brown and yellow cock hackle fibres
Body:	Wide gold tinsel or lurex
Wing:	Four well-marked cree hackles
Hackles:	Rear, long-fibred orange cock; front, bright yellow cock

Streamer flies — never intended in the first place for casting — have the annoying habit of tangling in the wing around the hook point, and so David Collyer has given us a matuka version of the Geronimo. This involves the removal of the underside of the wing feathers, their binding on top of the hook shank with a rib, and a reduction of their projection beyond the hook point.

Fish this pattern as you would a Muddler.

Gerroff

This pointed exclamation of a name was directed by Brian Clarke at the little trout which insisted on grabbing this fly created by John Goddard. As he attempted to withdraw it from their mouths his cries of "Get off" degenerated into "Gerroff" and he thus insisted that this is what the fly should henceforth be called.

Hook:	D/E 10-14, slightly longer shank than a standard hook
Silk:	Brown tied short
Body:	Olive brown and fluorescent pink seal's fur mixed — three brown to one pink
Wing case:	Strip of PVC or latex

Gerroff

The fly was originally designed as a shrimp pattern for the Kennet when it was very sluggish, and so only half the length of the hook was used in combination with the buoyant material in order to achieve a slow rate of sinking. It is recommended for small stillwaters using a floating line, when it should be cast out to trout seen feeding underwater or alongside weed beds. As it gradually sinks, trout will close in and take.

The Ghost Swift Moth *(Hepialus humuli)*

This is quite a large moth with a wing span of almost one and a quarter inches (30mm) whose male has white wings and a darkish body, and is found throughout the British Isles. As it is often found flying at dusk it is considered to have a ghost-like quality. It is not found usually near water and thus there are few dressings. General representations of moths in different sizes and coloured white are probably adequate.

There is one specific pattern which was invented by Richard Walker for fishing the little River Oughton near Hitchin where he lived as a boy. A guest once watched him take a 4lb trout on it and, on examining the fly, exclaimed that he had seen fish caught on chicken feathers but never on a whole bloody chicken! From then on all his friends called it 'the chicken'. Certainly one of Richard's specifications is that it be tied fat.

Hook:	L/S 8
Silk:	White
Rib:	A stiff cock hackle cream-coloured
Body:	Cream ostrich herl tied fat
Wing:	Swan secondary wing feathers tied across the back
Hackles:	One cream and one pale ginger cock hackle

The Ghost Swift Moth

This pattern once took eight out of twelve fish for Richard Walker and Peter Thomas on a windy day at Church Hill Farm in broad daylight, and not evening for which it was originally devised. Some were taken dry. Others swirled round the fly without taking but responded as soon as the fly was drawn under by a pull of the line.

Golden Olive

A traditional and well-known wet fly, particularly good for sea trout, but very useful in smaller sizes as a representation of a lake olive. This dressing is given by David Collyer.

Hook:	8-12
Silk:	Olive
Tail:	Optional: golden pheasant crest or golden-olive cock hackle
Tag:	Orange floss silk
Rib:	Oval gold tinsel or gold wire
Body:	Golden-olive seal's fur
Wings:	Bronze mallard with optional underwing of golden pheasant tippet fibres
Hackle:	Golden-olive cock

Golden Olive

A popular fly from May to July on loughs in Ireland like Arrow, Mask and Owel.

Goldie

Goldie

The curiosity, belligerence — or pugnacity as Skues called it — of trout, especially rainbows, is aroused by lures of different colours. Most fishermen, depending on the time of year, ring the first changes through black, white and orange. Lures like Leprechaun which is green show fish responding to other colours as well. Goldie offers us a black and yellow combination.

Hook:	D/E L/S bronze 6-10
Silk:	Black
Tail:	Yellow hackle fibres
Body:	Gold tinsel ribbed with gold wire
Underwing:	Yellow goat or skunk hair
Overwing:	Black goat or skunk hair
Hackle:	Yellow hackle fibres, beard only
Head:	Black varnish

It is used in a very large size by Bob Church with an American lead core line when trolling at Rutland Water which has a large area of water where this is allowed.

Gold-Ribbed Hare's Ear

Gold-Ribbed Hare's Ear

The use of hare's ear is as old as the art of fly dressing, but the Gold-Ribbed Hare's Ear goes back to about the 1880's. Not a specific imitation of anything, it is generally regarded as an excellent pattern for the medium olive, the teased-out hare's fur simulating the nymph shedding its shuck as it hatches into the dun. Skues had great confidence in the fly and Halford, who put a wing on it, said it was probably the most killing pattern of his day on the Test and other chalk streams. It has frequently been dressed with a wing since and used as a dry fly.

However, in its original version it is a most effective representation of both pond and lake olive nymphs on stillwater so that Taff Price says that if he had to have a limited number of flies the G.R.H.E. would be one of them. More recently, John Wadham in an article in *Trout Fisherman* stated that he considered that the G.R.H.E. was the best overall pattern for use on Rutland Water.

Hook:	14-16
Silk:	Yellow or primrose
Rib:	Fine flat gold tinsel or fine gold wire
Whisks:	Three strands of hare's ear
Body:	Dark fur from the root of the hare's ear spun on the silk
Hackle:	Long strands of the body material picked out with the dubbing needle

If it is to imitate the hatching olive it can be fished singly on a floating line and long leader slowly just below the surface. It is equally valuable from a boat when olives are about, fished on the middle dropper with an olive nymph imitation on the point and maybe a Greenwell on the bob.

David Collyer's version was taken from the American magazine, *Field and Stream*, and he has found it extremely successful on stillwater. The main difference from the home model is that it has a wing case of dyed-black turkey tail. He has taken fish with it both fairly deep and off the surface.

Hook:	D/E 10-14
Silk:	Brown or black
Tail:	Hare's body fur
Rib:	Oval gold tinsel
Body:	Hare's body hair
Wing cases:	Dyed-black turkey tail
Thorax:	Long fibres of hare's body hair

For the sinking pattern lead or lead wire can be added to the hook shank.

The Gosling

A famous Irish traditional pattern of the wet mayfly nymph. Writing recently, Arthur Cove observed that the orange and yellow fibres give the fly a lure-like quality.

The front hackle can be wound on in the usual way or tied in bunches around the hook shank, but either way the feathers should envelop the body.

Hook:	Mayfly 8-10
Tail:	Three cock pheasant tail fibres or brown mallard fibres
Rib:	Oval gold
Body:	Yellow or pale golden-olive seal's fur: or yellow and hot-orange seal's fur well mixed
Hackle:	Four turns of hot-orange cock, with grey mallard or yellow-dyed grey mallard in front

The Gosling

It may well be one of the oldest mayfly nymph patterns known.

The Governor

A traditional fly which goes back at least to the 1830's. As such it was designed for river fishing. However, it is considered to be a useful representation of a beetle for stillwaters. The pattern is little changed, and so I give one of the earliest, by T. C. Hofland.

Hook:	9
Tag:	Scarlet twist
Rib:	Gold twist
Body:	Copper peacock herl
Hackle:	Red or ginger
Wings:	Light pheasant

The Governor (F. M. Halford)

Halford's development of the pattern involved the replacement of the light pheasant wing with that of the woodcock.

Hook:	12-15
Tag:	Primrose floss silk
Body:	Copper-coloured peacock herl
Hackle:	Ginger cock
Wings:	Woodcock

The fly can be fished either dry or wet.

Grasshopper *(Orthoptera)*

Although imitations of grasshoppers go back a long way, dapping with the live insect has been the most popular way of tempting trout. Artificials are much more popular in the United States and Canada whereas in this country few writers evince enthusiasm for imitations of these lively, chirruping creatures which live in the meadow grass and are at their most vocal in the warm sunshine. Both Courtney Williams and Joscelyn Lane subscribe to the tradition that when these creatures accidentally jump into the water they appeal to the really big trout.

Grasshopper (Charles Cotton)

Charles Cotton's pattern was one of the earliest, and it still seems as good as any.

Hook:	Not given but suggest L/S 12
Silk:	Green
Rib:	Green silk
Body:	Green and yellow wool mixed
Hackle:	Red cock palmered

The materials of Taff Price's Green Grasshopper form an interesting contrast with Cotton's.

Hook: L/S 12
Silk: Green
Body: Clipped deer hair (dyed green or coloured with a waterproof pen)
Legs: Two knotted cock pheasant tail fibres
Wings: Two slips of green-olive-dyed swan or goose
Head: Peacock herl

He also has a brown version:

Hook: L/S 12
Silk: Brown
Body: Clipped deer hair left natural colour
Legs: Cock pheasant tail fibres
Wings: Oak turkey slips
Head: Peacock herl

He recommends that his patterns be tried on those dog days when trout need something different. They can be fished dry or waked as for sedges and moths but more slowly, or cast at a cruising trout or even dapped.

For those who would like to try an American pattern, here is one by Joe Brooks which he calls Joe's Hopper:

Hook: 6-14
Silk: Black
Tail: Red fibres
Rib: Brown hackle, trimmed with the widest part at the tail end
Body: Yellow chenille
Wing: Mottled turkey extending to the tail and tied flat to the body
Hackle: Brown and grizzly

It was included by Dan Bailey, the famous fly tyer from Montana, in his list of five best dry flies to fish the Yellowstone River, and there is no reason why it should not work on stillwater. Indeed, grasshopper imitations are an area which might well repay further research in this country.

Gravel or Pebble Caddis

Halford was not the only one to take the principle of exact imitation seriously! Here is a representation of the caddis in its shelter, case and all, by Taff Price, to give the trout a real mouthful.

Having listened to him, I am sure that he has his tongue in his cheek as he heaves this fast sinker into the water. Like most of his patterns, however, it has caught fish for him.

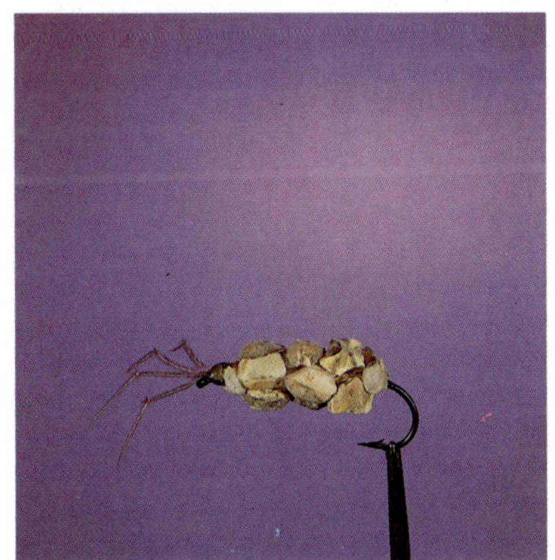

Gravel or Pebble Caddis

Hook: L/S 8-14 (weight hook towards the head)
Silk: Green
Body: Green or yellow floss. Minute pebbles or gravel stuck on with Araldite and allowed to dry

The photograph shows the Caddis with legs or feelers as in the illustration in Taff Price's *Stillwater Flies, Book 1.*

Great Diving Beetle

See under Dytiscus Beetle

Great or Large Red Sedge
(Phryganea grandis and striata)

Great or Large Red Sedge
(Taff Price)

The two species are the largest sedges in the British Isles, and the length of their anterior wings can be three quarters to over an inch (20 to 27mm). The wings are a dark reddish-brown and the antennae are pronounced. Hatching of the two species covers from May to the beginning of August. Any number of dressings have been invented to imitate them.

John Henderson's pattern employs a traditional sedge palmered body and shoulder hackle but omits a wing.

Hook: 9
Silk: Nylusta, brown
Rib: Gold tinsel
Body: Yellowish-brown seal's fur mixture
Body hackle: Red cock
Shoulder hackle: Red cock followed by a Rhode Island hen hackle or a feather from the breast of a Rhode Island cock or hen

In Ireland this fly is known as the Murragh or Peter, and the dressing is that given by J. R. Harris in his *An Angler's Entomology*, having a traditional feather wing. It is very popular on loughs like Conn, Corrib and Carra in August especially.

Hook: 5-7
Body: Dark grey-black or black-claret mohair or seal's fur
Wing: Dark brown speckled hen wing feather tied to lie close to the hook
Hackle: Two dark red cock hackles tied in front of the wing

Richard Walker uses cock hackle or pheasant tail fibres for his wings. He considers it a very reliable pattern especially if carried in both the big size L/S 8 and the small ordinary size 10.

Hook: U/E 8-12
Silk: Brown
Tag: Fluorescent orange wool
Body: Cock pheasant centre tail fibres
Wings: A bunch of red cock hackle fibres square at the tips, or a bunch of pheasant tail fibres
Hackle: Two red cock hackles

Finally, a dressing by Taff Price which uses a whole body feather for wing.

Hook: L/S 8-10 or U/E Mayfly 8-10
Rib: Gold oval
Body: Grey-brown polypropylene or fur
Body hackle: Natural dark red
Wing: Red hen body feather lacquered, tied flat
Hackle: Two natural red cock hackles, stalks left untrimmed to represent antennae

A slow, steady retrieve can be used to represent the natural striving to reach the bank. Another method I find effective is to employ a greased leader with either a swift skating retrieve or short periodic jerks.

Green Aphis *(Aphididae/Homoptera)*

Green Aphis (Derek Bradbury)

Gardeners are only too familiar with the greenfly which sucks the life out of their plants. It has long been recognised that if they are blown onto the water trout appreciate them. Leonard West in his *The Natural Trout Fly and its Imitation*, a pioneer book of imitative fly dressings written in 1921, speaks of how he was fishing one day and not a fish rising when a sudden squall struck the trees on the bankside, and immediately fish were rising by hundreds. He found that thousands of small green aphis had been blown onto the surface of the water.

There are two early imitations by F. M. Halford and Eric Taverner which they called Green Insect.

Hook: 15-16
Body: Two or three strands of peacock sword feather twisted together
Hackle: Pale blue dun

Roger Woolley's dressing is similar.

Eric Taverner's pattern is:

Hook: 15-16
Body: Bright green peacock herl
Hackle: Soft silver-grey hen hackle

The problem of evolving a satisfactory dressing is compounded by the tiny size of the natural. Taff Price has attempted to overcome this by tying the body short in the manner of John Goddard's Gerroff.

Hook: 16
Body: DFM green silk built up to insect body-shape and tied short to approximate nearer to the size of the natural
Hackle: Pale blue dun. A tuft of DFM white floss can be tied in across the back for a winged version

An even more ingenious solution is that of Derek Bradbury who, having observed that in heavy falls of aphis they tend to drift together in clumps, devised a dressing which combined two or three flies on the same hook shank.

Hook:	14-16
Silk:	Olive
Wings:	White DRF floss, two strands per wing. Two or three pairs tied spent down the hook shank
Hackles:	One for each set of wings. Tiny light olive cock hackles with all fibres removed from the underside of the hook

Green and Yellow Nymph

Green and Yellow Nymph

Another of Tom Ivens' nymphs designed to fish high in the water when fish are taking nymphs from just below the surface or even taking the fly on the surface.

Hook:	10-12
Body:	Two strands of green-dyed swan herl from tail to halfway. Two strands of deep yellow-dyed swan herl to one eighth of an inch from the eye
Head:	Two strands of peacock herl twisted together and wound about four times

In a small dressing with the leader greased down to the last two or three inches, Tom Ivens says that fished with virtually imperceptible movement it is most effective.

Green Beast

Green Beast

Alan Pearson, the big fish specialist, devised this dressing which is intended to represent the larva of one of the larger water beetles. It has been very successful for him on many waters, and other anglers have found it a good pattern, too.

Hook:	R/B wide gape 10-12
Silk:	Dark green
Tail:	Short grass-green hackle fibres
Rib:	Fine silver wire
Body:	Grass-green floss silk to create a fat carrot-shape
Hackle:	Brown partridge long in fibre, with all fibres on one side of stalk cut off, two turns only

It can be tied in scarlet, grey, brown, black and orange. The green version can be tied with a rib of hot-orange DRF silk.

Alan Pearson recommends that it be fished with an occasional tweak and long pauses. Richard Walker thinks that drawn slowly and steadily through the water it might resemble a damselfly nymph. I have fished it fairly well-down on a number of small stillwaters and taken fish. I don't know what insect they take it for.

Greenbottle *(Lucilia caesar)*

Another of those once-in-a-lifetime patterns, designed by Taff Price, to represent those glossy green flies known as greenbottles and near-relatives of the bluebottles.

Hook:	14
Silk:	Green
Body:	Built up of green seal's fur close ribbed with green lurex
Wing:	Grey hackle points
Hackle:	Dark green

I have seen naturals blown onto the water, but have never observed one taken by a trout.

Greenbottle

Green Corixa

Richard Walker's corixa pattern takes into account that some of the stages of the development of the adult are of a green hue, and this represents the larva stage.

Hook:	14
Rib:	Silver
Body:	White floss (fat)
Back & legs:	Olive swan dyed a pale shade

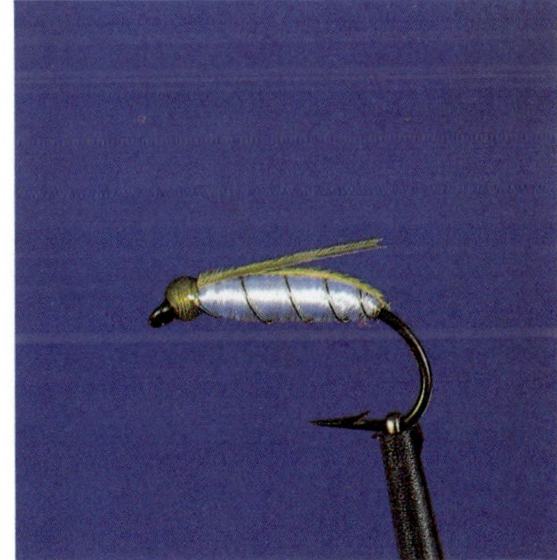

Green Corixa

The Green DF Partridge

As Richard Walker, its inventor, points out, this is an easy pattern for the tyro to tie, yet can be a very effective fish taker. He suggests that it can be used in either a leaded or unleaded version. Four or so layers of wine-bottle lead foil bound on top of the hook shank before the body material is added will enable the fly to fish hook-point up. Either pattern should be fished slowly with one-foot retrieves:

Hook:	10-12
Body:	Lime-green DF wool, tied rather fat
Rib:	Silver thread
Hackle:	Sparse brown partridge
Head:	Black

The Green DF Partridge

This is a pattern recommended by Alan Pearson, the big fish specialist, in his book, *Catching Big Trout*. He uses a long shank 8 hook and spins on a slim body as compared to the original's fat one. He specifies that the length of the body should not exceed one inch, thus leaving an amount of bare shank. He has in mind the stalking of an individual trout, and his dressing is calculated to sink at his desired rate, and says that with an accurate cast the trout rarely refuses.

He uses it mostly when patches of green algae have floated up from the bottom of the lake and big rainbows seem to cruise in its vicinity feeding on what he believes is a tiny green worm, no doubt a chironomid larva. This is when the Green Partridge is at its best.

Green Nymph

Tom Ivens recommends that this nymph pattern of his be fished well down when fish are not showing. The fly is retrieved six inches at a time, with pauses in between, and the angler must be vigilant to watch for his line drawing. On other occasions fish hook themselves. In smaller sizes the partridge hackle can be omitted.

Hook:	7-11
Body:	Pale green nylon monofilament over white floss, thicker at the thorax
Hackle:	Two turns of brown partridge hackle
Head:	Two strands of bronze peacock herl twisted together

Green Nymph (T. C. Ivens)

Roy Masters has developed this pattern further by using an underbody of lime fluorescent floss silk covered with light green monofilament.

Richard Walker has also devised a Green Nymph dressing which is as follows:

Hook:	12-18
Body:	Swan herl for sizes 16 and 18. Ostrich herl, short in the flue, for sizes 12 to 14. Colours from brown-olive to greenish-olive
Tail:	Suitably dyed feather fibres tied short

The pattern can be weighted with an underbody of fine copper wire (two layers and a built-up thorax) if required.

The Green Palmer

Green Palmer

A palmer pattern suggested to Richard Walker which is probably taken for a dragonfly larva though it seems a bit too green to me.

Hook:	6-10
Body:	Green seal fur dubbed on green silk
Hackle:	A big cock hackle dyed light grass-green, wound palmer-style
Rib:	Fine gold thread. This is wound last to cross the turns of hackle

The fly can be weighted to start with by whipping four or five layers of lead foil on top of the hook shank. The pattern should be allowed to sink and then retrieved steadily at a slow to medium pace.

Green Peter

Green Peter (Wet)

A favourite old Irish pattern dressed to represent a sedge pupa. Sedges in Ireland are commonly called Peters or Rails, and this pattern with its slip of dark green-olive goose feather and hen pheasant wing tied along the body probably represents the cinnamon sedges which are abundant on the Irish lowland limestone lakes. The abdomens of the naturals are often of a greenish hue.

Hook:	9-10
Rib:	Gold tinsel to give a segmented effect
Body:	Green seal's fur, and a slip of dark green-olive goose feather, tied in at the head
Wing:	Dark mottled hen pheasant wing, tied to lie along the side of the body — not the top
Hackle:	Two turns of ginger hen hackle
Beard:	A few fibres of mallard scapular fibres

It can be fished wet or dry. The wet pattern has the hen hackle behind the wings as in the dressing above, whilst the dry has a cock hackle in front of the wings.

Lough Owel is famous for its big sedge fishing or, as it is known locally, Green Peter fishing, which usually begins about the middle of July. The pattern is used extensively in that month and August on loughs like Mask, Arrow, Corrib, Conn and Carra.

Variations of the Green Peter are the Dark Peter with a black seal's fur body, and the Blue Peter with a blue seal's fur body.

Green Peter (Dry)

Green Sedge Pupa

One of the early dressings for sedge pupa was that given by J. R. Harris in his book *An Angler's Entomology*. Various sedge pupae tend to reflect the colour of the ultimate adult, and Harris's Green Sedge Pupa may possibly represent the pupal stage of the cinnamon sedge.

Hook: 11-13
Body: Tail half, light green floss silk tied thickly
Thorax: Brown ostrich herl or copper-coloured peacock herl, wound to occupy about half of the hook shank
Wings: Very short brown mallard tied to reach only the end of the thorax
Hackle: Two turns of red hen or cock
Swimming legs: Two cock pheasant tail fibres tied sloping back towards the tail, underneath the hook

Green Sedge Pupa
(A. R. C. Howman)

Another good pattern is that of Major A. C. R. Howman (Alastair Ross), and was based on a study of the insect life of his own lakes.

Hook: 10
Body: Olive floss
Rib: Silver tinsel
Wing cases: A blob of olive seal's fur
Legs: Furnace cock, clipped
Head: Orange silk

Fish on a floating line and long leader with slow, steady pulls.

Greenwell's Glory

Greenwell's Glory (Dry)

C. F. Walker wondered sceptically whether the enormous popularity of this fly owed as much to the alliteration as to its practical attributes! Certainly, even non-fishermen have heard of this fly whose name was probably given to it by its inventor, James Wright of Tweedside, and not by the learned Canon Greenwell himself who inspired its tying. The original dressing is now invariably ribbed with fine gold wire, and the Canon himself said that this could be added.

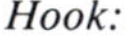

Hook:	10-14
Silk:	Yellow, well waxed
Rib:	Fine gold wire
Body:	Yellow silk
Wing:	Paired slips of blackbird wing
Hackle:	Coch-y-bonddu

Starling primary feather can be used instead of the blackbird wing, and an excellent non-winged version has a furnace cock and medium blue dun cock for hackle and a few fibres of furnace cock for tail. Fished dry, this has taken many trout for me on both rivers and lakes.

In an era of specialist patterns, Greenwell's Glory remains, in my view, the best general representation of an olive nymph or dun. Teamed up with a Gold-Ribbed Hare's Ear on the droppers with a nymph pattern on the point, it can form an unbeatable combination when olives are about. It is no less potent when fished singly as a dry fly and cast to rising fish.

The Flyfishers' Club possesses a Greenwell's Glory tied by Canon Greenwell himself.

The Grenadier

Another amazingly simple pattern devised by Dr. Bell, that early pioneer of imitative fishing, with particular reference to Blagdon. Unfortunately, there is no written evidence of what this fly was intended to represent, but this is no handicap to its effectiveness.

Hook:	D/E 13
Rib:	Oval gold tinsel
Body:	Hot-orange floss or seal's fur
Hackle:	Two turns of light furnace cock

It sinks easily because it is only lightly hackled, and should be retrieved slowly. The hot-orange makes it more effective in the latter half of the season. It can be used on the top dropper when boat fishing in the traditional style, in which case it is better to make the hackle thicker so that it tends to bounce on the ripple. It was one of the patterns used by Robert Cobbledick, the West Country fisherman, when he won the Brown Bowl for the heaviest bag of any angler in the Fifty-Fifth International Flyfishing match held at Rutland Water in May 1983. He had twelve trout for 23lb 5oz.

Tom Stewart caught fish with the Grenadier used as a dry fly.

The Grenadier

Grey and Red Matuka

See under Matukas

Grey Duster

I have had a regard for this dry fly ever since I used it regularly on the River Wharfe, and it has gone on to prove its versatility on stillwater also. For one thing, it is very easily seen by the angler. Another virtue is that it can be used throughout the season. If an angler is to catch anything in a caenis hatch it may well be with a small Grey Duster. In its larger sizes it can be used during the mayfly season. Dressed with a whisk, it can be used as a representation of a lake olive dun which has pale grey tails.

Grey Duster

Hook:	12-14, larger for mayflies and lakes
Silk:	Brown
Body:	Dubbing of light rabbit's fur mixed with a small amount of blue under-fur
Hackle:	Badger hackle, well-marked with a black centre and white list
Tail:	Optional

David Collyer recommends that in a caenis hatch the fly should be cast well ahead of a rising fish, if possible one with a regular route pattern, and left quite still on the top.

Preben Torp Jacobsen, the Danish fly dresser, has experimented successfully with a parachute hackle instead of the traditional one and calls his fly the Parachuting Badger. John Goddard expresses a preference for this dressing in his *The Superflies of Still Water*, as he feels it caters more adequately for the disposition of lake trout to feed in or under the surface film rather than on top of it.

Grey Ghost

Grey Ghost

Here is another spectral pattern to join its compatriots, the Black and White Ghosts. There are actually two distinct patterns known as the Grey Ghost. The first is a popular New Zealand matuka style lure which can be effective on the larger reservoirs as an attractor:

Hook: L/S 6-10
Body: Flat silver tinsel
Rib: Oval silver tinsel
Tail: None
Wing: Two light grey cock hackles, bound down to the body by ribbing tinsel
Head: Black varnish
Hackle: Light grey (optional)

The second is an American streamer pattern in origin which is popular for trout and sea trout all over the world:

Gray Ghost

Hook: L/S 6-10
Body: Orange floss or orange wool
Rib: Flat silver tinsel
Throat: Strands of bronze peacock herl tied on directly under the head, then white bucktail, both as long as the wing, then yellow cock hackle fibres or a golden pheasant crest
Wing: Four medium blue dun cock hackle fibres tied streamer style
Cheek: Lady Amhurst tippet feathers or silver pheasant body feathers or barred widgeon throat feathers
Eyes: Jungle cock (optional)
Head: Black varnish

Probably works best as a fry imitator.

Grey Goose Nymph

Intended by Frank Sawyer for use on the chalk streams to represent the pale wateries. He used it during late evening on lakes with light quick-actioned tackle, and fished very slowly on a floating line. One of his techniques was to cast to an area where fish were feeding and wait until about half the leader had sunk. Then he would slowly lift the rod tip and thus simulate an ascending nymph.

Hook:	14-16
Body:	Gold-coloured wire tied in the manner of Sawyer's Pheasant Tail Nymph
Tails, body, thorax:	Lightish grey, green, yellowish wing feathers of a farmyard grey goose. The darker butt end of the herls create a well-defined thorax and wing cases.

Grey Goose Nymph

Until the 1983 season, I had used the Grey Goose Nymph only on rivers, but I had several successes with it on stillwater by casting to individual fish and raising the rod tip as prescribed. The quick, clean entry of the pattern into the water helps this type of fishing.

Grey Midge Pupa

A midge pupa which is extremely easy to tie devised by David Collyer. This is a tiny midge pupa imitation for very calm conditions and those minute, almost imperceptible, rises.

Hook:	D/E 14-18
Silk:	Black
Body:	Stripped peacock herl
Thorax:	Mole's fur

David Collyer belongs to the school of thought which believes that the pupa should be fished very slowly indeed using a knotless tapered leader greased right up to the fly.

Grey Midge Pupa

Grey Squirrel Mayfly

Another fine dressing from John Henderson which has much in common with the American Grey Wulff. In this dressing, however, the wing hairs are divided into two and fixed in an upright position with figure-of-eight turns of the tying silk. The hackle, though tied in by the stem in front of the wings, is brought down and up behind them where the three turns close up to the wings keep them almost upright. One turn is taken between the wings and two or more in front.

Hook:	L/S 9-10
Silk:	Pale yellow
Tail:	Three fibres from a cock pheasant's tail
Rib:	Flat silver tinsel or silver lurex
Body:	Fur from the flank of a grey squirrel
Wings:	Fibres from the grey squirrel's tail
Hackle:	Light Plymouth Rock (grizzle) dyed light olive

Grey Squirrel Mayfly

The substitution of a few grey squirrel hairs in place of the cock pheasant fibres for the tail whisks gives the fly harder wearing properties.

Grey Wulff

This is an American pattern devised by Lee Wulff to simulate the transitional stage in the mayfly from nymph to dun. The fly first became popular in the 1950's following its use on the Houghton Club water by Lewis Douglas, the then United States ambassador.

Hook:	8-10
Silk:	Yellow
Tail:	Natural brown bucktail
Body:	Dubbed grey squirrel fur
Wing:	A bunch of brown barred squirrel tail fibres or grey squirrel tail fibres tied as a single forward wing
Hackle:	Two blue dun cock hackles and one dark red Indian game cock hackle

Grey Wulff

The Small Grey Wulff has small brown barred squirrel tail fibres for whisks and for wing, and a medium blue dun cock for hackle.

Peter Deane, the well-known professional tyer, who had much to do with the fly from the outset, attributes its success to the single forward wing which represents the stage of the hatching nymph when the wings have emerged from the thorax but are still stuck together. This is a pattern which is always worth trying during a mayfly hatch and should be cast to rising fish.

Grizzly Beetle

Grizzly Beetle

This is a pattern used by Alan Pearson, the big fish specialist, and is what Taff Price terms a broad spectrum fly. Fished wet, it can be taken for a shrimp or a corixa, and dry and well-waterproofed for terrestrials blown onto the water like horseflies or houseflies. Alan Pearson says that he has taken fish with it when they did not appear to be feeding and had rejected other patterns. One of the drawbacks of the pattern is its poor hooking capacity caused probably by the long stiff hackles near the hook point:

Hook:	Wide gape R/B 10 quite heavy in the wire
Silk:	Black
Rib:	Three black ostrich herls
Tail:	Half a dozen or more fibres projecting backwards of the body hackle
Body hackle:	A black, white and grey (grizzle) cock hackle from tail to head on opposing spiral to the rib
Back:	Seven to ten cock pheasant tail fibres from tail to behind head
Head:	Black varnish

Apart from the back, it has much in common with old flies like Ronald's Black and Red Palmer and Halcyon's Grizzled Palmer. The latter used a grizzled hackle over gold ribbed peacock herl.

Grouse Series

Grouse and Green

The chief variation in the dressing of the traditional lake flies is the wing, and in this series a feather from a grouse tail is used. The Grouse and Green was Courtney Williams' favourite and Eric Taverner recommends it as one of the best tail flies for Highland lochs.

Grouse and Green

Hook:	8-12
Tail:	Brown mallard or a few fibres of golden pheasant tippet
Rib:	Gold or silver wire
Body:	Green wool or seal's fur
Wing:	Brown mottled feather from a grouse's tail
Hackle:	Red

The most popular in the series in use today in Scotland from May to August is the Grouse and Claret. It may be taken for a sedge pupa or even a sepia or claret nymph or dun.

Grouse and Claret

Hook:	8-12
Tail:	Golden pheasant tippet
Rib:	Gold or silver wire
Body:	Claret wool or seal's fur
Wing:	Brown mottled feather from a grouse's tail
Hackle:	Natural red cock or one dyed claret

One which is almost certainly taken as an imitation of a sedge is the Grouse and Orange.

Grouse and Orange

Hook:	8-12
Tail:	Three or four fibres of golden pheasant tippet
Rib:	Gold wire
Body:	Orange wool or seal's fur
Wing:	Brown mottled feather from a grouse's tail
Hackle:	Red or dyed-orange cock

Most commonly these flies are fished in a traditional team of three from a boat or from the bank.

Grouse Wing *(Mystacides longicornis)*

This is a common sedge fly with very long antennae whose grey wings, covered with yellowish down normally, but not always, have three brown transverse bands. These markings with some similarity to a grouse wing feather explain its name and the use of grouse feather in the dressing of its imitative patterns. Not only has it a long season from May to September but it frequently flies in the late afternoon and early evening.

Unfortunately, it is not generally considered to be of much significance to the trout. However, Taff Price has given us a dressing.

Grouse Wing (Taff Price)

Hook:	14
Body:	Brown polypropylene or fly body fur
Wing:	Thin strips of grouse wing extending beyond the hook
Hackle:	Dark ginger
Antennae:	Dark mallard fibres

Another dressing is by Richard Walker.

Hook:	L/S 12
Silk:	Black
Tag:	White fluorescent floss tied very small
Body:	Dark chocolate ostrich herl or dyed swan herl clipped down
Wing:	Grouse wing or tail fibres, or dark sepia and brown speckled turkey
Hackle:	Dark furnace or dark coch-y-bonddu

Other useful imitations of the natural are the Grouse and Orange and the Grouse and Yellow.

Hair Sedges

These patterns arose from experiments by Richard Walker to produce flies for someone allergic to feathers. The hair is laid along the hook shank with the butts projecting forward. These are then divided and set at right angles to the hook shank with a figure-of-eight binding.

Hair Sedge (Red)

Red Sedge

Hook:	10
Silk:	Chestnut
Body:	Rabbit belly fur dyed chestnut with a very little orange DRF wool at the rear
Wing:	Goat or similar hair dyed chestnut. Figure-of-eight dubbing, as body

Small Black Sedge

Hook:	14
Silk:	Black
Body:	Mole fur
Wing:	Black squirrel fur. Dubbing as body

These patterns catch fish, are very hard-wearing and quick to dry.

Hairy Minnow

A bucktail pattern devised by Taff Price as a fry imitator. It has been described by him as looking like "a sparse grotesque motheaten shaving brush" when dry, but taking on a very minnow-like appearance when in the water. It has been used with some success by anglers at Blagdon and Chew.

Hook:	L/S 8-10
Tail:	Small tuft of DFM red wool
Rib:	Oval silver
Body:	Flat silver
Wing:	Dark green bucktail, white bucktail underneath
Underwing or hackle:	Hook reversed in the vice, white bucktail tied in to the bend of the hook, then a small tuft of red bucktail at the throat
Head:	Black, with white painted eye, black pupil

Hairy Minnow

Hare's Ear

This is another fly of ancient vintage, designed originally for the river, which has made a highly successful transition to the era of stillwater. For instance, it is considered by John Wadham, probably Rutland Water's finest bank fisher, to be the best overall pattern for that water.

It is generally accepted to be a general representation of an olive, and I prefer Alfred Ronalds' model from the last century. It omits the starling wing, and can be used as the wet fly simulating the nymph with only a little of the dubbing picked out, and as the dry fly or dun with the dubbing prominent and acting as a hackle.

Hook:	13
Silk:	Fine yellow
Body:	Fur of a hare's ear or face, spun thinly and wound thickest at the shoulder. Some of the dubbing is then picked out to form legs
Tail:	Two fibres of a dun hackle

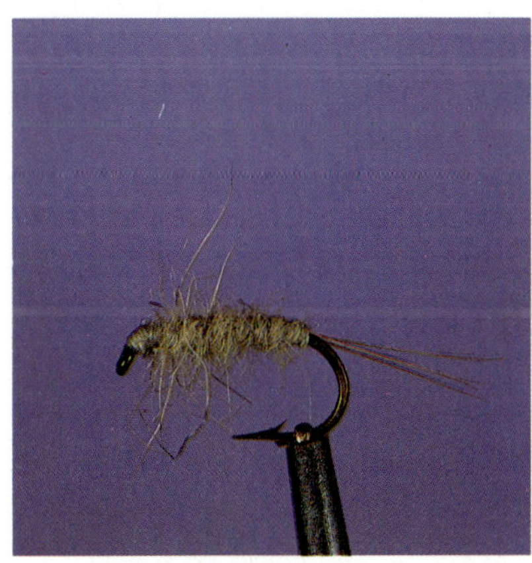

Hare's Ear (Alfred Ronalds)

Ronalds added that if not sufficient of the dubbing could be picked out two or three turns of a ginger dun hackle could be added.

The standard version of the fly is Halford's, which he stated was Ogden's original pattern.

Hook:	15-17
Body:	Pale primrose silk
Whisk:	Four or five strands of a ginger cock beard hackle
Legs:	The lightest fur from a hare's face spun on pale yellow tying silk, and worked as a hackle
Wings:	Pale starling

John Ketley, the fishing international, fishes the Hare's Ear in loch style. With little hackle he uses it on the tail, and with more on the dropper. He has a high opinion of the fly for warm, cloudy days when sedges are about.

A dressing given by Steve Parton which he calls a Hare's Ear is used by him as a shrimp imitation.

Body:	Pale ginger hare jaw fur mixed with hare's face fur. Dressed large, pale and carrot-shaped. Better if picked out on the underside after ribbing
Rib:	Fine gold wire
Tail:	Protruding well round the hook bend — buff tipped hare's face guard hairs. Can be leaded underneath

Harlot

An out-and-out attractor—in fact a scarlet woman. Tied by David Collyer in an idle moment at his fly-tying bench and turning out — somewhat to his surprise — to be a good fish taker. Aptly named by him the Harlot.

Hook:	D/E 6-8
Silk:	Black
Tail:	Blue gallina
Butt:	Bronze peacock herl
Body:	In three sections: black, scarlet and black floss silk
Wing:	Married strands of scarlet, black and scarlet goose
Hackle:	Blue gallina, tied as a beard

Harlot

He does not say how it should be fished, but I should imagine a fast retrieve is the best.

Hanningfield Lure

A pattern invented by Richard Walker to imitate the colours of a small perch for use at Hanningfield Reservoir. The tail is a wound hackle rather than the usual hackle fibre or wool tag style to be found on most lures.

Hook:	L/S 8, tied in tandem
Silk:	Black
Tail:	Hot-orange cock, wound and clipped
Rib:	Silver thread (oval silver tinsel)
Bodies:	White fluorescent wool or nylon
Wing:	White goat hair with speckled turkey over
Hackles:	Orange and blue cock tied as beard
Sides:	Jungle cock or substitute

Hanningfield Lure

The inventor states that it is the best lure he knows for catching perch, thus underlining the cannibal instincts of that fish for its smaller brethren. As far as trout are concerned he says that it only does well when they are attacking concentrations of small coarse fish. David Collyer is more sanguine of its merits, averring that he would be happy to confine himself to three multi-hook lures: the Black and White lures and the Hanningfield Lure.

The Hatching Mayfly

Hatching Mayfly (John Goddard)

A pattern devised by John Goddard to imitate the mayfly dun as it comes out of its nymphal shuck in the surface film.

Hook:	L/S fine wire 8
Silk:	Yellow
Tail:	Tips of three pheasant tail fibres
Rib:	Gold wire or narrow gold lurex
Body:	Tail half — cock pheasant tail fibres. Head half — cream seal's fur
Wings:	V-shaped hackle fibre wings using a large pale blue dun cock
Hackle:	Small furnace cock tied thickly

It is recommended that the tail section be fished submerged. John Goddard says that not only does this pattern work well but it also has excellent hooking properties.

Another excellent representation of the insect at this stage of its development is by C. F. Walker which he called the Hatching Nymph.

Hook:	Suggest L/S 8
Rib:	Gold wire
Body:	Dubbing from the paler parts of a hare's ear
Thorax:	Two turns of darker hare's ear
Hackles:	Two wound very sparsely. The first a partridge feather dyed in picric acid. The second an undyed partridge feather. Both tied so as to slope along the body, the idea being to imitate the wings emerging from their cases

Commander Walker said that it would sometimes take even when fish were feeding on newly hatched flies. He also considered his pattern an excellent hooker because of its slim, soft hackles.

Hatching Midge Pupa

See Chironomids

Hatching Olive Nymph

Hatches of olives often take place in the hours around mid-day, and trout often seem to be partial to the emerging nymph rather than the adult dun. A number of artificials have thus been devised to represent them at this stage of their lives.

One of the pioneer patterns in this respect was that of Joscelyn Lane. It has much in common with the Gold-Ribbed Hare's Ear.

Hook:	10-12
Silk:	Golden-olive
Tail:	Four strands of hare's ear fur, about one quarter of an inch long
Rib:	Gold wire on body only
Body:	Dubbing from root of hare's ear, wound on primrose silk. Rather thin and tapered at tail end
Thorax:	Same fur but thicker
Hackle:	A few strands of the fur picked out with a dubbing needle from the lower part of the thorax to point in all directions

Hatching Olive Nymph
(Geoffrey Bucknall)

Geoffrey Bucknall's pattern represents either a lake or pond olive nymph hatching into an adult.

Hook:	12-14
Tail:	Slim strip of light olive goose feather
Rib:	Fine gold tinsel, oval or flat, up to thorax only
Body:	Light olive goose feather wound from butts of tail strip
Thorax:	A knob of dark olive seal's fur
Wing cases:	A strip of waterhen or any dark wing feather, over thorax only
Hackle:	A clipped medium or light olive cock hackle

John Goddard's pattern which he calls the Hatching Olive is as follows:

Hook:	13-16
Silk:	Brown
Body:	Olive-green condor — three fibres. One eighth of an inch of the tips left projecting to form tail, a silver lurex rib tied in and body covered up to thorax with a strip of olive-dyed PVC
Thorax:	Peacock herl with three dark pheasant tail fibres doubled and redoubled to form wing cases
Hackle:	Two turns of pale honey or dark red

All three patterns can be used to represent either of the hatching olives and should be fished very slowly on a floating line.

The Hawthorn Fly *(Bibio marci)*

Sometimes known as St Mark's Fly because hatches begin around the 25th April which is St Mark's Day. These continue for a few weeks into May. It is a black, terrestrial fly nearly half an inch long and characterised by a pair of long trailing rear legs. It is not usually found on water but in a strong wind it can be blown onto the surface and trout may eagerly take it.

The hawthorn fly has been imitated since the very earliest times with starling wings and ostrich herl for the body. Joscelyn Lane's dressing omits the ostrich herl from the body as he found that the natural's body had a particularly smooth, shiny surface.

Hawthorn Fly (David Collyer)

Hook:	10
Silk:	Black
Rib:	Finest silver wire, rather widely spaced
Body:	Black silk tapered finely at the tail end. The body varnished
Thorax:	Conspicuous. Tied in last, using two strands of black ostrich herl
Hackle:	Three to four turns of glassy black cock hackle, tied in behind the thorax, with fibres as long as the hook and sloping well backwards

David Collyer has an excellent dressing which incorporates the trailing legs of the natural.

Hook:	U/E 10
Silk:	Black
Body:	Peacock herl
Legs:	Dyed-black swan, knotted and trailing back and below the fly
Wings:	Pale blue dun hackle tips in an acute V low over the back
Hackle:	Black cock, a pair back to back

Another good pattern which omits the wing is that of Preben Torp Jacobsen.

Hook:	U/E 12
Silk:	Brown
Body:	Three strands of black-dyed condor or peacock herl
Legs:	Two strands of black-dyed condor or peacock tied with points trailing back
Hackle:	Two natural black cock wound on so that the convex sides are turned against each other
Head:	Single strand of black-dyed condor or peacock

The long trailing legs which are a feature of the latter two patterns exaggerate or caricature a recognition point and hopefully trigger a reaction from the trout.

Though generally considered to be a river fly, prolific hatches occur on some stillwaters including Chew Valley Lake and Siblyback Reservoir in Cornwall. When fish are rising to the natural the artificial should be cast to them and allowed to lie on or in the surface film.

The Heather Fly *(Bibio pomonae)*

Heather Fly — York's Favourite

This is a cousin of the hawthorn fly and is very similar in appearance except for a smattering of red on the legs which, no doubt, gives rise to its other name of Bloody Doctor. It commonly occurs in Wales and Scotland as it is often found near heather, and there it can be a more important fly than the hawthorn. In warm weather in August it swarms over the water and produces frenzied rises.

Dressings of the hawthorn with the black hackle replaced by the red one will prove effective, but Taff Price with his usual resourcefulness has given us two patterns, one of his own and the other Welsh from his home county of Gwynedd.

Hook:	12
Silk:	Black
Legs:	Red/brown horsehair
Body:	Black polypropylene
Wings:	Blue dun hackle tips or grey starling
Hackle:	Dark furnace

York's Favourite

Hook:	12
Tail:	Red ibis or substitute
Body:	Black seal's fur or ostrich herl
Hackle:	Dark furnace or coch-y-bonddu

Heavy hatches of the fly occur in Wales at such places as Llyn Brenig and at Lake Vyrnwy in August.

This Scottish version of the heather fly by Duncan Macalpine is claimed to be a more lifelike imitation by virtue of the red hackle which represents the scarlet or red colouration of the legs.

Hook:	11-12 light wire
Rib:	Fine flat silver tinsel
Body:	Black ostrich herl
Wing:	Young starling's outer covert feather folded and tied on flat
Hackle:	Black and white badger hackle dyed pillar-box red or marked with a red Pantone pen

Fished dry and cast to rising fish.

Heather Moth

A pattern given by Donald Overfield in his section on modern flies added to Courtney Williams' *A Dictionary of Trout Flies*. He states that it is a pattern for salmon and sea trout made popular by Peter Deane from a dressing given to him by the Hon. Edward

Davies in 1950. Donald Overfield recommends it as a good pattern for reservoir and lake trout tied in small sizes.

Hook:	Suggest 10-14
Tag:	Fine silver oval
Rib:	Flat silver tinsel and wire
Body:	Grey squirrel fur, well picked out
Hackle:	Plymouth Rock cock hackle palmered from the tag to the head

Heather Moth (Tom Stewart)

Eric Taverner includes the heather moth in a list of flies likely to be blown onto the water. Tom Stewart says that heather moths come out and are blown onto the surfaces of northern lochs of Scotland in July and August, and that trout will take a fully hackled pattern. He adds that it is also used by anglers who fish it dry on a floating line when sedges are hatching in Scottish lowland lochs. It is usually fished in this way on the bob of a wet fly cast. He gives the following dressing:

Hook:	8 for nothern lochs. 10-12
Tail:	A few fibres of barred teal plumage tied in short
Rib:	Oval or round silver tinsel
Body:	Grey monkey fur or grey dun seal's fur or grey wool
Hackle:	Grizzle hackle tied in at eye and wound down to the tail, and secured by the ribbing tinsel which is wound up the body in evenly spaced turns between the hackle fibres. A further hackle can be tied in at the throat to give the fly a better tapered appearance

Heron and Yellow

A pattern by Arthur Dew recommended by Donald Overfield in his scholarly additional section to Courtney Williams' *Dictionary of Trout Flies* as an original general dry fly for stillwaters.

Hook:	D/E wide gape 12-14
Silk:	Brown
Body:	Natural heron herl in two equal parts, divided by a narrow ring of dyed-yellow swan's herl
Hackle:	Top quality coch-y-bonddu cock, preferably two

Heron and Yellow

Hoolet

John Goddard considers that the Windermere moth pattern called the Hoolet represents the aquatic china mark moth. Tom Stewart says its name comes from its winging with an owl feather, and that 'hoolet' is the Scottish name for that bird which is nocturnal. Geoffrey Bucknall's Hoolet is a very successful artificial of many years standing which will represent this or any other dusk-flying whitish moth.

Hook: 8-10
Body: Bronze peacock herl wound over a strip of cork
Wings: Owl or woodcock wing feather tied low over the body, either rolled or flat
Hackle: Two light red cock hackles wound over wing roots

Hoolet

Geoffrey Bucknall commonly fishes it as a wake fly on either calm or rippled surfaces. He describes the fish pursuing it as "like a dog after a rat".

Horsefly *(Tabanidae spp)*

It is more likely that you will be bitten by this fly than the fly by the trout! And very painful bites they can be too. The female which sucks blood, is the main offender. The angler is probably better off without them around, but Taff Price points out that some species have larvae which live totally in water and therefore can be imitated, as fish may take them. He gives us both a larval and adult representation.

Horsefly Larva

Horsefly Larva

Hook: L/S 12 weighted
Silk: Olive
Rib: Ostrich herl — colours to match the body
Body: Pale olive or cream or brown wool tapered

The Horsefly

Hook: 12
Silk: Green
Rib: Grey silk
Body: Grey polypropylene fur mixed with white DFM
Wings: Grizzle hackle tips
Hackle: Blue dun
Head: Fluorescent green silk

The larva leaves the water to pupate in the ground two or three inches below the surface. The larva pattern is thus best fished on a long leader slowly on the bottom.

Invicta

Invicta

'Glorious Invicta' Geoffrey Bucknall calls it. I am never without it when sedges are hatching from June onwards. It was invented by the renowned Cheltenham fly dresser, James Ogden, and has had a renewed lease of life on stillwaters. Though considered a traditional fly, in its successful modern role it is highly regarded as a good representation of a hatching sedge fly.

It is not as difficult to tie as it looks. A tip given by Geoffrey Bucknall many years ago to his fly-dressing students wanting a saucy upturn to the golden pheasant crest feathers for the tail is to damp them with saliva and stick them inside a wine glass to dry. It works!

Hook:	D/E 10-14
Silk:	Brown
Tail:	Golden pheasant crest feather
Rib:	Oval gold tinsel
Body:	Yellow-dyed seal's fur
Body hackle:	Red game cock palmered sparsely
Wings:	Hen pheasant centre tail
Throat hackle:	From wing of blue jay

Its strength is its versatility. It catches fish on large and small waters; it is used by both boat and bank anglers; it can be used singly just breaking the surface when trout are sticking their nebs out of the water for sedges hatching; it can be used in any position in a team of flies although bob fly is the most popular position. I recently put on an Invicta to fish rising to hatching sedges, only to find it taken by what proved to be an 8lb carp which took fifteen minutes to get to the net with darkness falling and my fishing time running out!

David Collyer asks the same question about the Invicta as Skues did about Kingsley's Alder. Fished wet, why do the trout take a fully-winged adult which is swimming under water? This has prompted David to devise what he calls an Invicta Sedge Pupa whose dressing is as follows:

Hook:	10
Silk:	Olive
Rib:	Oval gold tinsel
Abdomen:	Yellow wool
Thorax:	Mixed dark green-brown wool or yellow wool
Wing cases:	Oak turkey wing strip
Hackle:	Blue jay tied as a beard

Variations of the Invicta include the Silver with a silver tinsel body and oval silver rib, the Olive with olive seal's fur and olive hackle, and the Red Tailed with scarlet ibis or swan or goose tail.

Jack Frost

Jack Frost

Another lure devised by Bob Church, probably our foremost authority on lure fishing. Its effectiveness is enhanced by the generous spray of marabou which is so responsive to the slightest movement and by the polythene body creating a translucent impression.

Hook:	D/E L/S 6-10
Silk:	Black or white
Tag:	Crimson wool
Body:	White Sirdar baby wool covered by a one eighth wide strip of polythene
Wing:	Generous spray of white marabou
Hackles:	Long-fibred crimson cock followed by long-fibred white cock

Fishing the fly slowly with pauses makes the most of the marabou feather and the semi-transparent body makes it a splendid imitation of fry in the latter part of the season. I have found it effective fished in this way on both small and large waters. It took a nice trout for me at Croxley Hall recently on the wettest and windiest day I have ever fished. In large sizes it is also successful fished very deeply on the large reservoirs.

Jassid

Jassid

The reed smut or black fly is commonly referred to as the Black Curse because it is so minute, and yet it hatches in such numbers that trout become preoccupied with it and almost impossible to catch. Its larva only lives in water which has some movement, and so it is confined to lakes which have a reasonably strong inflow.

The Jassid is an attempt to produce an artificial small enough to deceive the trout. Originated by the American, Vince Marinaro, after observation of the insect life of the Letort River, a famous Pennsylvanian limestone stream, it imitates a tiny terrestrial called the jassid. Marinaro's dressing concentrates on the silhouette by using a flattened jungle cock wing. Though tiny, the jungle cock eye makes the fly visible to the angler.

Hook:	20
Silk:	Black
Body:	Black hackle tied palmer-fashion and clipped away on top and below
Wing:	One jungle cock or substitute tied in at the eye and flat along the body over the hackle

Joe Brooks, the American angler, on a visit to this country, took fish with the Jassid on the River Dove, and he also recommends it for stillwater in the late evening when there are often hatches of small flies, midges or smuts. John Goddard tells me that he obtained some Jassids many years ago tied on size 20 or 22 hooks, and he has had some success over the years using them to represent the reed smuts.

Jersey Herd

Jersey Herd

A first-generation stillwater lure produced by the original thinking of Tom Ivens, and still commonly used despite the spawning of other and more modern fry-imitating progeny. It was produced by Tom Ivens on Whit Monday, 1951, to fish fast yet not come to the surface, and he took bag limits on three successive days stripping it very quickly through the water. Here is another name that caught the imagination, and it arose because the originator tied the fly in a hurry and the only 'gold tinsel' available came from the top of a bottle of Channel Island milk.

Hook:	D/E L/S 6-10
Silk:	Black
Tail & back:	Twelve strands of bronze peacock herl
Body:	Wide, copper-coloured, flat tinsel over a floss silk underbody
Hackle:	Dyed rich orange cock hackle — two turns

I have had most success with the Jersey Herd fished in the manner advised by the designer, but in that superb reference book, *Stillwater Flies — how and when to fish them*, Syd Brock's approach is to fish it slowly on a slow sink line near the bottom usng a smaller size.

The pattern can be weighted or unweighted. Geoffrey Bucknall devised a tube version of about one inch using gold lurex with a tuft of orange goat's hair in place of the hackle to deal with trout attacking shoals of minnows. He uses the Jersey Herd in sunlight and another of Tom Ivens' patterns, the Green and Brown Nymph, when it is cloudy.

Other body materials are now sometimes used including mylar tubing and goldfingering.

John Storey

John Storey

Donald Overfield gives the history of this fly pattern in his *50 Favourite Dry Flies* and of how it was originated by the grandfather of the present keeper of the Ryedale Anglers' Club, Arthur Storey. The slant forward of the wing seems to have been initially the result of the inexperience at that time of Arthur Storey which did not at all detract from its effectiveness. I have always found the device particularly useful in helping me to see the fly on the water, especially fast-running water.

Hook:	14-16
Silk:	Black
Body:	Three strands of copper-tinged peacock herl
Wing:	Small feather from the breast of an adult mallard tied with a pronounced forward slope over the eye
Hackle:	Sharp bright Rhode Island Red cock

It is, of course, a general dry fly pattern. Arthur Storey confirms that it was never intended to represent any particular insect although David Jacques says that on the Yorkshire Derwent it is a good imitation of a beetle larva native to the river. However, on lakes, use it as a dry sedge imitation and it takes fish.

The original dressing used a down-eyed hook when the wing was tied wet fly fashion. With the forward wing and fished dry, an up-eyed hook may be preferred.

Ke-He

Ke-He

A general pattern invented by Messrs Kemp and Heddle, hence the name Ke-He, when fishing Harray Loch to represent great numbers of small black bees which had been blown onto the water. It is still a killing fly there, with or without the bees, and is also fished extensively in the Shetlands and on Highland lochs.

Hook:	10-14
Tail:	Golden pheasant tippet fibres
Body:	Bronze peacock herl fairly thick
Hackle:	Medium red/brown

Kingsmill Moore reflects on whether it is taken for a lure or a food form. He suggests that it might be taken for a black beetle. It is a pattern which continues to be fished on Lough Melvin and was recently used by Arthur Cove when he fished there.

Knotted Midge

Knotted Midge (Traditional)

Small black flies are on the water during most parts of the season. Whatever their species, fishermen loosely term them black gnats or midges although the former is the more appropriate name. They can often be seen over and on the water in pairs as they mate, and in so doing they kick up quite a fuss which sometimes attracts trout.

Hook:	12-14
Body:	Black tying silk
Hackle:	Black cock, one at tail end of hook and one at the shoulder

I am quite happy to use the above dressing, but the one by G. F. G. Rivaz is strictly a better representation as it takes into account the different colour of the male from the female.

Hook:	U/E L/S 16
Tails:	Three long cree hackle fibres cocked up at almost ninety degrees to the hook shank
Rib:	Very fine silver wire
Body:	Black silk
Front hackle:	Short-fibred badger cock
Rear hackle:	Red cock, wound at rear of body near the bend of the hook

Cast to rising fish and allow to lie motionless with the occasional twitch.

Lacewings *(Neuroptera)*

Green Lacewing (Taff Price)

There are many species of lacewings, only two of which are aquatic. Green and brown are the most common. They are exquisite creatures with bright orange eyes which, as Ronalds says, possess wonderful brilliancy. As their names imply, their wings are gauze or lace-like in delicacy. The green lacewing *(chrysopidae)* is most imitated although it is terrestrial. Ronalds' pattern is as good as any.

Gold Eyed Gauze-Wing

Hook: L/S 13
Silk: Pale yellowish-green
Body: Very pale yellowish-green floss silk
Wings: Any transparent feather, stained slightly green
Hackle: Palest blue dun procurable

T. E. Pritt also designed a pattern called Greensleeves which is also probably a lacewing imitation.

Greensleeves

Hook: 14
Body: Bright green silk
Wings: Hackle with a feather from the inside of a woodcock's wing, or from a hen pheasant's neck
Head: Bright green silk

A splendidly lifelike pattern is that of Taff Price. I have not fished it, but my only query is as to how well the green raffene will stand up to wear even though treated with artist's fixative.

Hook: 12-14
Silk: Green
Rib: DFM green silk
Body: Bright green polypropylene
Wing: Green raffene coated with artist's fixative to make more durable. Can be tied roof-like, over the back, or spent
Hackle: Lime green

David Jacques points out that many species are dusk-fliers, and certainly it requires a windy day for them to be blown onto the water. Peter Lapsley reports falls of the creatures on his lakes as early as February, and these will probably be *Chrysopa carnea*, the only species to live through the winter. Lacewings enter my caravan at dusk in the summer, during my fishing trips, where they continue to live quite happily. Taff Price suggests that if the trout do rise to a fall of lacewings nothing but a fly to match the natural will do, fished dry.

Ladybird *(Coccinellidae)*

Everyone is familiar with the ladybird which is a terrestrial small beetle. There can be times, however, when they get onto reservoirs and lakes, and Taff Price notes that this was particularly the case in 1976 following two mild springs.

In his imitation the back is dotted black so that at least the fisherman can see that it is a ladybird!

Hook: 14-16
Silk: Black
Body: Black polypropylene
Back: Yellow or orange raffene or dyed swan, varnished and dotted black
Hackle: Black

Richard Walker takes the view that there is no need to imitate the spots. In *More Fly Dressing Innovations* he specifies that the hackle be clipped short though the photograph has longish fibres. I also show it with longish fibres.

Hook:	14
Body:	Bronze peacock herl tied fat
Wing covers:	Bright chestnut pheasant tail fibres
Hackle:	Short, sparse natural black cock (clipped short)

Richard Walker advocates soaking his pattern in fly floatant and fishing it dry.

Ladybird (Richard Walker)

Lake Olive Nymph *(Cloeon simile)*

Lake Olive Nymph (C. F. Walker)

The lake olive is one of only two olives, the other being the pond olive, to be found on stillwaters. The nymphs of both species are similar in size at around a quarter of an inch (7mm) — with six legs, seven pairs of gills and three tails. The thorax of the lake olive is almost black, the pond olive dark brown; both have yellow and brown abdomens.

There are conflicting opinions about their habitats. C. F. Walker and John Goddard say they are nearly always found in deeper water, whilst J. R. Harris considered they could be found in the shallow bays of larger lakes. He said they delighted in a lake bottom clothed in moss or other aquatic plants which do not grow very high. All agree that they commonly hatch in numbers in May and June, and again in late August and September.

One of the earliest patterns which is still highly regarded is that of Joscelyn Lane.

Hook:	12
Silk:	Golden olive
Tail:	Four or five cock hackle fibres dyed olive, nearly one quarter of an inch long
Rib:	Fine gold wire
Abdomen:	Olive silk or 3X nylon, very thin at tail end and thickening gradually to thorax
Thorax:	Darker and thicker than body, but not ball-shaped, weighted if required
Hackle:	A small bunch of cock hackle fibres dyed olive, tied in under throat with most of the fibres lying back close below the body

C. F. Walker devised a dressing which would serve for both the lake and pond olives which he called the Cloeon Nymph.

Hook:	13-14
Tail:	Fibres from any brown speckled feather
Rib & tag:	Silver tinsel
Abdomen:	Brown and ginger seal's fur mixed and kept fairly smooth
Gills:	Pale yellow-brown condor herl wound as ribbing
Thorax & wing pads:	Dark brown seal's fur
Leg hackle:	Medium honey dun hen

Another good imitation based on careful observation of the natural is that of John Henderson.

Hook:	13
Silk:	Olive
Body & tail:	Three fibres from a blue game cock's tail, dyed light olive, the points forming the short whisks, the remainder being wound up the shank to form the body
Rib:	Fine gold wire or yellow silk
Thorax:	Dark olive seal's fur mixture
Hackle:	Two turns of small dun hen

The vicinity of weed beds is a good place to fish the nymph remembering that it is an agile darter if dislodged or moving from an aquatic plant, and so some movement must be imparted to the artificial. The other obvious time to use the pattern is when the nymph is coming to the surface to hatch into the adult. There are, of course, specific imitations of the nymph at the point of ecdysis which can be found under Hatching Olive.

On a larger reservoir where droppers are allowed a good lake olive team would be a Lake Olive Nymph on the tail, a Greenwell Nymph on the middle dropper and the Gold-Ribbed Hare's Ear on the bob.

Other patterns which can represent the lake olive nymph will be found under Gold-Ribbed Hare's Ear, Hare's Ear, Hatching Olive Nymph, PVC Nymph, Suspender Nymph.

Lake Olive Dun *(Cloeon simile)*

The dun of the lake olive is very similar to the pond olive in size — around a quarter of an inch (7mm) — and in looks. It is duller in appearance with a greyish tail compared with the pond olive's black ringed one. Lake olives hatching in spring tend to be slightly larger than those appearing in late summer or autumn. Hatches occur in the middle of the day and are often rather sparse. It is only when they are more prolific that the imitation of the dun comes into its own.

J. R. Harris calls the early duns Green

Lake Olive Dun (Peter Lapsley)

Olives and the later ones Golden Olives because of the differences in colouration. His pattern takes this change in colour later in the season into account.

Hook:	13-15
Tail:	Brown olive cock
Rib:	Gold wire
Body:	Palest blue heron herl or white swan dyed brown-olive
Wing:	Dark starling tied forward
Hackle:	Green-olive or brown-olive cock. For later in the season use the brown-olive hackle and the swan herl dyed brown-olive on a size 15 hook

C. F. Walker's dressing is tied in smaller sizes as the season progresses.

Hook:	13-14 reducing to 15 in September
Tail:	Grey-brown mallard fibres
Rib:	Gold tinsel
Body:	Pale grey condor herl lightly stained in picric acid
Wing:	A bunch of fibres from a medium blue-grey waterhen or coot body feather, tied upright
Hackle:	Pale honey dun cock (or dyed pale yellow-olive)

Peter Lapsley's hackled pattern omits the wings, and I must say that I have never found this to be a disadvantage from the trout's point of view.

Hook:	U/E fine wire 14
Silk:	Brown
Tail:	A small bunch of light dun cock hackles
Rib:	Silver wire
Body:	Dark olive condor herl
Hackle:	Two medium blue dun cock hackles

The artificial needs to ride high in the water and should be cast out to rising fish or allowed to float dormant in the vicinity of weed beds.

Other good patterns to use for the lake olive dun can be found under Olive Dun, Sooty Olive, Super Grizzly.

Lake Olive Spinner *(Cloeon simile)*

It is not too often that fishing a dun pattern is successful, possibly because the natural hatching adult comes very quickly off the water, but in the evening the spent female spinner, having perpetuated the species by laying her eggs, may lie in some numbers on the water. Trout may then be observed taking them in with a slow sipping rise.

Few commercial patterns are available, and this is where the fly tyer can come into his own. Here are four excellent representations of the spinner, each designer having his own ideas on how to create the spent wing characteristics.

Lake Olive Spinner (C. F. Walker)

The first comes from J. R. Harris.

Hook: 14-15
Silk: Orange
Tail: Rusty dun or reddish cock hackle fibres
Rib: Gold wire
Body: Deep amber or mahogany seal's fur
Hackle: Good quality rusty or pale grizzled dun cock tied spent or half spent (hackle flattened beneath the hook but left upright on the upper side)

How fortunate we are that John Henderson and the Fly Fishers' Club gave John Veniard permission to reproduce a booklet of articles Henderson wrote for the club Journal! This was printed in *Reservoir and Lake Flies*, and so his observations on the natural and his dressings were made available to a wider public.

Here is his Lake Olive.

Hook: 13
Silk: Nylusta, tan shade
Tail: Five fibres from a medium cock spade feather
Rib: Fine gold wire
Body: Light fiery-brown mixed with ginger seal's fur
Hackle (wing): Light dun cock (four or five turns divided into two bunches by the tying silk in a figure-of-eight fastening)
Hackle (legs): Medium red cock

C. F. Walker's method of tying the spent wing is a slight modification of Henderson's.

Hook: 13-14
Tail: Fibres from a medium blue dun cock spade or saddle hackle
Rib: Gold tinsel
Body: Dark red seal's fur
Wing: Pale brassy dun cock hackle (fibres divided laterally by two cross lashings of silk but without bunching them closely as in the Henderson style)
Leg hackle: Optional. Pale brown or honey dun cock

Lastly, a fine modern pattern by David Collyer.

Hook: U/E 12
Silk: Brown (sherry spinner)
Tail: A few strands of ginger cock hackle
Rib: Fine gold wire
Body: Scarlet wool very thin
Wings: Two light grizzle hackle points, dull outside (sloping back then secured vertically by the tying silk and separated with figure-of-eight turns to hold in semi-spent position)
Hackle: Ginger or light red cock tied sparse and finished behind the wings

You can take your pick of the kind of wing you wish to use according to your inclination and level of skill.

The patterns are designed to cast out to rising fish and be left still on the surface.

The female spinner of the lake olive is also effectively represented by Cliff Henry's Port Spinner, Lunn's Particular and Pheasant Tail which are listed separately.

Lamb's Wool Damsel Nymph

This is a damsel nymph pattern devised by Richard Walker which uses mixed lamb's wool for the body.

Hook:	L/S 8 loaded with three longitudinal strips of lead foil
Tail:	Four or five strands of pale pheasant tail fibres, dyed green, short
Rib:	Pale brown 'silk' in terylene
Body:	A mixture of equal parts of bright orange and cobalt-blue lamb's wool. The thickness of the dubbing increased as it is wound from tail to head to produce a carrot-shaped body
Hackle:	Sparse grey partridge (speckled) dyed grass-green

Lamb's Wool Damsel Nymph

The originator first tried this pattern out with great success at Damerham. He allowed the nymph to sink all the way to the bottom and tweaked it back quite slowly.

Large Brown Corixa

An imitation by Richard Walker of the ubiquitous corixa, this time one of the larger ones. September is one of the best times for using corixa patterns as the trout often move into the shallow water late in the evening. This is where the lesser water boatman with his little paddles is most likely to be found operating.

Hook:	10
Rib:	Silver thread
Body:	White or olive floss
Back & legs:	Brown speckled turkey

Large Brown Corixa
(Richard Walker)

Another good dressing for the Large Brown Corixa is that of David Collyer:

Hook:	10
Rib:	Poroven silk
Body:	White floss silk dressed very fat
Wing case:	Strip of woodcock wing fibres tied in at tail, brought over to lie on top of the body and tied in at the head
Legs:	A few fibres of white hen hackles tied in under the head

Sink and draw on a floating line best simulates the frequent journeys to the surface of the lesser water boatman in his quests for that vital air bubble.

Large Brown Sedge

Large Brown Sedge

A general representation of a larger brown sedge using a bunch of feather fibres or hackle fibres close to the body to form a wing. Clip the ends of the fibres flush with the bend of the hook. Richard Walker emphasises that the two long stiff cock hackles are tied ahead of the wing and that no spiral body hackle is to be used.

Hook:	L/S 10
Silk:	Orange
Tag:	Yellow fluorescent wool or floss
Body:	Mahogany-brown ostrich herl, very fine, with the flue clipped close to the body to achieve a velvety appearance
Wings:	Light brown cock hackle fibres
Hackle:	Light brown cock — two

Large Red Sedge

See under Great Red Sedge

Large Summer Dun Nymph
(Siphlonurus lacustris)

Large Summer Dun Nymph
(C. F. Walker)

These are the nymphs of large up-winged flies which J. R. Harris says are sometimes mistaken in Wales for mayflies. He gave them the colloquial name of summer mayfly, but C. F. Walker felt that this was confusing and so re-named them the large summer dun. They hatch most commonly in July and August. They occur largely in the hilly areas of Wales, Scotland and Northern England although John Goddard mentions that he has observed hatches at Darwell Reservoir.

The nymphs are similar to those of the lake olive except that when fully grown they are nearly twice as large. Walker says that they are the strongest swimmers of their kind. Not only can they dart about with great rapidity but they can stop abruptly. This is achieved by the use of their large gill-plates.

C. F. Walker's pattern is designed for when duns are hatching and fish are taking the mature nymphs as they rise to the surface.

Hook:	Long mayfly 11-12
Rib & tag:	Silver tinsel
Abdomen:	Brown and ginger seal's fur mixed and kept fairly smooth
Gills:	Pale yellow-brown ostrich herl with a good flue or condor herl wound as ribbing
Thorax & wing pads:	Dark brown seal's fur
Leg hackle:	Medium honey dun hen

Taff Price has also given us a dressing:

Hook:	L/S 12-14
Silk:	Brown
Tail:	Brown-olive fibres
Rib:	Gold wire and palmered olive hackle
Body:	Brownish-olive seal's fur
Thorax:	Olive and yellow seal's fur mixed
Wing case:	Brown feather fibre
Hackle:	One turn of dark olive hen or cock hackle

C. F. Walker advises allowing his nymph pattern to sink a short distance and then bringing it up by raising the tip of the rod. Remembering the acceleration and braking power of the natural, a fast, sometimes erratic retrieve, on a floating line may be worth trying.

Large Summer Dun
(Siphlonurus lacustris)

Large Summer Dun (Taff Price)

The angler, if he does encounter these flies, will hardly mistake them as they are the only ones of this size, apart from the mayfly, which he is likely to see on stillwater. They are at least half an inch (13 to 15mm) long with only two tails compared with the mayfly's three. The body is olive marked with brown, and the four wings are of a greenish-olive tinge.

C. F. Walker's dressing is:

Hook:	Long mayfly 11-12
Tail:	Brown mallard fibres
Rib:	Gold tinsel
Body:	Medium grey-brown condor herl lightly stained in picric acid
Wings:	A bunch of grey fibres from near the tip of a mallard scapular feather
Hackle:	Brown-olive dyed cock

Taff Price says that the flies hatch at both Darwell and Powdermill in Sussex, and gives us this pattern:

Hook:	12
Tail:	Dark olive cock hackle fibres
Rib:	Yellow silk
Body:	Brownish-olive seal's fur or polypropylene dubbing
Wing:	Partridge dyed pale olive
Hackle:	Brown-olive and light olive cock hackle mixed

He advises that the artificial be cast near the margins as this is where the fly hatches in the vicinity of weed. Mayfly patterns can be used as alternative artificials.

Large Summer Spinner
(Siphlonurus lacustris)

The spinners of the large summer dun hover close to the shore or even over the shore line and fly during late afternoon or in the evening. C. F. Walker's pattern is intended to be used when the spinners are on the water, simulating the female after she has laid her eggs.

Hook:	L/S 11-12
Rib:	Gold tinsel
Body:	A mixture of grey-green, dark brown and yellow seal's fur, the last showing towards the tail
Wings:	Medium brassy dun cock hackle with fibres divided laterally
Hackle:	Optional. Medium brown cock

Large Summer Spinner
(C. F. Walker)

Walker gives no tail in his dressing, which is an omission as his photograph of the artificial certainly shows one. It would appear to be teal or mallard fibres. I show it with these added, but no hackle, which is how he preferred it.

Taff Price, one of the few writers who has seen hatches of the fly, gives us this dressing:

Hook:	12
Tail:	Long dark olive fibres
Rib:	Yellow silk or nylon
Body:	Polypropylene dyed brown (light)
Wing:	Light partridge tied spent
Hackle:	None, or dark olive clipped at the bottom

Cast to rising fish or leave motionless on the surface.

Last Hope

I was reading an article recently in *Trout Fisherman* on what to do if there was a caenis hatch. The author suggested that the best thing was to pack up and go home!

Before you do this, try the aptly-named Last Hope. John Goddard designed the fly in the first place to imitate a pale watery dun and then found that it was a good last resort for the Angler's Curse. He emphasises the need to use a very short-fibred hackle.

Hook: U/E fine wire 17-18
Silk: Pale yellow
Body: Two or three Norwegian goose or condor herls grey-buff
Tail: Honey dun cock, six to eight fibres
Hackle: Dark honey, very short in the fibre

Last Hope

The pattern should be fished dry for the dun, and retrieved very slowly for the hatching nymph.

It will also serve as a representation of the small spurwing, sometimes called the little sky blue.

Leaded D.F. Doll

This is a modification by Richard Walker of Bob Church's Baby Doll, designed to make it sink faster and lie with the hook point upwards, thus avoiding snags when fished on or near the bottom. It is important when the fly is finished to rub the body all over with fine glass-paper to fluff up the wool and give it a velvety effect which emphasises the fluorescent quality.

Hook: L/S 6-8
Silk: White
Tail: White wool
Body: Daylight-fluorescent white wool over a hook shank which has been varnished with Vycoat. Use the wool to produce a fish-shaped body and tie in three strips of wine bottle lead foil lengthwise along the top of the body, binding firmly with the final layer of white wool
False hackle: Crimson or orange-dyed cock hackle tied in above the body and very short in the fibre

Leaded D.F. Doll

This pattern took my last fish of the 1983 season at the end of October on a desperately cold day when nothing seemed to be taking. Its sinking quality is extremely useful for searching various depths of water, and in dark water is is splendidly visible.

The Leadhead

The Leadhead

This is the precursor of the Dog Nobbler which has proved exceedingly popular in recent seasons. Richard Walker, having tried out a selection of what are called in the U.S.A. 'fly rod jigs' used by Americans for catching 'panfish', developed the idea further and adapted it for British stillwater fishing. He corrected the two faults of the American pattern which were poor hook penetration and hook straightening by using normal hooks, properly hardened and tempered, and pinched a deeply cut split shot just behind the hook eye which made the fly fish point up. He described his Leadheads in *Trout and Salmon* as early as 1974 but they never became popular, largely he felt, because their dressing did not commend itself to either professional or amateur fly tyers.

Hook:	R/B 8-10 forged or flattened
Head:	Pinch a split shot, BB or a little smaller, just behind the eye. Use pliers to pinch the shot on firmly. Between the eye and the shot, and also behind the eye, build up tapered bindings of tight turns and soak these with PVC varnish (Vycoat)
Body:	Floss ribbed with tinsel
Wing:	A bunch of suitable hair. The head painted with plastic paint and when dry coated with clear PVC varnish
Useful colours:	Yellow wing, light brown head, arc chrome DF wool or floss body, ribbed silver thread; natural grey squirrel wing, brown head, red DF wool body; black wing, black head, red DF wool body

Fished either with a series of short pulls with a pause between each, thus producing an up and down action, or retrieved at a steady speed they proved most effective.

Angling writers like C. F. Walker have commented on the effect a name can have on a fly's popularity. Dog Nobbler sounds exciting; Leadhead dull. Richard Walker himself says he has never been good at names. Undue modesty from the creator of Sweeny Todd, Barney Google and Nell Gwynne!

Leech *(Hirundinae)*

Few anglers would consider fishing a leech pattern. Yet these creatures which look like worms with suckers at each end can move rapidly with their aid and also by swimming with an undulating motion. However as most are bloodsuckers and eat large meals, they spend a great deal of their time motionless. The medicinal leech is the only one capable of penetrating human skin and is now very rare. Leech gathering was once a very profitable business.

About eleven species of leech are found in freshwater in Britain. They vary in length, when at rest, from under half an inch (13mm) to three or four inches (76 to 102mm). When extended they may be three or four times this size. Their colour varies from brownish-green to greenish-grey to yellow. The horse leech (*Haemopis sanguisuga*), the most common, is one to one and a half inches long, and is found usually in mud at the lake bottom. Its colour is either dark green or light green or brown.

The Leech (Thom Green)

As far as I can see, only Taff Price has given us a dressing, using marabou to simulate the undulations.

Hook:	L/S 6
Tail:	Black or brown marabou
Body:	Black fur
Wing:	Black or brown marabou (two: one near the tail and the other near the shoulder)
Hackle:	A false hackle of yellow marabou

Leech patterns are more popular among the Americans, and I give one evolved by Thom Green after a good deal of experiment with imitations. He contends that leech artificials have a reputation for taking big lake trout. As the leech moves so slowly it must be fished slightly slower than you feel is too slow. It is imperative that the rod be aligned exactly with the line to detect soft, almost imperceptible, takes.

Hook:	L/S 2-10, 3X long, bent so that the eye is horizontal
Silk:	Pre-waxed black, brown, tan or olive-green to match the body-colour
Tail:	Same colour as body, marabou generous spray, cut straight and two thirds length of body
Body:	Mohair dyed olive-brown, black, olive, brown or dark brown, thick at rear tapering towards the eye. Rear third of hook wrapped with lead wire
Hackle:	Same colour as body, a soft-fibred body hackle wound as collar but very sparse

You should remember that leeches will occasionally release their hold on the weeds or other objects on which they normally move, and by a series of contractions swim through the water rapidly. This movement can be imparted with a short, twitchy pull very occasionally with each retrieve.

Is the Black Lure, fished slowly on the bottom, taken for a leech? David Collyer rejects this theory because he feels that its outline is basically fish-shaped.

Leprechaun

Green has become a more popular colour of recent times. I have found Alan Pearson's Green Beast and David Collyer's Green Nymph very successful. Peter Wood's Leprechaun lure utilises fluorescent lime-green chenille for the body which appears to enhance its deadliness.

Leprechaun

Hook:	L/S 6-10
Silk:	Black
Tail:	Green hackle fibres
Rib:	Silver tinsel
Body:	Fluorescent lime-green chenille
Wing:	Four matched green cock hackle feathers
Throat hackle:	Green hackle fibres

I have not had much success with it from the bank at Grafham even in July, but Bob Church strongly recommends it fished from a boat amidst the profuse blooms of daphnia often encountered at the windward end of the reservoir.

A variation by John Ketley ties the four green hackles matuka style which gives it a strong resemblance to the New Zealand lake fly called the Green Orbit.

Lesser Water Boatman

See under Corixa

Light Sedge

Anglers of a less purist nature prefer to fish their sedge patterns in colour shades rather than dress imitations of specific sedge flies. David Jacques, when not sure of the type of sedge hatching, always used his Pale Sedge first.

Hook:	11-14
Silk:	Hot-orange
Rib:	Stiff ginger hackle with over-rib of gold twist
Body:	Two or three herls from a cinnamon turkey tail
Wings:	Wing feather of a hen pheasant, bunched and rolled, and tied sloping back over the hook bend
Hackle:	Bright ginger cock in front of the wings

Light Sedge (Terry Thomas)

Terry Thomas's pattern to achieve the same effect is called the Light Sedge.

Hook: 14-4 as required
Body: Light cock pheasant tail fibres wound on as thickly as possible
Body hackle: Ginger cock
Wing: Brown deer hair tied on flat with cut ends to the rear and splayed out triangular fashion
Front hackle: Ginger cock

To be fished in the manner of all sedge patterns.

Little Brown Sedge

Little Brown Sedge

So-called by Courtney Williams to distinguish it from the popular Brown Sedge which has a brown floss silk body. He contended that the mixed-wool body made all the difference, and that from June to September on river or stillwater, in daytime or evening, it was a most killing pattern. He ranked it with Skues' Little Red Sedge as one of the most effective representations of the natural insect.

Hook: D/E 14
Silk: Orange
Rib: Fine gold wire
Body: Dubbed mixture of fawn and brown wool
Wings: Red hen (Rhode Island)
Hackle: Red cock, carried down the body from shoulder to tail and in front of the wing

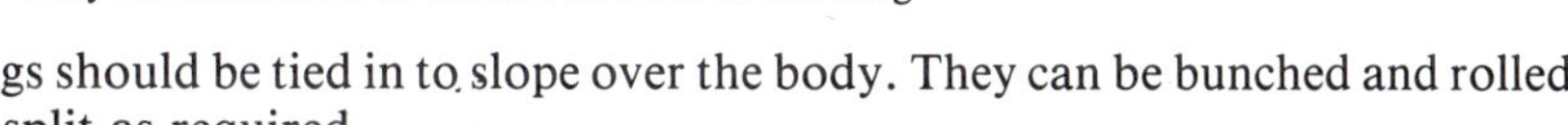

The wings should be tied in to slope over the body. They can be bunched and rolled or double split as required.

Generally fished dry in the sedge manner, but Courtney Williams said it could also be fished wet.

Little Marryat

I have decided to include this dressing of the classic chalk stream fly by G. S. Marryat devised to represent the pale watery dun as, according to John Goddard in his *Trout Flies of Stillwater*, it serves as a good imitation of the small spurwing. Previously known as the little sky blue, John Goddard says that it is found on stillwater and may be more common than is supposed.

Marryat's original dressing is given in Skues' *Silk, Fur and Feather* as follows:

Hook:	U/E 16
Silk:	White or pale straw colour
Tail whisk:	Ginger cock
Body:	Fur from flank of opossum
Wing:	Pale starling
Hackle:	Ginger cock

Halford gives the hackle and whisk as pale buff Cochin cock. Skues' modified version is:

Hook:	15-16
Silk:	White or pale straw
Tail whisks:	Creamy dun
Body:	Cream fur from a baby seal
Wings:	Pale starling wing feather
Hackle:	Creamy dun

Fished dry and cast to rising fish.

Little Marryat

Little Red Sedge

Though Skues is renowned for his work on nymph fishing, he always matched the natural on the water, including the dry fly where appropriate. He thus devised this imitation of the small red sedge, and it was one of his favourite patterns when ephemeropterans were not about.

The small or little red sedge *(Tinodes waeneri)* is one of the smallest of the sedge flies but common from May to October. The wings, of course, have a distinct red shade.

Hook:	14
Silk:	Hot-orange waxed with brown wax
Rib:	Fine gold wire binding down the body hackle
Body:	Darkest hare's ear
Body hackle:	Long deep red cock with short fibres tied in at the shoulder and carried down to the tail
Wings:	Landrail wing (or substitute), bunched and rolled, and tied on sloping well back over the tail
Front hackle:	Like body hackle but larger, and long enough to tie five or six times in front of the wing

Little Red Sedge (G. E. M. Skues)

Skues' dressing uses landrail wings which are now virtually unobtainable. Donald Overfield suggests the use instead of dyed hen wing fibres, preferably light brown. Another suggestion, from John Veniard, is the pinkish-brown feather of the mavis thrush.

Joscelyn Lane also devised a Little Red Sedge pattern which he tied with his favourite wing method.

Hook:	12-13
Silk:	Hot-orange
Body:	Long ginger cock hackle in close coils from bend to eye and clipped close
Wing:	A bunch of pale ginger cock hackle fibres tied to lie in contact with the body
Hackle:	Red cock hackle

Fish in the manner of most sedge fly imitations.

Loch Ordie

Loch Ordie

An extraordinary fly invented by the Duke of Atholl and a real killer in the far North of Scotland. John Veniard says that dressed in the Harray style it has nine or ten hen hackles starting with black at the tail through all shades from reddish brown to honey dun topped off with white at the head. In *Dick Walker's Trout Fishing* he describes Hardy's Loch Ordies as a solid mass of cock hackles looking like miniature hedgehogs. He believes that their considerable success is due to their ability to float longer than any other pattern. He also mentions that they were poor hookers and that one version had a trailing treble hook to remedy this fault. I show a photograph of a dressing using this device.

Hook:	10-12
Silk:	Black
Hackles:	Brown hen or cock palmer-fashion and thick, with a white hackle at the head. Other-coloured hackles can be added

In the Harray style it is designed to work sub-surface, and the dapping version is tied more fully. Whichever way it is used it appears to be very successful. *Trout and Salmon* reported it as the best fly in the Shetlands in August, 1983. Bruce Sandison, who writes whimsical and amusing articles for that journal, fished the Shetlands recently and commented that the Loch Ordie does better than any other fly. He says that the Shetlands anglers fish it throughout the season in different sizes according to the conditions ranging from a size 16 to one as large as a small helicopter!

It also produced fish when the Autumn International Fly Fishing match between the four home countries took place on Loch Harray on the Orkney mainland in 1983.

Richard Walker is convinced that far more scope exists for big floating flies like the Loch Ordie, Red Sedge and Ghost Swift Moth than is at present exploited.

Longhorns Pupa

An effective and well-tried imitation of a sedge pupa coming up to hatch for whose body Richard Walker originally used ostrich herl but which he has now replaced by dyed natural lamb's wool. This needs degreasing first in tepid water with plenty of detergent. There are four colour combinations to cover most species of sedges.

Hook: 10-12 normal shank
Silk: Pale yellow
Body: Rear two-thirds amber or pale sea-green; front one-third sepia or chestnut, all of dyed natural sheep's wool
Rib: Fine gold thread on rear half only
Hackle: Two turns of short brown partridge
Horns: Two strands of pheasant tail fibres slanting back over the hook cut to twice the length of the hook

Longhorns Pupa

The sepia and amber is the originator's best fish taker. The sepia and green scores in May when not so many sedges actually hatch.

When numerous sedges are present but not being taken on the surface, the Longhorn is most effective moved fairly quickly with a sink and draw action just below the surface where one would expect to find hatching sedge pupae. It can also be fished from a boat in a team of sedge representations with a sedge pupa on the point and a G. & H. Sedge or a Walker Sedge on the bob.

The Longhorns
(Oecetis lacustris, Oecetis ochracea)

The angler is likely to encounter these sedges in most localities he visits from June to mid-September. *Lacustris* has a wing length of about one quarter of an inch (7 to 8mm) and *Ochracea* over half an inch (11 to 13mm). Both have ashy-yellow to light fawn wings with greenish bodies, but their most distinguishing feature is their long antennae, in some cases three times as long as their wingspan.

This dressing was devised by John Goddard and Cliff Henry:

The Longhorns

Hook:	L/S 12-14
Silk:	Green
Body:	Two or three strands of dull green-dyed ostrich herl tied thickly along the body and trimmed cylindrically, long at the bend and close at the eye to simulate the wings of a sedge
Hackle:	Pale cream dun cock, tied along the body palmer-fashion, but the butt attached at the bend and not the eye as is normal. In this way the hackle does not break down the tapered outline of the body herl

This is a very buoyant fly which will skate along the water surface nicely. It can also be cast out to lie motionless or be retrieved in short jerks.

Lucky Alphonse

Lucky Alphonse

Richard Walker has extended the principle used in the dressing of the Knotted Midge or Gnat to the problem of fishing for caenis-eating trout. The idea, also used in Derek Bradbury's Green Aphis, is to simulate more than one fly on the same hook as a means of overcoming the tiny size of the natural.

Hook:	L/S 12
Silk:	Dark brown and allowed to be shown a little on each side of each hackle
Body:	Undyed swan herl
Hackles:	Four cream hackles set at intervals along the hook shank from tail to shoulder

It is fished as a dry fly but is intended to sit in the surface film rather than on the water. Though it by no means solves the problem of the caenis hatch, it offers another way of tackling it and has been satisfactorily taken by trout at such times.

Lunn's Particular

William Lunn, river-keeper of the Houghton Club for forty-five years and immortalised in J. W. Hill's book, *River Keeper*, came to fly dressing late in life, yet managed to produce a number of patterns which became famous. The Particular is one of his best known.

His flies were designed for the chalk streams but the Particular can be used for a number of spinners on stillwater, notably the lake olive and, at a pinch, the sepia and claret spinners, though it may be a little on the light side. John Goddard recommends it also as a representation of the little amber spinner.

Hook:	14-16
Silk:	Crimson
Tail:	Fibres from a large Rhode Island Red cock hackle
Body:	Undyed hackle stalk of a Rhode Island Red cock hackle
Wings:	Two medium blue dun cock hackle tips put on flat
Hackle:	Medium Rhode Island Red cock hackle

Cast to rising fish and allow to lie motionless.

Lunn's Particular

Mallard and Claret

Regarded as one of the most versatile and killing of all the traditional lake patterns, few anglers even today would not have it in their box. The fly is generally considered to have been invented by William Murdoch of Aberdeen, also the originator of the Heckham Peckhams. He probably used the mallard feather in dressing a large Grouse and Claret, grouse feathers being rather short in the web whereas mallard are long.

Hook:	D/E 10-14
Silk:	Black
Tail:	Golden pheasant tippet feathers
Rib:	Fine gold wire
Body:	Dark claret seal's fur
Wings:	Dark bronze speckled feathers from a mallard
Hackle:	Claret or natural red cock

Mallard and Claret

It is commonly used on the bob in smaller sizes in early season when it may be taken for the first buzzers. The strength of the pattern, however, lies in its being able to be used throughout the season, and though it represents no particular food form it may be taken for many such as claret and sepia nymphs and duns, sedges, etc.

Later in the season it is fished in a larger size rather slowly from bank or boat. It is generally fished on the point, but some prefer it on the dropper.

Other patterns in the series are Mallard and Yellow, Mallard and Red, Mallard and Silver, Mallard and Green, but the Claret is by far the most effective.

Marabou Flies

Marabou feather, first publicised by Bob Church, is an important addition to the fly fisherman's armoury, and many flies now make use of it. Whilst it appears bulky and fluffy when dry, it becomes very fine and supple when wet. It has been used with devastating effect on a number of lures of which I give two. The first is David Collyer's dressing:

Black and Orange Marabou

White Marabou

Hook:	L/S 6-10
Silk:	Black
Rib:	Oval or round tinsel
Body:	Flat silver tinsel or lurex
Wing:	White marabou with five strands of peacock sword feather over
Hackle:	Scarlet cock fibres
Cheeks:	Jungle cock or substitute

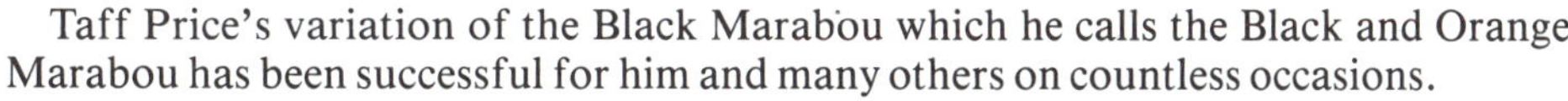

Taff Price's variation of the Black Marabou which he calls the Black and Orange Marabou has been successful for him and many others on countless occasions.

Black and Orange Marabou

Hook:	D/E L/S 8
Silk:	Black
Tail:	Orange cock fibres
Rib:	Oval gold tinsel
Body:	Flat gold tinsel or lurex
Wing:	Bunch of black marabou
Cheeks:	Jungle cock or substitute
Hackle:	Bunch of orange cock hackle fibres

A variety of colours can be utilised including black, yellow and green.

The patterns can be fished in a number of ways as long as they take advantage of the suppleness of the marabou. They can be retrieved deep on a sinking or slow sinking line, and worked slowly to utilise the liveliness of the marabou. I have found a white and orange marabou on a slow sinker at the back end of the season, worked fairly quickly with short sharp pulls, extremely effective. It imparts a most lifelike wiggle action which fish chase and take with great relish.

It is advisable to wet marabou lures before casting, otherwise the fragile fibres can be damaged by false casting.

March Brown *(Rhithrogena haarupi and Ecdyurus venosus)*

The natural insects of which there are two species, *R. haarupi* which hatches in large numbers in March and April, and *E. venosus* which appears less profusely in May

March Brown (T. E. Pritt)

and June, are confined to rivers, and generally Northern and Welsh rivers at that. The male is darker than the female, both having brownish bodies and mottled brown wings.

W. H. Lawrie says that the artificial was the very first fly on Dame Juliana Berners' list of twelve, but J. W. Hills states that it was first mentioned by Chetham who called it the Moorish Brown.

Why include it in a stillwater list of flies at all? The clue lies, I think, in Skues' remark that the artificial was an excellent dry fly which was a poor imitation of the natural but quite a passable one of almost anything else! In this respect, it is generally regarded as a useful imitation of a hatching sedge and is often used as a bob fly in a team of three. It is considered by some to represent a shrimp.

I give T. E. Pritt's dressing as a traditional Dales' fly which has taken fish for me on rivers when the natural was present, but also on stillwaters in the North and South where the March Brown never appears.

Hook:	12
Silk:	Pale orange
Tail:	Two strands from a partridge tail
Rib:	Yellow silk
Body:	Dubbed with a little hare's ear and yellow mohair
Wings:	Tail feather of a partridge (or inner quill feather of a hen pheasant's wing)
Legs:	From the back of a partridge

Roger Woolley thought the March Brown was taken later on for a sedge, and he advocated that orange tying silk should always be used in the dressing. I find that his tying of the March Brown Nymph is ideal for stillwater and most effective.

Hook:	11-13
Silk:	Orange
Tail:	Three short strands of brown mallard feather
Rib:	Gold wire
Body:	Brown dubbing or brown quill or pheasant tail fibres
Wing cases:	Woodcock wing feather
Legs:	Small brown speckled grouse hackle, one turn only

See also under Silver March Brown.

Matukas

The matuka style of dressing flies originated in New Zealand. They usually have chenille bodies, but their particular feature consists of the two feathers used for wings with fibres stripped from one side of the hackle for the length of the hook shank, and the upright fibres being bound to the hook by the ribbing. The tips of the hackles are left intact to protrude past the hook bend to form a tail. The initial demand for matuka feathers was said to have had an adverse effect on the number of these birds in New Zealand, and now many different common feathers are used.

Red and Black Matuka

Two outstanding qualities of matuka dressings are that they avoid the annoying habit of long-feathered lures insomuch as the wing feather does not get caught up under the hook, and they move cleanly and straight through the water.

David Collyer's Ace of Spades is the outstanding example of a matuka fly, and there are countless others of varying colour and feather. I give three of the most popular dressings, the first two by David Collyer.

Grey and Red

Hook:	L/S 6-10
Silk:	Black
Body:	Silver-grey chenille
Rib:	Oval silver tinsel
Wing:	Hen pheasant body feather
Hackle:	A bunch of scarlet cock hackle fibres

White and Orange

Hook:	L/S 8-10
Silk:	Black
Body:	White chenille
Rib:	Oval silver tinsel
Wing:	White hen hackles
Hackles:	Orange and white cock hackles wound together

Red and Black

Hook:	L/S 6-10
Silk:	Black
Body:	Red chenille
Rib:	Oval gold tinsel
Wing:	Two black hen hackles back to back, and tied down on top of the body with ribbing tinsel
Head:	Black varnish

Whether matukas simulate small fish or attract trout out of curiosity or belligerence, they are most versatile and can be fished in a number of ways. Two techniques to be used are periodic pauses fished deeply on a sinking line or long steady retrieves just below the surface on a floater.

I have found the Red and Black Matuka an effective pattern. On a dour day at Ladybower Reservoir in Derbyshire it took me two nice trout fished in a series of short, sharp pulls on a floating line. Curiously, having broken the hook extracting the fly from the second fish, I found I had no replacement in my box. I used instead a Grey and Red Matuka with no success.

Mayfly Nymph
(Ephemera danica and vulgata)

Mayfly Nymph (Richard Walker)

Every angler has heard of the mayfly which is the biggest and most fascinating of all the upwinged flies. There are a number of stillwaters where the mayfly is present, and the artificial nymph is a pattern that every fisherman should have in his box.

The nymph or larval form grows up to one inch (20 to 25mm) in length, is of a creamy-fawn colour with six strong legs, three tails and prominent brownish wing cases. It burrows in the bottom for most of its life, but leaves its security prior to hatching to swim to the surface when it becomes vulnerable to the trout.

Richard Walker describes the colour of the *E. danica* nymph as being predominantly ivory and the dressing of his pattern reflects this.

Hook:	L/S D/E 8-10 (weighted with strips of lead if required)
Silk:	Brown
Tail:	Four or five strands of pheasant tail fibres
Underbody:	Floss silk if pattern not weighted
Body:	Lemon-yellow angora wool or very pale buff knitting wool or white wool
Rib:	Medium warm-brown nylon thread — five close turns near rear end followed by a space, then four close turns, then open ribbing to thorax. The close turns of thread represent the dark bands on the natural near the rear of the abdomen
Thorax:	As body
Wing case & legs:	A bunch of pheasant tail fibres doubled and redoubled over thorax. The fine ends of the fibres are then divided into two backward sloping bunches to form legs

Richard Walker says that mayfly nymphs have a curious habit of emerging from their burrows and rising to the surface then going down again. They do this in the evening a fortnight before any considerable hatch. Trout take the nymphs at all levels, and so leaded versions fished sink and draw are most effective. Trout will often take the artificial nymph, not only when no naturals are about, but even in water where none exist. Though effective throughout the season, the pattern works best in April, May and June.

Derek Bradbury, Taff Price and John Veniard all have excellent dressings. Apart from Richard Walker's, the only pattern I am familiar with is that of Peter Lapsley.

Hook:	L/S 8-10
Silk:	Brown
Tail:	Cock pheasant tail fibre points
Underbody:	Fine lead wire flattened horizontally
Abdomen:	Rear half buff condor herl; front half dull yellow seal's fur
Rib:	Black nylon monocord
Thorax:	Dull yellow seal's fur
Wing case:	A slip of speckled brown hen's quill
Legs:	One turn of brownish partridge hackle

A mayfly nymph pattern has been developed by Brian Clarke, John Goddard and Neil Patterson which will remain in the surface film for as long as is required. It involves a ball of ethafoam or plastazote contained in nylon mesh to support the head above the surface whilst suspending the rest of the fly at a natural angle in the water.

Hook:	Keel hook L/S 12
Silk:	Brown
Tail:	Three tips of cream ostrich herl kept well apart with a dab of varnish
Body:	Seal's fur mixed half white, a quarter tan and a quarter yellow
Rib:	Brown monocord or silk
Wing cases:	Ethafoam or plastazote ball enclosed in nylon mesh and coloured brown (use Pantone 464M pen)
Thorax:	As body wound either side of the ball and picked out with a dubbing needle

The ball may look conspicuous from above, but it is partially obscured from the trout's point of view and might even be taken for an expanding shuck. The pattern should be fished slowly on a floating line with perhaps an occasional twitch. The dressing is taken from the absorbing book, *The Trout and the Fly*.

For a traditional Irish pattern see under Gosling.

Mayfly Dun
(Ephemera danica and vulgata)

Mayfly Dun — Nevamis

The mayfly has been imitated at least since Dame Juliana Berners and Charles Cotton, and there is a vast angling literature on the subject. The countless dressings would fill this guide on their own.

Because of its size, yellowish-white body, markedly veined wings and three tails, the dun can hardly be mistaken for any other fly. The males and females are slightly different, and the duns generally are not so popular with the trout as the spinners. The anglers' popular name for the dun is the Green Drake, arising from the traditional practice of imitating the wing of the insect with the feathers of the mallard drake. The two species mentioned are most common, hatching in late May and early June. Some stillwaters have hatches including Lakedown in Sussex and Lapsley's Trout Fishery in Hampshire.

Traditional fan wings have been largely superseded by hackled patterns, some of the most effective being the straddle-bug dressings.

Hook: L/S 10-12, suggest Mayfly hook
Silk: Brown
Tail: Two or three black cock hackle fibres or three fibres of brown mallard
Body: Natural raffia
Rib: Brown silk or fine gold wire
Hackle: Summer duck, long with a shorter inner hackle of hot-orange
Head: Peacock herl

This can be very killing because, for some reason noted by several angling writers, the hot-orange is extremely attractive though it bears no resemblance to the colour of the natural.

David Jacques has devised an interesting imitation which he calls the Green Drake Upright. He has found that the posterior of the natural dun is elevated and so he incorporates a large tail hackle to achieve this effect.

Hook: Mayfly as light as possible
Silk: Olive or straw colour
Body: Shape built up with floss silk, then covered with natural raffia
Head hackle: Two short stiff cock hackles, dyed green drake
Tail hackle: Two or more long cock hackles, as stiff as possible, the same shade as the head hackles

Finally, from John Goddard, a pattern called the Nevamis Mayfly, developed to overcome the bad hooking properties of some mayfly artificials.

Hook: L/S U/E fine wire 8
Silk: Yellow
Tail: Three long pheasant tail fibres
Rib: Oval gold tinsel
Body: Cream seal's fur wound thickly — body hackle large honey cock tied in at tail and wound to shoulder and then clipped to one quarter of an inch of body at shoulder sloping to one eighth of an inch at tail
Wings: V shaped hackle fibre wings using a large pale blue dun cock
Hackle: Small furnace cock with half inch fibres

Casting to rising fish is the usual technique.

For other mayfly patterns see under Grey Squirrel Mayfly, Grey Wulff, Hatching Mayfly, Shadow Mayfly and Walker Mayfly.

Mayfly Spinner
(Ephemera danica and vulgata)

The frustration experienced when trout sometimes ignore the dun artificial may be because spinners are present, and there is a consensus of opinion that not only are trout more interested in them but are easier to deceive with a representation of the spinner.

The female spinner as she floats dying on the water after laying her eggs is often referred to as the spent gnat. Whilst she is still flitting over the surface dropping her eggs she is named the grey drake.

There are many excellent modern patterns, one of which is David Collyer's Hacklepoint Mayfly with which he has taken many fish.

Hook:	L/S U/E 10
Silk:	Olive or grey
Tail:	Cock pheasant centre tail fibres
Rib:	Oval gold tinsel
Body:	Natural raffia, varnished
Wings:	Two or four badger cock hackle tips
Hackle:	Iron-blue cock

Richard Walker's Hairwing Spent Mayfly uses black squirrel hair tied in two bunches. Its advantages are that it is buoyant and durable and will not spin in the air like some hackle-point patterns.

Hook:	L/S 8
Tail:	Pheasant tail fibres dyed sepia
Rib:	Sepia tying silk
Body:	Ivory-coloured wool, with two bands of dark brown wool near the rear of the body
Wings:	Black squirrel tail hair, secured in two horizontal bunches with figure-of-eight binding
Thorax:	Sepia pheasant fibres

Mayfly Spinner (Neil Patterson)

An excellent and killing pattern which Neil Patterson first published in *Trout Fisherman* is called The Deerstalker. It uses a bunch of deer hair tied along the shank of the hook which gives it strong floating properties and yet the fly rests on the water just like the natural.

Hook:	Extra L/S 10
Silk:	Black
Tail:	Twelve to fifteen cock pheasant tail fibres
Rib:	Fine silver wire criss-crossed
Body:	A bunch of deer hair tied along the shank and whipped down with black silk
Wings:	Very long-fibred furnace hackle tied spent
Thorax:	Black seal's fur over the figure-of-eight whipping

As with the dun pattern it is best to cast in the path of a rising fish and leave the fly motionless.

Medium Sedge *(Goera pilosa)*

This is a day-flying sedge with an anterior wing amost half an inch long (10 to 12mm), sombre yellow in colour, most common in May and June, and widely distributed. Unfortunately, not a great deal seems to be known about it as far as stillwater is concerned.

Halford's pattern is one which can be used to imitate several sedges:

Hook:	11-13
Body:	Unstripped condor herl dyed medium cinnamon or cinnamon turkey tail fibres
Body hackle:	Short-fibred ginger cock hackle
Wing:	Well-coloured red hen wing quill
Front hackle:	Ginger cock wound in front of wing over the wing roots

Medium Sedge (Joscelyn Lane)

Joscelyn Lane also devised a medium sedge pattern:

Hook:	D/E 12
Silk:	Straw-coloured
Body:	Dark honey dun cock hackle tied along the whole body and clipped short
Wing:	Medium honey dun cock hackle fibres tied in a bunch low over the body
Hackle:	Ginger cock

Medium Stonefly *(Diura bicaudata)*

Medium Stonefly

For the perfectionist requiring a specific imitation of the medium stonefly which is found only in the North and West, and usually on high ground, here is a pattern by Taff Price.

As these long thin flies with the hard glossy wings found from April to June are generally considered to be non-flyers and the only appearance of the adult on the water is when the female jettisons her eggs, it is hardly surprising that Courtney Williams quotes an old Swaledale angler as saying that the very best of artificial patterns are "as near useless as dammit is to swearing". However, let us remember that he was talking about stonefly patterns on rivers.

Hook:	12-14
Silk:	Brown
Tail:	Two short pheasant tail fibres
Rib:	Fine yellow silk
Body:	Brown polypropylene
Wing:	Brown partridge hackle varnished and tied flat over the back
Hackle:	Brown

Mickey Finn

This is an American lure, origin unknown, but named by Gregory Clark. It has become popular on the British reservoirs. The wing has yellow bucktail on the bottom followed by red, and the yellow on top should be equal in amount to both the other layers.

Hook:	L/S 6-12
Silk:	Black
Rib:	Oval silver tinsel
Body:	Flat silver tinsel
Wing:	Small bunches of yellow bucktail, then red bucktail in the middle and yellow bucktail on top
Throat hackle:	Red cock hackle fibres (optional)

Mickey Finn

It is particularly good when algae soar to the top levels of the water along with the temperature. At these times, swiftly retrieved orange-coloured lures in windy conditions will often provoke exciting aggression from rainbows. The showy Mickey Finn with its yellow and red has a similar effect.

Minnow Streamer

A lure designed by Taff Price specifically to represent the minnow.

Hook:	L/S 6-10
Silk:	Olive
Tail:	Blue dun hackle fibres
Rib:	Silver oval tinsel
Body:	White floss or wool
Wing:	Olive hackles
Cheek:	Barred teal or mallard
Hackle:	Red beard hackle. Female minnow uses blue dun
Eye:	Two jungle cock or substitute tied short, or painted eye
Head:	Olive on top, white underneath

Minnow Streamer Female

It should be fished as nearly as possible to simulate the movement of a minnow; that is to say that there are times when it should be virtually stationary and others when short, quick pulls will imitate the darting motion of the little fish.

Missionary

Missionary (Dick Shrive)

The original fly was invented by Captain J. J. Dunn for use on Blagdon. Courtney Williams' dressing is based on a pattern used successfully in New Zealand.

Hook:	8-10 (standard hook originally given, but a L/S can be used)
Tail:	White cock hackle
Body:	White wool, pulled and spun on
Wings:	A few fibres of black turkey tail feather extending well beyond the hook with strips of dark teal on each side
Hackle:	White cock

Dick Shrive's version employs a whole grey mallard feather or a teal breast feather, and is commonly used. The wing set low over the body vibrates as the fly sinks, and this is when the fish often take.

Hook:	L/S 6-8
Silk:	Black
Tail:	Dark ginger or red cock hackle fibres
Rib:	Flat silver tinsel or lurex
Body:	White chenille
Wing:	Whole grey mallard or teal breast feather, set flat, one and a half times the hook's length
Hackle:	Dark ginger or red cock hackle

Bob Church uses the fly at the back end when trout are feeding on small fry which have now left the comparative safety of the margins and are gathering in weedy areas. From a boat he will use extremely long hooks of up to three and a half inches. As a further variation he substitutes a bunch of barred teal feathers taken off the quill for the whole wing feather, and this should be retrieved much more quickly.

Trout will often attack a shoal of fry or minnows, leaving a number wounded. They may return to pick up these stragglers. The Missionary, slowly sinking with a slight to-and-fro motion caused by the flat wing, perfectly simulates the wounded little fish.

Montana Nymph

There are countless overseas fly patterns which would be worth trying on British stillwaters, but their very number would swamp the essentially national character of this guide. I have therefore confined myself to those commonly used by home anglers or recommended by eminent angling authors or where there appears to be no satisfactory British pattern.

The Montana Nymph is recommended by both Taff Price and David Collyer, and I give the dressing from Terry Hellekson's *Popular Fly Patterns* where it is referred to as the Montana Stone. Hellekson says it is also very effective when tied with dark olive chenille rather than black.

Hook:	L/S D/E 6-10
Silk:	Black
Tail:	Two black hackle tips tied in a V
Body:	Black chenille
Wing case:	Black chenille
Thorax:	Yellow chenille
Legs:	Black hackle wrapped through the thorax

Montana Nymph or Stone

It is doubtful whether it imitates any living creature either in the United States or here, but it may be considered a useful representation of a large stonefly creeper. Taff Price thinks that on our waters it could be taken for a large dragonfly nymph. David Collyer caught fish on it retrieved quickly on a floating line and very long leader. As it was such a sunny and bright day he put a small split shot about four feet up the leader to avoid line wake.

Mosquito Pupa *(Culicidae)*

If you are bitten at the waterside, the chances are that it is by a female mosquito. They breed in water, of course, and their pupae have much in common with those of the chironomid and the phantom midge. The larvae are inactive and the adults fly quickly off the water, so that if there are mosquitoes about it is the pupae that are best imitated.

David Collyer and Taff Price have both given us dressings.

Hook:	12
Silk:	Black
Body:	Stripped peacock herl, taken from the eye feather
Thorax:	Dubbed mole or muskrat which should be a pronounced ball

Hook:	Wide gape 14
Silk:	Grey
Rib:	Black silk
Body:	Grey silk carried round the bend
Thorax:	A full ball of mole or grey rabbit underfur

Mosquito Pupa
(E. H. Rosborough)

Imitations are very common in the United States where they probably have a lot more mosquitoes than we do, and I particularly like the look of E. H. ('Polly') Rosborough's dressing.

Hook:	14
Silk:	Grey
Tail:	Small bunch of finely-speckled guinea fibres tied short
Rib:	Grey thead
Legs:	A small bunch of finely-speckled guinea fibres tied in at the throat and extending to the centre of the belly

From my observation of naturals I have collected, the pupae will hang motionless head-downwards with its breathing tube just penetrating the surface, but when alarmed in any way will jack-knife downwards like lightning but only for a short distance. The artificial is thus best fished on a greased leader ultra slowly and with the merest of short movements occasionally.

G. E. M. Skues, in his book *The Way of a Trout with a Fly*, describes how he took two fish feeding on what he called mosquito nymphs with an improvised mosquito nymph imitation.

Moths *(Lepidoptera)*

There are a number of moth patterns devised according to species or colour which will be found under Brown Moth, Ermine Moth, Ghost Swift Moth, Hoolet, Wainscott Moth, Wave Moth, White Moth.

Mottled Sedge
(Glyphotaelius pellucidus)

The mottled sedge is bigger than the cinnamon sedge and has heavily mottled wings. It is usually about from June onwards. On initial hatching the adults are of a pale colour.

An early dressing by Leonard West includes a simulation of the fairly pronounced antennae.

Hook:	10
Rib:	Yellow wool
Body:	Cock pheasant
Wings:	Woodcock or bittern
Hackle:	Furnace cock
Horns or antennae:	Cock pheasant

Mottled Sedge (Joscelyn Lane)

Joscelyn Lane's representation is what he calls the mottled or marbled cinnamon which is a different species from *pellucidus* but can serve as an imitation. He regards it as a grand fly for the evening sedge rise, it having presented him with more fish than any other sedge pattern. He says that it is the most reliable sedge in his box for "the undoing of large trout''. His methods of tying sedges are well worth studying and can be found in his book, *Lake and Loch Fishing for Trout*. I find them very effective, especially for skating the pattern over the water surface.

Hook:	10
Silk:	Golden olive
Tail:	Rusty dun cock hackle fibres bunched with butts level and cut off fan-shaped. These help to support the fly on the water
Body:	Red cock hackle, long and halfway along the shank. All fibres clipped off above shank and level with hook point below and at sides
Thorax:	Large red cock hackle trimmed to a conical shape
Wings:	Rusty-dun cock hackle fibres, a broad bunch tied in by the butts halfway along shank and lying flat
Leg hackle:	Red cock four to five turns tied with fibres radiating at right angles to the shank

John Goddard says that the body of the natural is sometimes a dull green, and Taff Price's version takes this into account.

Hook:	10
Rib:	Yellow silk
Body:	Pale ginger hare's fur mixed with green seal's fur
Wing:	Cock pheasant wing extending beyond the hook, and clipped to shape. A felt-tipped pen can be used to add further markings
Hackle:	Ginger cock (two)

Mrs Palmer

When this lure was originally devised by Richard Walker he anticipated that the fly would be attractive to trout at the back end of the season in bright conditions. He considers that because goat hair is fine and mobile in water it is preferable to bucktail which is stiffer.

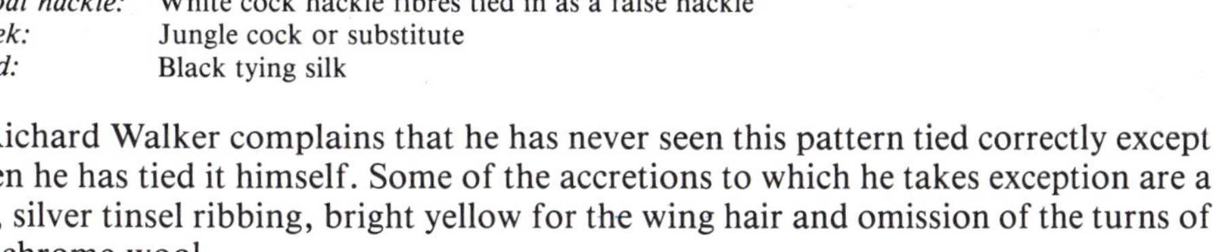

Mrs Palmer

Hook:	L/S 6-8
Silk:	Black
Rib:	Fine silver thread
Body:	White DF wool with a few turns of arc chrome DF wool just behind the wing and hackle roots
Wing:	Pale yellow goat hair twice the hook length
Throat hackle:	White cock hackle fibres tied in as a false hackle
Cheek:	Jungle cock or substitute
Head:	Black tying silk

Richard Walker complains that he has never seen this pattern tied correctly except when he has tied it himself. Some of the accretions to which he takes exception are a tail, silver tinsel ribbing, bright yellow for the wing hair and omission of the turns of arc chrome wool.

A dressing given by Bob Church seems to incorporate several of the features of which Richard complains. He says that Mrs Palmer is a lure pattern that can stand beng fished more slowly than any other lure he knows and still catch fish, whereas Bob Church has found it an attractor par excellence to be fished fast in high summer. Both, however, agree that it is one of the very best lures for fishing cloudy or stained water.

Mrs Simpson

Mrs Simpson

I include this New Zealand lure because it involves a type of winging not common in this country, and which some fly dressers might like to try. This is the whole feather kind of lure also known as the Killer Style. As well as in New Zealand, it is commonly fished on the lakes in the Eastern Highlands of Zimbabwe.

I assume that the fly was named after the Duchess of Windsor whose name this was before her marriage to the Duke, formerly King Edward VIII.

Hook: L/S D/E 6-12
Tail: Black squirrel tail fibres
Body: Black, yellow, red or green chenille
Wing: A minimum of four pairs of brown partridge, the smallest pair at the tail end tied in first, the others tied in consecutively overlapping along
Head: Black varnish

Muddler Minnow

Muddler Minnow (Original)

One day, as Don Gapen was fishing the Nipigon River in America, he saw an Indian nearby lift a flat rock at the edge of the river and quickly stab down at something with a fork. He came up with a minnow impaled on the tines. The minnow had a flattened head, the body tapered back from the wide head and narrowed towards the caudal fin, and it had very wide pectoral fins. Don recognised it as a member of the numerous sculpin family, also called darter or muddler minnow. The

Indian had another name for it. "Cocatouse minnow," he said. "The best thing to catch big trout." Gapen took the minnow home and set to work to tie a fly that would resemble it in the water. The result was the Muddler Minnow. Its potential was recognised by Dan Bailey at Livingston who began to tie it commercially.

The Muddler industry in this country has flourished since 1967. The dominating feature of the pattern is the deer hair used as body material, and this is the most difficult part of the fly to dress. How to do so is explained in John Veniard's book, *Reservoir and Lake Flies*, and by David Collyer in his *Fly Dressing I*. The original dressing was:

Hook:	D/E L/S 6-12
Silk:	Black
Tail:	Small section of turkey wing quill (oak) slightly longer than the gape of the hook
Body:	Flat gold tinsel ribbed with gold wire in larger sizes
Wing (inner):	Substantial bunch of grey squirrel tail hair, or on large hooks black and white bucktail or brown and white calf tail, extended almost to the tip of the tail
Wing (outer):	Two large sections of mottled (oak) turkey wing feather to reach to the bend of the hook
Head:	Natural deer hair spun on the shank and clipped
Ruff:	Small bunch of natural deer hair spun and unclipped to form a hair hackle

The deer hair head can be clipped either ball-shaped or cylindrical or cone-shaped. The latter shape, as recommended by Richard Walker, is now much favoured.

The versatility of the fly makes it a must for every angler's fly box. Even where there are no small fish present it can be taken for a sedge or a moth or even a damsel. Weighted versions can be fished slowly, sunk deep. Generally, it is most effective retrieved just below the surface at a medium to slow pace especially if there is a good ripple on the water.

The incorporation of marabou in the dressing was first appreciated by Dan Bailey of Montana among others. The White Marabou given here is typical, utilising marabou for the wing, and a tinsel or mylar body. Brown, olive, yellow, black and orange are other popular colours.

White Marabou Muddler

Hook:	L/S 6-8
Silk:	White
Tail:	Scarlet-red hackle fibres tied short
Body:	Silver tinsel chenille
Head:	Natural deer hair spun on shank and clipped
Wing:	Spray of white marabou with about six strands of peacock herl over

There have been many other variations of the original. Paul Drake and George Bodmer of Colorado Springs introduced a lead-shot head with the deer hair in front of the shot and folded back over it to form both a head and a hackle. The weight up front in what they called the Bullet Head Muddler makes the fly dip up and down with the rod action in a manner reminiscent of the later Dog Nobbler.

Another colloquial name for the Cockatouse minnow is 'sculpin' and David Whitlock of Oklahoma attempts to imitate that fish in his dressing which gives a flat-headed outline of the fish from the trout's point of view with the wings dressed flush with the hook shank.

Sculpin Muddler

Hook:	L/S 4-8
Silk:	Brown
Rib:	Oval gold tinsel
Body:	Dark brown wool yarn
Wing:	Single brown partridge tail feather tied in on top with the fibres stripped from the area that contacts the body
Fins:	A brown partridge feather at each side. Tips of these feathers should curve outwards
Hackle:	Collar of dyed-brown deer body-hair. Clip on top and bottom so the hair has more of a flair to each side
Head:	Dyed-brown deer body-hair clipped to shape

The range of colours in the standard Muddler includes black, orange, brown, yellow and white. The latter colour is known as the Mizoolein Spook.

One of the most popular colour variations of the standard Muddler in this country is that of Richard Walker called the Texas Rose Muddler.

Texas Rose Muddler

Hook:	L/S 8
Silk:	Orange
Rib:	Fine oval silver tinsel
Body:	Orange floss silk
Wing:	Yellow bucktail
Head:	Natural deer hair spun on shank and clipped. The length of the head should be equivalent to one third of the body

Finally, a fly included in Richard Walker's book, *Fly Dressing Innovations*, and based on the principle of the Muddler Minnow.

The Spuddler

Hook:	L/S 6-10
Tail:	A bunch of brown calf-tail hair
Body:	Cream wool with a thorax of DRF fire-orange fuzz wool
Wing:	Four long cree (barred) cock hackles, dyed brown or olive-green, tied in two pairs, overlaid with a bunch of Canadian fox squirrel tail hair, about half the length of the wing hackles
Head:	Muddler Minnow style of spun and clipped deer hair, but cut shorter than usual on the underside and stained mahogany with a Pantone marker pen

This is particularly effective in waters where there are numerous small perch present. It can be fished on the surface with a floating line when fry are being attacked by trout or fished deeply on a fast-sinking line.

The Murk-Meister

The Murk-Meister

Any new fly should be devised for a specific purpose, and there are always sound underlying reasons behind any new pattern introduced by Richard Walker. This one, created by Richard Aylott, who has originated a number of effective patterns, is designed for use in stillwater fisheries whenever the water is opaque due either to an excess of suspended matter or to a plethora of algae. The fly is thus dressed to be highly visible and to create a certain turbulence apparent to the fish:

Hook:	L/S 6-10
Silk:	Hot-orange
Bodies:	Arc chrome (yellowish-orange) wool teased out and dubbed on the silk, built up fat
Tail:	A tuft of white fluorescent wool
Hackles:	Stiff ginger cock hackles

The tail should be tied in first and the wool wound over the hook shank to provide a base for the body.

It is intended to be fished with short, quick pulls with pauses in between each pull.

Mylar Minnow

Mylar Minnow

Another member of the artificial fish shoal which includes the Polystickle, Sinfoil's Fry, etc. Syd Brock's fly, however, uses mylar for the body rather than polythene. In this respect, and because of its tail and back, it has some resemblance to the Jersey Herd. It can have a throat hackle added of orange fibres.

Hook:	L/S D/E 10-14
Silk:	Black
Underbody:	Wool or floss
Body:	Silver or gold mylar piping cut to length
Back & tail:	Peacock herl
Head:	Bold head of tying silk, varnished and eye detail added

As a fry imitation, the usual fishing tactics should be used.

Mylar is a glittering non-tarnishable material, and is particularly suitable for the bodies of streamer and bucktail flies.

Nailer Fly

Nailer Fly

The name speaks for itself. A lure recommended by Bob Church for fishing deeply from a boat on the big reservoirs in early season or later when daphnia are multiplying in their millions and a big lure like the Nailer will be attacked with relish by rainbows.

Hook:	L/S 6-10
Silk:	Black
Tail:	Red cock hackle or hair fibres
Rib:	Gold wire (optional)
Body:	Gold lurex or tinsel
Wing:	Underwing of bright red hair (goat or skunk). Overwing of brown hair. Or four red cock hackles with brown mottled turkey over
Throat hackle:	Chocolate-brown cock or natural brown, long in fibre

Needle Fly *(Leuctra fusca and L. hippopus)*

See under Dark Spanish Needle

Nell Gwynne

Nell Gwynne

Richard Walker likes to describe patterns which are easy to tie, and this is a good example. This fly is a development of the Baby Doll and so-called by him as Mistress Gwynne was a 'doll' who sold oranges at the theatre.

Hook:	L/S 6-8
Silk:	Black
Body:	White DRF wool
Back & tail:	Orange wool
Hackle:	Orange-dyed cock

It can be fished very much like the Baby Doll. In the first Bewl Bridge Flyfishing Championship the largest fish, a 5lb 3½oz brown trout, was taken on a Nell Gwynne.

Oak Fly *(Leptis scolopacea)*

Oak Fly (Taff Price)

A common terrestrial fly nearly a third of an inch (8mm) in length and with yellow-orange and black-brown body giving it a wasp-like appearance. The two wings are veined and spotted and held flat over the body. Fishermen have been imitating this fly since Dame Juliana Berners, yet as early as 1747 Richard and Charles Bowlker had it on a list of flies seldom found useful to fish with. The Downlooker, from its habit of facing downwards at rest, or Canon Fly, to give it its other names, has continued to have the thumbs-down from such eminences as Courtney Williams and John Goddard. Skues said that he never caught a trout with it.

However, if you find this admittedly strong flyer on the water and not on yourself or your surroundings, as it is quite friendly despite its appearance, there are dressings. Alfred Ronalds said its season was May and June and that his imitation could be used with most success on windy days.

Hook:	12-13
Body:	Orange floss silk tied with ash-coloured silk which may be shown at the tail and shoulders
Wings:	Scapular feather of the woodcock
Legs:	Furnace hackle with a black list up the middle and black at the extremities tied palmered, and the fibres snipped off nearly up to where the wings are set on, leaving a sufficient quantity for the legs

Roger Woolley agreed that the pattern was most useful on breezy days and gave the following dressing:

Hook:	11
Rib:	Dark quill from the stem of a peacock tail feather
Body:	Raffia dyed orange
Wings:	Two small dark grizzled cock hackles or from a woodcock wing feather, tied flat on back
Hackle:	Furnace cock

Taff Price has caught the insect on several reservoirs, and gives a dressing as follows:

Hook:	L/S 14
Silk:	Black
Rib:	Black silk
Body:	Yellow polypropylene
Wings:	Pale grey hackle tips tied spent
Hackle:	Pale yellow or ginger

Olive and Gold

Olive and Gold

David Collyer offered this pattern which he devised with a note of apprehension, as there are already so many standard-type wet flies. However, from the moment he tied it he felt it would be a good fish-killing dressing, and so it proved to be. The ribbing wire is suggested as a safeguard against the cutting of the tinsel by the trout's teeth.

Hook: 6-12
Silk: Brown (sherry spinner)
Tail: Golden pheasant crest
Body: Flat gold tinsel or lurex, ribbed with gold wire if necessary
Wing: Married strips of goose feather, gold-dyed in the middle and olive-dyed on the outside (six strands)
Hackle: Ginger cock

David does not tell us how he fishes it, but no doubt a traditional wet fly retrieve will be the best method.

Olive Dun

Olive Dun (Cliff Henry)

The olive dun is the most common of all our river flies but not, of course, found on stillwater. However, the river fisherman, coming on to a stillwater and seeking a representation of a lake olive dun could quite happily use either of these patterns.

Hook: 14
Tail: Three whisks, same colour as the body
Body: Medium olive seal's fur
Wings: Starling's wing feather, primary
Hackle: Cock hackle dyed the same shade of olive as the body

Cliff Henry's dressing is strongly recommended by John Goddard.

Hook: 14-16
Silk: Green
Tail: Grey-blue whisks
Body: Hen hackle stalks from a light olive cape
Wings: Mallard duck quill feather
Hackle: Pale gingery-olive

Fished dry and cast to rising fish.

A number of patterns have been devised for the lake olive dun and will be found under that heading. Some fishermen may well plump for a dry Greenwell's Glory or an Olive Quill.

Olive Quill

Another imitation of the natural olive dun which will serve very well to represent a pond olive dun. The traditional dressing is:

Hook:	14-16
Tail:	Three whisks as hackle
Body:	Peacock quill dyed olive
Wings:	Medium or dark starling's wing feather
Hackle:	Dyed medium or dark olive cock

Halford had a hackle dressing which he called the Hackle Dark Olive Quill.

Hook:	14-16
Tail:	Gallina dyed green-olive
Body:	Peacock or condor quill, dyed green-olive
Shoulder hackle:	Dyed green-olive
Head hackle:	Medium or dark blue dun hen

Olive Quill (Traditional)

Bob Church has a wet fly adaptation of Halford's pattern which he fishes successfully drifting from a boat at Chew Valley among other places. He regards it as one of the best deceiver (imitative) patterns fished in a team of three loch-style.

Hook:	14-16
Tail:	Four fibres of medium olive cock hackle
Body:	Stripped peacock quill dyed olive
Wing:	Dark starling wing feather
Hackle:	Two or three turns of dyed medium olive cock

The Olive Sun Nymph

This is a general-purpose nymph invented by Richard Aylott, creator of Aylott's Orange, which is good when olives are about and particularly good, as Richard Walker points out, when there is bright sunshine with the surface either broken or calm.

Hook:	D/E 12-14
Silk:	Pale green
Tail:	A golden pheasant topping
Rib:	Fine gold thread
Body:	Greenish-yellow DF floss, tied thin
Head:	A few turns of peacock herl

It should be fished a few inches below the surface on a floating line and long leader. Cast out and then retrieved ahead of a cruising fish, it can be very effective.

The Olive Sun Nymph

The Ombudsman

Wittily so-called by Brian Clarke because of its all-round appeal to trout. He set out to devise something that would suggest a number of creatures that live on the lake bottom, such as alder larvae or caddis.

Hook:	L/S 8-10 (one or two layers of copper wire if required)
Rib:	Copper wire for strength (optional)
Body:	Bronze peacock herl wrapped around the shank from start of the bend to about three sixteenths of an inch behind the eye
Overbody:	Several fibres from a dark mottled domestic hen's wing or any large, dark brown mottled wing feather sloping back along the peacock herl and forming an almost tubular shape over the top two thirds of the hook, with tips coming together almost as a point, well behind the hook bend
Hackle:	Two turns of softish brown cock hackle in front of the feather fibres
Head:	Brown tying silk, tied long and prominently

The Ombudsman

The fly is designed to be fished slowly on the bottom on a floating line and long leader.

The dressing is given in Brian Clarke's book, *The Pursuit of Stillwater Trout*, a book written with real style and panache and one which radically altered my attitude to stillwater trout fishing, and interested me in attempting more seriously to imitate the natural insect in or on the water.

Orange Bucktail

Orange Bucktail

A first cousin to the Whisky Fly and included in Taff Price's book on lures before the Whisky Fly details had been published.

Hook:	Normal or L/S 6-8
Body:	Largish oval gold tinsel in tight turns
Wing:	Orange bucktail not too heavily dressed or goat or calf tail
Hackle:	None

A dressing by John Goddard gives a black head with white painted eye and black pupil.

As with most orange lures it should have striking appeal to rainbows on the larger reservoirs from August onwards.

Orange John

Orange John

A fly devised by John Ketley for when he fishes in traditional loch style at the back end of the season, and he wants a sedge fly to skip along on his top dropper. It needs a large front hackle to ensure it stays well up in the water and at times to break through.

Hook:	D/E 10
Silk:	Orange or brown
Rib:	Goldfingering
Body:	Hot-orange seal's fur
Body hackle:	Light brown
Wing:	Flat hen pheasant
Hackle:	Honey

Another tactic John Ketley finds useful is to grease the top dropper so that the bob fly stays on top throughout the retrieve. The pattern is notably good for those warm September evenings.

The Orange Nymph

This is an ingenious imitation of those tiny creatures, daphnia, which are generally regarded as beyond imitation. Taff Price, after fishing a southern lake to no avail, finally took a fish on a small Partridge and Orange. His friend caught a fish on a Grenadier nymph which also has orange in its dressing. On examining the fishes' stomach contents, they were found to be full of orange-coloured daphnia. The Orange Nymph was devised as a result of this experience.

Hook: 14-16
Silk: Orange
Rib: Gold tinsel
Body: Pinkish-orange seal's fur
Back & antennae: Orange-dyed swan or goose

The Orange Nymph

Taff Price usually fishes the nymph as a dropper with a larger nymph on the point. Alternatively, it can be cast directly in the path of fish cruising through shoals of daphnia.

Orange Quill

The blue-winged olive is primarily a river fly, but John Goddard includes it in his list in *Trout Flies of Stillwater* as perhaps being present on lakes more often than is suspected. This might happen if a lake is fed by a stream or river. I therefore include Skues' Orange Quill as the classic representation of the sherry spinner as the best pattern to imitate the spent female spinners of the blue-winged olive.

Orange Quill (G. E. M. Skues)

Hook: U/E 13-14
Silk: Hot-orange
Tail: Bright red cock or paler from spade feather
Body: Pale condor quill, stripped, so as to show no dark edge, and dyed hot-orange. Stripped ostrich herl is equally effective, condor being difficult to strip
Wings: Pale starling, rather full, as the natural insect has wings longer than the ordinary olive duns
Hackle: Bright red cock

David Jacques' methodical investigations showed that the Orange Quill will not take as an imitation of the blue-winged olive dun, and he devised an effective representation of the male dun as follows:

Hook:	U/E 14
Silk:	Hot-orange
Tail:	Dark dirty-olive cock
Body:	Plastic dyed in picric acid over ostrich herl dyed yellow
Wings:	Two pairs from the wing feather of a coot
Hackle:	Dark dirty-olive cock

Whichever pattern is used, it should be fished dry and cast to a rising trout.

Orange/Silver Midge Pupa
(Chironomus plumosus)

John Goddard considers that the orange-silver midge is one of the most common and far-flung species of all the chironomids, and I have found Brian Harris's version of the pupa particularly good, having taken fish with it at Ardleigh Reservoir among other places. The natural has a dark thorax, orange wing cases and bright silver body segments ringed with dark red. I include a tiny amount of mole's fur to darken the thorax slightly.

Orange/Silver Midge

Hook:	D/E 10-12
Rib:	Silver lurex in close turns so that the body floss shows only in thin spaces. Coated liberally with clear fly head varnish
Body:	Hot-orange floss silk, one strand
Thorax:	Orange seal's fur or ball of orange wool teased out and dubbed on silk
Tail & breathing tubes:	Tufts of white nylon floss

Although the artificial should be fished slowly on a greased leader, remember that the naturals occasionally go down from the surface, and so a little action to the fly at intervals sometimes repays.

John Goddard has now acepted the suggestion of Bob Carnill that a more appropriate angler's name for the orange/silver midge should be grey boy. It is a good early season fly, stretching from early April to June.

Orange Streamer

Orange Streamer

An orange streamer pattern by Taff Price to reinforce your Whisky Flies, Orange Muddlers and Bucktails when fish are going for orange later in the season.

Hook:	L/S 8-10
Silk:	Orange
Rib:	Gold oval tinsel
Body:	Orange floss
Wing:	Two hot-orange hackles with two badger or grizzle hackles outside
Hackle:	None

In his book, *Lures for Game, Coarse and Sea Fishing*, Taff Price adds a cheek of jungle cock.

Painted Lady Streamer

Painted Lady Streamer

This streamer lure has been described by Taff Price, its originator, as a pretty fly that catches fish, and no more than a tarted-up version of the Black Lure tied with odd scraps of feather left on his fly bench after he had been tying some salmon flies. He said that he was surprised when it caught fish. Nevertheless, it now figures in a number of fly dressing lists:

Hook:	L/S 6-8
Silk:	Black
Body:	Black silk
Tail:	Blue guinea fowl (gallina)
Rib:	Oval silver tinsel
Wing:	Four black hackles (or black hair for hair wing version)
Cheek:	Jungle cock (or substitute)
Hackle:	Magenta cock hackle

It is most successful for reservoir trout early in the season or any time in the season late in the evening.

It should not be confused with the brightly-dressed American Painted Ladies so successful in Washington and British Columbia waters.

Pale Sedge

See under Light Sedge

Palmered Sedge

Palmered Sedge

Some years ago, Peter Lapsley became a little disillusioned with the G. & H. Sedge because, while it rose a good many fish, it often failed to hook them, largely, he felt, because the spun deer hair body seemed to be too bulky for the fish to take easily. He went to the drawing board and designed the following pattern:

Hook: U/E 10-12
Silk: Brown
Body: Four to six furnace cock hackles closely palmered one after the other from a point about one third of the way round the bend of the hook to one eighth of an inch behind the eye; clipped into a wedge shape like the G. & H. Sedge
Hackle: One or two stiff, short-fibred brown or furnace cock hackles
Antennae: The stalks of the last two hackles used (optional)

It has taken a great many fish for him, his friends and others. It floats well, and can be left sitting static on the water or it can be used as a wake fly.

Palmer Flies

For other patterns involving palmer dressings see under Black Palmer, Bi-Visibles, Bumbles, Conrad Voss Bark Palmer Nymph, Green Palmer, Loch Ordie, Palmer Nymph, Red Palmer.

Palmer Nymph

Palmer Nymph

This is a favourite nymph of Donald Overfield's devised by Conrad Voss Bark. It is weighted and the palmered body gives an impression of the gills and legs of a nymph.

Hook: 8-12
Silk: Primrose
Tail: Golden pheasant tippet
Rib: Fine gold or silver wire used to bind down the palmer hackle
Body: Copper wire with thorax covered by the tying silk. Two short-fibred cock hackles, one golden-olive and one red tied palmer-fashion down the body
Head hackle: Reddish-coloured feather

It can be fished either just below the surface or deeper if required.

For the theory behind Conrad Voss Bark's nymphs and their connection with Kingsmill Moore's Bumble flies, see under Conrad Voss Bark nymph.

Parmachenee Belle

Parmachenee Belle

A real dazzler of a fly emanating many years ago from America where it is regarded as an absolute killer. It was fished on the Maine lakes and the Parmachenee Lake in particular. It looks like nothing living or dead, and is just the kind of fly to use when desperate on a hot summer's day pulled fast just below the surface, in the hope of seeing that thrilling bow wave of a pursuing trout.

Hook:	6-10
Silk:	Black or scarlet
Tail:	White and scarlet or red goose or duck feathers
Rib:	Silver or gold tinsel
Body:	Lemon-yellow seal's fur or mohair or yellow floss silk
Butt:	Black ostrich herl (optional)
Wing:	White striped with scarlet using goose or duck feathers
Hackle:	White and scarlet cock or hen hackle fibres

Advice regarding special flies for desperate moments is freely given but rarely works. However, on a hot sunny day in July at Grafham when nothing was moving and no one was catching, the Parmachenee Belle did work the oracle for me with a 3lb brown trout. As I removed the hook, it struck me that the fly when wet has the gleam of a perch fry.

The Parmachenee Belle can be tied in a hair-wing version using scarlet and white bucktail for the wings.

Partridge and Orange

To remove the Partridge and Orange from my flybox would be rather like expelling one of the original members from the Football League. It imitates the february red which is the 'dun fly' of Dame Juliana Berners' *Treatise* according to J. W. Hills although W. H. Lawrie identifies the 'dun fly' with the march brown.

Hills says that the dressing has hardly changed over the centuries from the original "body of dun wool and the wings of the partridge". The february red is a smallish red-brown stonefly found mainly in the North of England, Wales and Scotland, and the Partridge and Orange is a proven killer in these areas.

A great deal of my early fly fishing was on the River Wharfe and so I was prejudiced in favour of the fly, but I did wonder how it would fare in the South. It soon proved its effectiveness on the Amwell Magna stretch of the River Lea when I came to Hertfordshire, but doubts about its stillwater potential remained. It certainly is no killer, but it has taken fish for me both as a single fly and as part of a team when olives have been about. It is the easiest of flies to tie but the hackle must be sparse.

Partridge and Orange

Hook:	14
Body:	Orange silk
Hackle:	Well-dappled feather from the back of a partridge

Fished very slowly, the natural movement of the partridge hackle is what makes it effective. It could be taken for a nymph or a midge pupa or a shrimp. William B. Currie in his *The Guinness Guide to Game Fishing* mentions taking loch trout with it when flying ants had been blown onto the surface.

A specialist development of the Partridge and Orange is the Short Orange Partridge devised by Richard Walker to take big fish on the smaller stillwaters. The illusion of a smaller fly is produced by tying for only half the body length, and the bigger hook helps the fly to sink more quickly without the necessity of weighting.

Hook:	D/E L/S wide gape 6-12
Silk:	Brown
Body:	Orange floss silk tied short to only half the length of the hook
Hackle:	Brown partridge

Richard recommends that the pattern be used for tackling big trout found cruising a few feet from the surface. For later in the season when algae scum is breaking to the surface in hot weather a green version should be tried which has a body of phosphor-yellow wool instead of the orange floss silk. Phosphor-yellow is a misnomer as it has a lime-green appearance. The algae at this time often brings with it green and brown larvae of a midge species.

The Short Orange Partridge is one example of Richard Walker's original thinking to appear in his book of *Modern Fly Dressings* sub-titled *More Fly Dressing Innovations*.

Pearly

The Pearly is an extremely buoyant lure which lends itself to the same kind of fishing technique used for the Plastazote Corixa. With a twelve-foot leader and a fast sink line, a pull on the line when it has sunk will cause the floating lure to dive. Even after it has sunk, pauses in the retrieve will allow it to rise again. Fish may take it either on the rise or the dive.

Hook: D/E L/S 8-10
Tail: Cock fibres of chosen colour
Body: Wool of same colour tied to within one quarter of an inch of the eye
Wing: Marabou of the same colour tied up to the eye and varnished
Head: Pearl or wooden bead painted in chosen colour then secured behind the eye with instant glue
Eyes: Black and white fast drying paint
Colours: Black, white or orange

Pearly

Another tactic with this pattern, especially later on in the season, is to use a floating line and retrieve at great speed in order to produce that exciting follow and take.

A variation of the Pearly is to leave out the wing, replace the wool body with chenille, and the tail of cock fibres with a generous spray of marabou. It then becomes the Pearly Nobbler.

Perch Fry

Of all the imitations of coarse fish fry, perch fry imitations seem the most popular and the most profitable. Some, like the Church Fry, are well known. Here are three others worth trying.

The first, given by John Veniard in his *Reservoir and Lake Flies*, incorporates the supple qualities of marabou.

Hook: L/S 4-6
Tail: Reddy-brown cock hackle fibres cut to shape
Underbody: Floss silk, fairly full
Body: Gold mylar piping marked with a brown felt-tipped pen to simulate bars. Alternatively, gold tinsel ribbed with wide brown floss silk
Wing: Brown marabou feather fibres, with one or two orange ones over the top to form a crest
Throat: Several white marabou feather plumes reaching about two thirds the length of the body
Head: Black, with a yellow eye black centred

Perch Fry (John Veniard)

Another pattern called the Perch Streamer has been devised by Taff Price.

Hook: L/S 6-8
Tail: Orange cock hackles
Body: Gold mylar marked with dark vertical lines with a felt-tipped pen
Underwing: Two white cock hackles as long as the wing

Wing:	Two grizzle hackles dyed a yellowish-green, two light grey hackles either side
Throat hackle:	Orange cock
Shoulder:	Hen pheasant body feather (dark centre, light buff outer)
Cheek:	Jungle cock or substitute

A further Perch Fry pattern is given in the *Sue Burgess Fly-Tying Library*. It makes use of cling film, that indispensable aid to the housewife for keeping food dishes airtight.

Hook:	Extra L/S 6-10
Silk:	White multi-strand
Tail:	Cream cock hackle fibres
Body:	White SB body floss covered in cling film to form fish-shaped body
Wing:	Two red/brown cock hackles barred with black Pantone pen
Hackle:	Beard of red hen hackle fibres

To be fished later in the season on the bigger reservoirs like all perch fry imitations.

The Persuader

A pattern designed by John Goddard originally for fishing Hanningfield Reservoir, but since found to be universally successful. He incorporated three elements in its make-up as a general attractor nymph: fairly large size to be visible, appealing colour combination and a body that looked appetising and tasty. The outline is aimed roughly to be that of a sedge pupa.

The Persuader

Hook:	D/E L/S 8-10
Silk:	Orange
Rib:	Round silver tinsel number 20
Body:	Five strands of white ostrich herl (trim after tying)
Thorax:	Orange seal's fur
Wing pads:	Three strands of dark brown-dyed turkey herl from the tail feather

It can be fished in various ways. Firstly, near the bottom on a sinking line and slowly. Secondly, pulled back fairly quickly and just below the surface on a floating line or sink tip. In his essential reference work, *Stillwater Flies and how to fish them*, John Goddard points out that the latter method will sometimes work with trout preoccupied with caenis. The Persuader can also be employed as a fry imitator cast in the path of trout beating up shoals of fry.

I had not used this pattern before I started working on this guide, but I tied a few and found that they did, indeed, persuade, fished on my local lake with a steady retrieve and just below the surface on a floating line when I think they were taken for sedge pupae.

Peter Ross

Peter Ross

Like Canon Greenwell, Peter Ross did not tie his fly but was a most able fisherman. He kept a general store in the lovely little village of Killin in Perthshire with Loch Tay on his doorstep. His suggested variation of the Teal and Red has become one of the best-known flies ever. Courtney Williams gave it the riband of the most killing lake fly in the British Isles, and even today, when so many flies have been invented based on a close study of underwater life, the Peter Ross has its place in most anglers' fly boxes.

Hook:	D/E 8-14
Tail:	Golden pheasant tippet
Rib:	Fine oval silver wire over the whole
Body:	Halved: the tail end of flat silver tinsel and the rest of red seal's fur
Wing:	From the breast or flank feather of a teal
Hackle:	Black cock or hen

It continues to be used as a point fly in a traditional team of loch flies well under the surface. If it is employed as a fry imitator later in the season, a floating line with the leader degreased is best to avoid line wake. It can be retrieved fairly quickly but with a variety of pauses and short pulls.

The Phantom Fly Larva
(Chaoborus flavicans)

Phantom Fly Larva
(Peter Gathercole)

It is not surprising that this fly is almost unknown to most fishermen considering that it spends most of its life in a near-invisible state! A fascinating study of the fly can be found in David Jacques' *The Development of Stillwater Fishing*. The larvae come from eggs laid on the surface by the female fly. They hatch out there or on the lake bottom. The larva when fully grown is about five eighths of an inch (16mm) long and lies horizontally in the water, being able to vary its depth by means of two swim bladders in the thorax and two in the seventh segment of the body near the tail. Covered with tiny black spots, the swim bladders are virtually the only items visible to the human eye. Its antennae form a grab-like device to capture minute aquatic creatures as food. Though generally stationary, the larva can move incredibly quickly by flexing its rear end aided by hairy bristles at its tail.

Very large numbers of phantom fly larvae exist in most stillwaters yet few have been found in trout autopsies. C. F. Walker, who was the first to mention phantom flies, asserts that trout eat the larvae in considerable numbers.

Taff Price has devised an artificial using marabou feather fibre.

Hook:	14-16
Silk:	White
Tail:	A small tuft of white marabou
Body:	Flat silver tinsel
Head:	Two turns of white ostrich herl

Peter Gathercole in a recent article in *Trout Fisherman* asserted that when *chaoborus* in any of its three stages occurs in any number, trout can become preoccupied with them to the exclusion of other food forms. His dressing, which makes use of polythene over a silvered hook, is similar to one given by David Collyer in his first *Fly Dressing* book except that it also simulates the swim bladders. I have dressed a few and they look very convincing in my box though I have not had any success with the trout. I have tried them under several conditions using a floating line and long leader, fishing them rather like a midge pupa.

Hook:	L/S 14 silvered or bronze with a layer of silver tinsel
Body:	Turns of light brown tying silk near the bend and at thorax to represent swim bladders. A quarter inch strip of clear polythene up and down the hook shank to produce a neat tapered body
Hackle:	Sparse short-fibred white or badger cock

Another pattern devised to represent the phantom fly larva can be found under Barney Google.

Phantom Fly Pupa
(Chaoborus flavicans)

The pupa of the phantom fly or midge probably offers the best opportunity to the angler as it is more visible than the larva and usually assumes a more vertical position. The prominent thorax is crowned by a couple of appendages of oval shape but pointed at the top which, David Jacques by experiment has demonstrated, almost certainly act as a depth control mechanism. The quarter inch (6mm) body is palish green and the thorax darkens to a light brown with maturity.

Phantom Fly Pupa
(Peter Gathercole)

There are a number of imitations, but I list first David Jacques' in view of his unrivalled knowledge of the natural.

Hook: D/E 15
Silk: Black
Body: A thin strip of PVC dyed lightly in picric acid tied tightly over white swan or goose herl or flat silver. The body must stop at the bend
Thorax: Cinnamon turkey tail or cinnamon wool or kapok

Another pattern which also uses PVC to attempt transparency is that of John Goddard.

Hook: D/E 16
Silk: Brown
Body: One strand of white marabou silk with a narrow silver lurex rib
Thorax: Formed from two strands only of orange marabou silk. The whole covered with clear PVC

The only one that I have dressed and used is Peter Gathercole's version.

Hook: 14
Tail filament: White feather fibre
Rib: Silver wire
Body: White floss covered with clear polythene
Thorax: Amber seal's fur with a back of light brown feather fibre
Head filament: White feather fibre

From the angler's point of view the important thing to note is that until the pupa is ready to change into the adult fly it never approaches the surface, remaining stationary except that every ten seconds or so it lashes the water with its tail. Thus artificials should be fished on a floating line with a long leader well down in the water and motionless with the occasional small twitch.

The Phantom Fly
(Chaoborus flavicans)

Phantom Fly (John Goddard)

The adult fly almost certain emerges only during the hours of darkness, and therefore is of little value to the angler. When the female returns to the water to lay her eggs, probably about dusk, then there are possibilities for deceiving trout.

The phantom, with its pale green hue and lightish grey-olive wings, six legs and antennae, is very like a chironomid or midge, and this is probably why it had never been mentioned in any fishing work before that of C. F. Walker. However, when the wings are at rest they almost cover the abdomen whereas the chironomid has the last few segments uncovered. The phantom wings are approximately elliptical, the chironomid's in the shape of a triangle.

Here is David Jacques' dressing for the adult.

Hook: D/E 16
Silk: Black
Body: A thin strip of PVC dyed lightly in picric acid tied tightly over white swan or goose herl or flat silver, very thin
Tail: Pale watery cock fibres, rather short. Although the natural is tail-less, they are included to give improved buoyancy, and to imitate the backward spread of the long hind legs of the natural
Wings: Pale starling, dipped for a few seconds in picric acid. Tied short, sloping well back
Hackle: Pale watery

A rather easier dressing is that of John Goddard.

Hook: U/E 14
Silk: Orange
Body: Grey condor herl with a wide rib of olive-dyed PVC
Wings: White hackle points tied spent
Hackle: Honey cock, tied in well back from the eye

Cast to rising fish in the traditional dry fly manner.

Pheasant Tail

Considered to be one of the best all-round dry fly patterns for representing a number of spinners on rivers. It is also valuable on stillwater whenever lake olive and sepia spinners are on the water.

The original dressing was devised at the turn of the century by Payne Collier for fishing in Devon.

Hook: 14
Tail: Three long herls from a saddle hackle
Rib: Four turns of gold twist
Body: A very dark herl of a cock pheasant's tail feather
Hackle: Honey dun, called in the West Country 'brassy'

Pheasant Tail (G. E. M. Skues)

The most popular dressing is that of G. E. M. Skues who said it was one you could use throughout the season. It is a favourite of mine and, although I may not use it very often, it is deadly for the right occasion. I once had a memorable and exciting hour, collecting my limit, during a fall of lake spinners. The dressing below is a rather more detailed one that Skues gave to a correspondent in March, 1947 to represent a number of rusty-coloured spinners.

Hook: 12-16 according to the size of the natural fly
Silk: Hot-orange
Tail whisks: Same colour as the hackle — stiff
Rib: Finest gold wire
Body: Four, three or two strands of one of the three centre feathers of a cock pheasant's tail, tied in with tips towards the eye of the hook
Hackle: Rusty or honey dun cock (sometimes a Rhode Island Red or even a ginger red makes a killing variation)

Cast the dry fly to rising fish.

Pheasant Tail Nymph

See under Cove's Pheasant Tail Nymph and Sawyer's Pheasant Tail Nymph

Plastazote Corixa

Plastazote Corixa

This was a revolutionary way of dressing a corixa using new materials and strategies invented by both Derek Bradbury and David Collyer.

Hook:	D/E 10-12
Silk:	Brown
Body:	White plastazote glued to the hook shank and then cut to shape, or polyethylene foam. The plastazote can either be slit halfway with a razor blade or pierced with a hot needle. With the foam plastic make sure that more of the body shape is above the hook than below
Back & legs:	Olive or brown feather fibre
Oars:	Two pheasant tail fibres

The method of fishing involves a sinking line settled on the bottom and a leader long enough to allow the buoyant fly to float on top. By means of long, slow pulls at intervals the fly is drawn downwards, and thus simulates the corixa on its way home after collecting its air supply.

David Collyer advises a leader of 5lb breaking strain as often the takes are extremely savage. At other times there may be difficulties in detecting the take.

Polystickle

Polystickle

There have been various attempts to imitate the humble little stickleback. Conrad Voss Bark in his book, *Fishing for Lake Trout*, refers to an imitation used by his grandfather on Blagdon many years ago. One of the earliest imitations was devised by Joscelyn Lane and given in his work, *Lake and Loch Fishing*.

However, Richard Walker's Polystickle was an entirely new conception and a significant landmark in the development of stillwater flies in the post-war era. The 'stickle' covered by polythene, a material first mentioned by Ken Sinfoil in *Angling Times*, combined with a back and tail of another new material, raffene, produced an exciting translucence through which the fish 'organs' could be seen. Hence 'Polystickle'.

There have been many versions of the original, but Richard Walker insists that the cardinal features must be a spiral binding of black silk over a silvered hook shank, or the alternative of silver tinsel in open spirals over a bronzed hook shank so that you get the appearance of a tiny, translucent fish with vertebrae showing through; a big, bold built-up head; a short tail, clipped square.

Hook:	D/E L/S silver 6-8
Silk:	Black
Back & tail:	Brown raffene
Body:	Shank ribbed with black silk two thirds of the distance to the eye, then a length of crimson floss silk is wound in up to the eye. This is then covered and built into a fish-shaped body with polythene strip
Throat hackle:	Hot-orange-dyed cock hackle fibres
Head:	Big and bold with black tying silk given several coats of cellulose

The many variations include the black, brown, green and white Polystickle.

The pattern can be deadly in July and August fished from the bank in the margins of lakes and reservoirs as the fry move into slightly deeper water. Various retrieves can be tried. David Collyer favours a slow build-up of speed. Sometimes a slow or a fast pull works, but remember that whatever action you impart you are imitating the movement of a tiny stickleback.

Pond Olive Nymph *(Cloeon dipterum)*

The nymph of this, the most important of the upwinged flies to the stillwater angler, is quite small with the usual three tails banded a darker shade of brown. Its colour varies but generally combines shades of brown and olive in the body. It is almost indistinguishable from the lake olive nymph.

Pond Olive Nymph (Brian Harris)

One specialist pattern is by Brian Harris.

Hook:	Partridge limerick 12-14
Silk:	Olive-green nylon
Tail:	Body fibres left projecting one eighth of an inch
Rib:	Fine gold wire
Body:	Three fibres of dark olive-dyed goose or swan wing feather fibre
Thorax:	Olive-dyed rabbit fur
Wing case:	Fibres of any dark feather

Another comes from Taff Price.

Hook:	14-16
Silk:	Brown
Tail:	Dark olive cock hackle fibres
Body:	Olive-brown fur
Thorax:	The same
Wing case:	Dark brown hen fibres

One of the best patterns remains that of C. F. Walker which serves for both the *cloeon* nymphs and will be found under Lake Olive Nymph.

David Jacques points out that though the nymphs which are weed dwellers are generally quiescent, living on algae, they can dart about in a very agile manner especially if disturbed. The artificial is thus best fished near to weed beds slowly but with periodic little jerks.

Three other excellent patterns to imitate the pond olive nymph are the PVC Nymph, the American Gold-Ribbed Hare's Ear Nymph, and the Hatching Olive Nymph.

Pond Olive Dun *(Cloeon dipterum)*

Pond Olive Dun (C. F. Walker)

C. F. Walker described the pond olive as the "bread and butter" fly of the lakes. Not only is it found in most parts of the country in considerable numbers but it flourishes from the beginning of May to the end of the season. It is a medium to large ephemeropteran decreasing in size as the season progresses. It has a darkish olive body with reddish blotches, two tails ringed black or dark red, and grey wings which are slightly spread at rest.

Both Walker and John Goddard think this may make the drying of the wings easier after emergence, and certainly the dun takes to the air very quickly. For this reason, the nymphs and spinner patterns are regarded as better fish takers than those of the dun. However, Commander Walker gave us a dressing.

Hook:	13-14 decreasing to 15 later in the season
Tail:	Grey-brown mallard feathers
Rib:	Gold tinsel
Body:	Pale grey condor herl lightly stained in picric acid
Wings:	A bunch of fibres from a medium blue-grey waterhen or coot body feather, tied upright
Leg hackle:	Pale honey dun cock (or dyed pale yellow-olive)

David Jacques has devised a dressing as follows:

Hook:	14-15
Silk:	Orange
Tail:	Olive cock
Body:	Olive PVC over conder herl, natural straw colour
Wings:	Starling
Hackle:	Olive cock

Taff Price has also given us an imitation of the dun although he says that he has never seen a trout take a pond olive dun on his local lake.

Hook:	14 or Yorkshire fly body hook
Silk:	Olive
Tail:	Blue dun
Rib:	Brown silk
Body:	Olive swan or goose herl
Wing:	Blue dun hackle fibres upright
Hackle:	Olive

Hatches often occur in the middle part of the day when trout may take the dun in which case these patterns should be fished dry and cast to rising fish.

Four other patterns which will serve well for a pond olive dun are Greenwell's Glory, Olive Quill, the Rough Olive and the Super Grizzly.

Pond Olive Spinner *(Cloeon dipterum)*

Pond Olive Spinner
(Richard Walker)

The female adult pond olive dips fleetingly over the surface of the lake late into the evening and night to deposit the minute larvae which she has already developed from eggs in her oviducts. She then lies spent on the water, when she is known as a spinner. She is often called the apricot spinner because of her distinctive overall colour. As she lies with her body tinged with red and outspread shining wings with marked yellow veins, her gossamer frame soon disintegrates or is taken by foraging trout.

Richard Walker says that in the dusk when trout are rising and yet refusing sedge and midge imitations, a Pond Olive Spinner will often take a fish as the natural often returns to the water at this time. His pattern is as follows:

Hook:	14
Silk:	Orange
Tail:	Four or five strands of grey mallard feather fibre (speckled)
Rib:	Clear nylon monofil, 2lb or 3lb
Body:	Swan secondary fibre dyed the colour of tinned peaches, and wound over a varnished silk whipping whilst the whipping varnish is wet
Thorax:	Chestnut pheasant tail
Wings:	A bunch of dun hackle fibres divided by a figure-of-eight binding. The pheasant tail is wound over this binding
Hackle:	None

C. F. Walker's dressing, like so many patterns given in his *Lake Flies and their Imitation*, has hardly been bettered.

Hook: 13-14 reducing to 15 in September
Silk: Grey-brown mallard feathers
Rib: Gold tinsel
Body: Seal's fur dyed Naples yellow, mixed with a little amber and red
Wings: Bright golden dun or pale ginger cock hackle with fibres divided laterally by two cross lashings of silk
Hackle: Pale honey dun or ginger cock, or none

Finally, John Goddard's dressing.

Hook: U/E 12-14
Silk: Orange
Tail: Fibres from a pale badger hackle
Body: Apricot-coloured condor or ostrich herl covered with pale olive-dyed PVC
Wings: Pale blue hackle tips tied spent
Hackle: Dark honey cock. A bunch of these fibres tied in under each spent wing in place of the traditional type of hackle

Trout feeding on spinners often do so with the minimum of fuss and a sound remarkably like that of a little kiss. Cast the artificial in the path of a feeding fish and allow it to lie perfectly still.

See also under Apricot Spinner.

The Poodle

The Poodle

Described by Bob Carnill in an article in *Trout Fisherman* as the nymph fisherman's answer to a lure, The Poodle, invented in 1978 by John Wadham, one of Rutland Water's most successful bank fishermen, has become an immensely popular pattern with the patrons of that water.

This is another fly exploiting the responsive qualities of marabou to the merest movement. Apart from a tail of marabou equal to the length of the hook shank, the fly has four spaced-out plumes of black marabou alternating with turns of chenille to create a marabou matuka effect.

Hook: New Partridge Black S.E.B. lure hook or Partridge wide-gape, size as required
Silk: Black Naples (waxed)
Tail: Black marabou plume or arctic fox
Tag: Two or three turns of DRF signal-green fuzz (optional) wool between the tail and start of the body
Body: Black chenille (leaded underbody if required)
Body plumes: Four or five, depending on hook size, black marabou plumes or arctic fox

A favoured technique is to fish the pattern in a crosswind, allowing the line to develop a wind-belly as it tows round then, as it approaches near-in, to retrieve as you would a nymph pattern with slow, short pulls. Takes are registered by a heaviness of the line, or the tip may be seen to submerge. In either case this is the cue to strike. With the wind behind him, the angler can cast straight out with a long leader and floating line, retrieving in a nymph-like fashion. Bob Carnill considers that the sinuous movement of the marabou may well mean that the trout take the fly for a black leech.

Popping Bug

Popping Bug

Another idea imported from America to our stillwater scene. Strangely enough, these bugs were used many years ago by American anglers for taking tarpon all along the Florida Keys, but are now regarded as mostly ineffective for this kind of fishing.

The heads of the bugs can be painted with enamel or coloured Vycoat to add eyes or even further detail. Some versions have hackles immediately behind the head and two or three strands of shirling elastic through the head to add further movement. A variety of colour schemes can be used.

Hook:	L/S 8-10
Tail:	A large spray of marabou
Body or head:	Pear-shaped cork, flat and concave at front end

This surface-skimming lure is fished on a floating line preferably downwind in short, quick jerks. The concave head, pulled sharply against the water, lets off a distinct popping noise, and considerable disturbance is created on the surface.

Popping Bugs have been very successful at Rutland and Grafham in the later hot months when fast-stripped surface lures and muddlers often attract rainbows. The takes are said to be spectacular.

Port Spinner

Port Spinner

An effective representation by Cliff Henry of the female spinner of the lake olive, so-called for obvious reasons.

Hook:	14-16
Silk:	Crimson
Tail:	Pale blue cock fibres
Body:	Hen hackle stalk from dark Rhode Island Red (Port wine colour)
Wings:	Pale blue dun hackle points tied spent
Hackle:	Two turns of light olive

Professor

Professor

A traditional lake pattern dating back to the 1820's and named after Professor John Wilson of Edinburgh University. It is a fly which has become well-known throughout the world with slight variations.

Hook:	6-12
Tail:	Two or three long fibres of red ibis feather (or substitute)
Rib:	Flat gold tinsel or black tying silk
Body:	Primrose yellow silk
Wings:	Mottled grey mallard
Hackle:	Natural ginger cock

Tom Stewart used the fly successfully for many years on Loch Awe and other Scottish waters especially on windy days as a bob fly. I have never caught a fish on it though this may be due to lack of confidence in the fly.

PVC Nymph

If I were restricted to a limited number of nymphs I should find it difficult to choose between David Collyer's triumvirate or the partnership of PVC Nymph and Sawyer's Pheasant Tail Nymph. I think I would settle for the latter because between them I should feel confident that I was covering any of the ephemeropteran nymphs to be encountered on stillwater. The Pheasant Tail Nymph will cover the darker end of the spectrum represented by the sepia and claret nymphs whilst the PVC Nymph will take care of the lake and pond olives. This is an arbitrary division, but certainly John Goddard had in mind when he devised the PVC Nymph that it was closer to the colour of some of the olive nymphs than the Pheasant Tail Nymph.

PVC Nymph

Hook:	D/E 12-17
Silk:	Brown
Tails:	Formed from the tips of the three strands of olive condor herl used for the body
Underbody & thorax:	Copper wire
Overbody & thorax:	Three strands of olive or olive-brown condor herl or substitute
Body covering:	A one eighth of an inch strip of PVC wound and overlapped up to the thorax
Wing pads:	Three strands of dark pheasant tail herl

Using the sink and draw method on a long leader, one or other of the nymph patterns has rarely let me down, whether at Damerham or Tenterden or Croxley Hall Waters. At Damerham and other crystal-clear waters, it can be used to stalk individual fish by means of the induced take. The vicinity of weed beds is a good place for either method. On bigger waters, on bank or in a boat, the PVC Nymph on the point together with a Greenwell and a Gold-Ribbed Hare's Ear forms a very strong team of flies if any olive nymphs are present.

Rat-Tailed Maggot

See under Drone Fly Larva

Red Ant

See Ants

Red Mite

See under Water Mite

Red or Green Larvae

See under Chironomid larvae

Red Palmer

Red Palmer

Palmer flies — that is flies with the hackle tied the length of the hook shank — are of ancient vintage. A dressing for the Red Palmer was given as early as 1651 in Thomas Barker's *The Art of Angling*, one of our earliest books to give instructions on the tying of flies. Its palmered red hackle, gold ribbing and orange cruel (thin worsted yarn or wool) body formed the basis of all future Red and Soldier Palmers. The names and dressings of the two flies seem to have been fairly interchangeable, but Blacker in 1843 gave the Red Palmer a red or orange mohair body and the Soldier Palmer one of peacock herl.

Hook:	9-12
Rib:	Flat gold tinsel
Body:	Red seal's fur or red wool or peacock herl
Hackle:	Red cock hackle from shoulder to tail

The fly, always popular in Scotland, has become much used in the expanding stillwater fishing scene. It is commonly employed for boat fishing as a bob fly in a team of three when it is generally accepted that trout take it as an imitation of a sedge. R. C. Bridgett who wrote *Loch Fishing in Theory and Practice* talks about using it as a point fly when he and a companion took forty-five trout on a northern Scottish loch. At the other extreme, it is sometimes used as a dapping fly. Tom Stewart said it killed more trout than any other fly on the remote lochs of the Scottish Highlands apart from its cousin, the Black Palmer. It is also used extensively in the Orkneys and Shetlands. In May 1983 it was used successfully by a number of the competitors in the 55th International Flyfishing match held at Rutland Water.

Other members of the Palmer family are the Black, Grey, Brown, Golden, and Black and Red. The Soldier Palmer can have a red wool tail added.

Red Sedge

See under Great Red Sedge

Red Tag

Primarily a river fly, especially for grayling, but recommended by the former captain of the English fly fishing international team, John Ketley, for the top dropper in a team of three when traditional boat fishing.

Hook:	14
Tag:	Bright red wool or scarlet ibis
Body:	Bright green peacock's herl
Hackle:	Bright red cock

Red Tag

Reed Smut Nymph *(Simulium)*

Although most species of reed smuts are found only in running water, John Goddard observes that they may be encountered in lakes with a strong inflow of water and adjacent to it. These tiny flies and their nymphs can completely preoccupy trout and are rightly called the Black Curse as they are so difficult to imitate.

This version of the nymph was designed by the well-known Danish fly dresser and entomologist, Preben Torp Jacobsen, and Donald Overfield says that it is an excellent pattern.

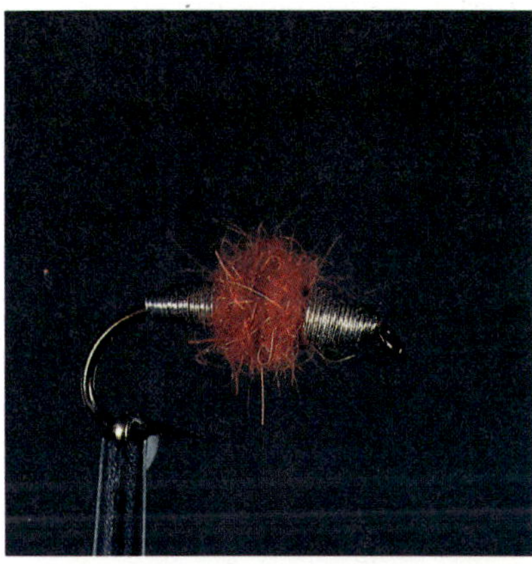

Reed Smut Nymph

Hook:	16
Silk:	Brown
Body:	Middle third copper wire wound backwards and forwards to create a shape tapering to the outside thirds consisting of fine silver wire
Dubbing:	The silk to be dubbed with blood-red cow hair wound over the middle copper base only

Reed Smut *(Simulium)*

The adult reed smut is smaller than one eighth of an inch (3mm), thickset and resembling a tiny house-fly in outline, and the wings are held flat along the body. Such flies are often taken for black gnats and, indeed, black gnat patterns can be used to imitate them. Jacobsen's artificial is a specific imitation and can be used by the desperate angler frustrated by the preoccupation of trout with these tiny creatures, the females of which, incidentally, bite both animals and humans.

Hook:	16-18
Silk:	Black
Body:	Black condor herl
Hackle:	Black parachute hackle

Reed Smut (Preben Torp Jacobsen)

Taff Price has also devised a dressing which he calls the Black Midge. He says that it is worth a try when trout are taking something in the surface impossible to distinguish and will accept nothing from your box.

Hook:	16-18
Silk:	Black
Body:	Black fur
Hackle:	Grizzle

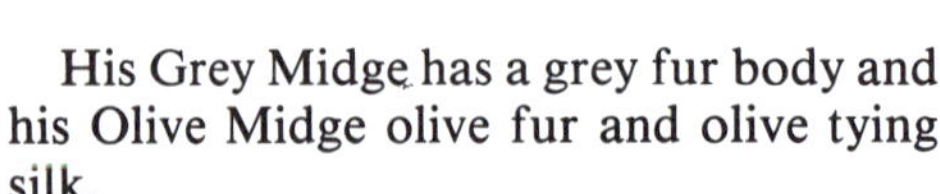

His Grey Midge has a grey fur body and his Olive Midge olive fur and olive tying silk.

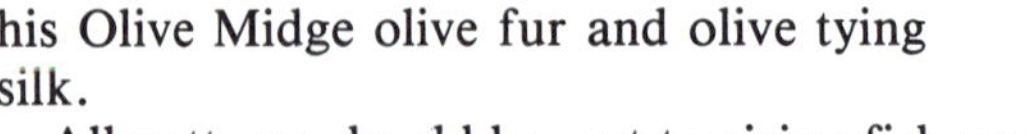

All patterns should be cast to rising fish and left motionless.

For another good pattern worth trying at this time see under Jassid.

Rees's Lure

Rees's Lure

Another lure making use of the fish-catching propensities of lime-green allied to a diving action produced by the weighted bead eyes. This fly was devised by Trevor Rees, secretary of the South Wales branch of the Fly Dressers' Guild.

Hook:	L/S all sizes
Silk:	Black
Tail:	DFM lime wool
Body:	Bronze peacock herl secured by the tying silk. A turn of lime-green wool is taken around the shank at the wing root
Wing:	Black marabou fibres with black squirrel over
Hackle:	Black cock
Eyes:	Bead chain silver

Taff Price says that this lure works wonders especially on the smaller put and take fisheries.

Roach Streamer

The introduction of the Polystickle spawned a host of fish fry and small fish imitations. Though perch fry are probably the most common of the coarse fish to be found in the large reservoirs, roach fry also figure in the trout's diet. Taff Price has devised a specific streamer imitation as follows:

Roach Streamer

Roach Streamer

Hook:	As required
Body:	White wool, flat silver rib
Tail:	Dyed-red cock hackles with an equal quantity of olive above
Wing:	Two white cock hackles flanked by two dark olive hackles
Underwing:	Two white cock hackles as long as the wing
Throat hackle:	Dyed-red cock hackle
Shoulder:	Lady Amhurst tippet either side of the wing
Cheek:	Jungle cock (or substitute)

Another ingenious roach fry imitation by Geoffrey Bucknall utilises small silver or gold beads under the shank of the hook near the head which gives rise to its name of

Roach Fry Optic

Hook:	Gold-finished Aberdeen 4-8
Body:	Open turns of red lurex covered with a strip of clear polythene, built up to the natural shape of the roach fry
Back and tail:	Dark green nylon raffia. The back being varnished
Hackles:	Dyed-red cock fibres, tied beard-fashion
Eyes:	A pair of beads tied in by the figure-of-eight method, under the shank of the hook at the head of the fly
Head:	Polyurethene varnish or Venglaze

Both can be fished in a variety of ways, but the angler should always remember that he is simulating a small fish and should retrieve his fly accordingly.

Rough Olive

The Rough Olive is a spring pattern dressed to imitate the large dark olive, a river fly. However, it serves as an excellent representation of olive duns on stillwater, especially the pond olive. The traditional pattern, popular in the West Country, is easier to tie as it omits the wings.

Hook:	14
Rib:	Yellow silk
Body:	Three strands of heron herl, first strand dyed brown-olive, other strands dyed greenish-olive
Hackle:	Green-olive with a brownish tinge

Most patterns including Woolley's and Halford's use heron herl for the body and starling wing. I give Skues' dressing with the hot-orange tying silk which I believe is an attractive feature to trout.

Hook: 14
Silk: Hot-orange waxed with clear wax
Rib: Fine gold wire
Body: Heron herl from a wing feather dyed brown-olive
Wings: Darkest starling
Hackle: Brown-olive hen hackle, with dark centre and yellowish-brown points

R. C. Bridgett, the Scottish angling writer, thought the Rough Olive was a superb fly not only to imitate olive duns but also small sedges. He dressed his flies with olive-dyed swan herl and a snipe wing. He frequently used it as a bob fly, and it makes an excellent component in a team of olive representations. It can, of course, be fished singly on a floating line and cast to fish rising to pond olive duns.

Rough Olive (G. E. M. Skues)

Rove Beetle *(Staphylinidae)*

Whilst the Black Palmer can serve to represent rove beetles or 'staphs' as they are commonly known, there are specific imitations of this very large family of terrestrial beetles which are often blown onto the water. They are black and vary in size from quite small to nearly an inch (25mm) in length, tending to be narrow in width.

John Henderson's pattern is as follows:

Hook: 13-15
Silk: Nylusta (gunmetal shade)
Body: Peacock herl, black ostrich herl or three fibres from a magpie's tail
Body hackle: Black cock trimmed from one eighth of an inch to one sixteenth of an inch
Shoulder hackle: Black or dark rusty dun cock, untrimmed

Rove Beetle (John Henderson)

Taff Price recommends small hooks as his pattern imitates the smaller beetles which have orange markings.

Hook: 14-16
Silk: Black
Body: Three parts black fur, orange fur, black fur
Hackle: Black

If there is a marked fall of beetles onto the water and trout are taking, then the fly should be cast dry to rising fish.

Rube Wood

Rube Wood

David Collyer described this as an American fly dressed in the traditional wet fly manner. He has made one small modification of Ray Bergman's fly by using fluorescent floss silk as the tag.

Hook:	6-12
Silk:	Black
Tail:	Teal breast fibres
Tag:	Scarlet floss silk or fluorescent scarlet floss
Body:	White chenille
Wing:	Grey mallard or lightly marked teal
Hackle:	Brown hen or cock

David uses a sink tip line from a boat when he is fishing this pattern in order to keep the line wake away from the fly. He retrieves it fairly quickly and has had at least four bag limits with it. Alternatively, one can use a long leader on a floating line, and I certainly prefer this from a casting point of view.

A fan-wing version of the Rube Wood can be used as a mayfly imitation.

Ruby

Ruby

Syd Brock has had excellent results with this scarlet-coloured lure. He believes it to be the only scarlet lure he has seen. There is, of course, that priestly wet fly called The Cardinal which has a scarlet floss silk body, dyed-red swan wings and a scarlet cock hackle. David Collyer's scarlet lady, the Harlot, also incorporates a good deal of that colour.

Hook:	L/S 6-10
Silk:	Black
Body:	Scarlet stretched plastic tape
Tail & throat hackle:	Scarlet cock fibres
Wing:	Four scarlet cock feathers
Cheeks:	Golden pheasant tippets

The originator uses a slow sink line which he pulls back in short, smooth retrieves.

Sawyer's Pheasant Tail Nymph

Sawyer's Pheasant Tail Nymph

Frank Sawyer visited and corresponded with G. E. M. Skues, a world authority on fishing the nymph in chalk streams. Sawyer, however, devised his own methods of fishing the nymph deeply to specific fish. He later discovered that his Pheasant Tail Nymph ' was extremely effective on lakes as well as chalk streams. He tied them without legs because he contended that swimming nymphs tuck their legs in closely to their bodies. He was also concerned with a clean entry into the water. When the pattern is wet the red of the copper wire glints and has a translucent effect. It was, of course, intended to represent olive nymphs.

Hook:	14-16
Silk:	None (brown silk is sometimes used now for tying off)
Body:	Fine red-coloured copper wire from bend to eye
Thorax:	Built up with the wire and taken to hook bend
Tail:	Four centre fibres of a browny-red cock pheasant,tied in with the wire, the tips of the fibres projecting one eighth of an inch
Rib & wing cases:	The four pheasant tail fibres spun on to the wire and lapped evenlyu to the hook eye. The fibres from the wire separated, taken over the thorax and redoubled back to the eye and tied off

Frank Sawyer was not in favour of speculative fishing or casting a long distance, but preferred to cast to individual trout and fish slowly. This can be done in stillwater, but much concentration is needed and the angler should tighten at the least sign. Generally this means a drawing of the cast and leader unless the fish is actually seen to take the fly.

Geoffrey Bucknall is in favour of distance casting with a nymph because he says that often the first signs of the evening rise come from fish feeding thirty yards away and the early part of the rise is often more profitable.

The Pheasant Tail Nymph was used extensively on river and lake by that great nymph artist, Oliver Kite. Anyone wishing to fish the nymph successfully should heed his advice that this depends above all on the lifelike employment of the artificial by the fisherman.

Sedge Flies *(Trichoptera)*

If the olives are the bread and butter flies of the lakes then the sedges are certainly the dessert, and often a substantial one at that.

Their life cycle is egg, larva, pupa, adult, and all but the egg stage is of use to the angler.

At the larval stage they are known as caddises — a name commonly used by the Americans for the whole life cycle — and dressings for these will be found under Caddis. Most stillwater caddises live in cases made of varying material ranging from vegetable matter, leaves and shells to gravel, sand and other debris.

The greatest point of danger for the aspiring sedge and one of the best opportunities for the angler occurs at the time of pupation. The larva, which may have lived for a year, makes a barrier of silk or vegetation over the end of its case which allows water in but effectively debars unwelcome visitors. After a period, the pupa cuts its way out of the case with its powerful mandibles, and the perilous journey to the surface begins. It has already assumed some of the characteristics of the adult, and it will now finally cast its pupal skin either in the water or on a plant or rock above water level. The second method might involve a journey of some distance through the water. Dressings are given under Sedge Pupae together with a list of other excellent imitations to which the angler may refer.

The adult sedges with their four roof-like wings and no tail vary in colour through pale yellow to brown to red to black, and in size from under half an inch to over one inch. With antennae of varying length they are difficult to confuse with any other fly. John Goddard points out, as a rule of thumb, that those hatching in the day tend to be smaller, darker and more hairy, and the night-hatchers (fortunately many after sundown) are generally larger and lighter in appearance. Their behaviour, whether emerging quickly from their shucks or struggling for some time in the surface film or skittering along the top of the water, has an important bearing on how the angler fishes his flies. Identification of some of the individual species and close observation of what is happening in the water contribute to success.

There are over two hundred species and consequently there are many imitations. There are particular representations of the fifteen main species and numerous general patterns dressed according to colour and size.

Dressings of the following adult sedge patterns are given in this guide:
Black Sedge, Black Silverhorns, Brown and Green Sedge, Brown Sedge, Brown Silverhorns, Caperer, Chris's Orange Sedge, Cinnamon Sedge, Cree Sedge, Delta Wing Caddis, G. & H. Sedge, Great or Large Red Sedge, Grouse Wing, Hair Sedges, Large Brown Sedge, Light Sedge, Little Brown Sedge, Little Red Sedge, Longhorns, Medium Sedge, Mottled Sedge, Orange John, Palmered Sedge, Silver Sedge, Small Buff Sedge, Wake Fly Sedge, Walker's Sedge, Welshman's Button.

Sedge Pupa *(Trichoptera)*

As I mentioned in my general comments on sedge flies, probably the most rewarding stage to imitate in the life cycle of these creatures is that of the pupa. As it ascends to the surface to hatch or makes its way to some object above water level or to the shore, it is at its most vulnerable.

Consequently, there are many dressings for the sedge pupa. Peter Lapsley says that the one which has given him the best results is:

Hook:	D/E 10-14
Silk:	Brown
Rib:	Fine gold tinsel
Underbody:	Fine lead wire covered with white floss silk — or simply white floss silk
Body:	Olive, yellow or fawn seal's fur, lightly dubbed
Legs/wing cases:	One turn of partridge breast feather, tied as a beard
Head:	Bronze peacock herl

Taff Price's pattern is based on American models and uses latex as a body material.

Hook:	L/S 10 to normal shank 12
Underbody:	Floss silk or wool
Abdomen:	Cream latex marked with a felt-tipped pen
Thorax:	Orange or green seal's fur mixed with hare's fur
Wngs:	Two short grey duck, or mottled hen, tied either side of the thorax
Legs:	Grouse hackle fibres
Antennae:	Brown mallard fibres or in larger sizes cock pheasant tail fibres

Sedge Pupa (John Goddard)

John Goddard provides a range of colours for his imitations of the pupae of diverse sedge flies in the early stages of their metamorphosis to adults.

Hook:	L/S wide gape 10-12
Silk:	Brown
Body:	Cream, dark brown, orange or olive-green seal's fur, the latter two colours may be covered lightly with fluorescent floss of the same colour
Rib:	Narrow silver lurex or oval tinsel
Thorax:	Dark brown condor herl or dyed turkey (light brown with brown-bodied pattern)
Wing cases:	Pale brown condor herl. Four strands are brought over the top of the thorax and tied in at the eye, and then doubled and redoubled to form the wing pads
Hackle:	Honey or rusty hen hackle, tied sparsely one and a half to two turns

In *The Superflies of Still Water* the wing cases are specified to be two or three pale-coloured feather fibres doubled and redoubled (dark brown for brown-bodied pattern).

I use the full colour range when sedge pupae patterns are required, and I can certainly confirm John Goddard's advice that the cream pattern is especially good in September, and I have also taken a lot of fish on the olive-green. Whilst sink and draw sometimes works, I take most of mine just below the surface on a floating line and long leader with medium, steady pulls. The pupae can also be used in boat fishing as the point fly in a team of sedge representations.

There are a number of sedge pupa imitations at the various stages of hatching which can be found under Amber Nymph, Aylott's Orange, Fiery Brown, Green Peter, Green Sedge Pupa, Invicta, Longhorns Pupa, Sharp's Favourite, Shorthorns and the Shredge.

Sepia Nymph
(Leptophlebia marginata)

Sepia Nymph (C. F. Walker)

The sepia nymph has a dark sepia body and distinctive gills and tails. The seven gill filaments are leaf-like and pointed, and the three tails are as long as the body and set wide apart. The nymph swims poorly and probably spends most of its time on or near the lake bottom before hatching into the adult either at the surface or on vegetation or bank. It appears early in the season when there is not too much insect food available to the trout.

In his *Lake Flies and their Imitation* C. F. Walker investigated the entomology of stillwater and then produced a whole new series of flies, a pioneering feat of great originality. Ironically, from choice, he never fished any of the patterns he devised. Many of them have worked for me, and this includes his Sepia Nymph. He always dressed his nymphs with silver tags, having observed a sepia nymph in his aquarium which, on the point of hatching, assumed a pale, dove-grey colour due to the presence of air under the skin. He described this air supply as endowing the insect with a silver halo.

Hook:	12-13
Tails:	Fibres from a black hen hackle as long as the body and well splayed apart with a turn of tying silk
Body:	Dark brown seal's fur mixed with a little ginger
Gills:	Body material well picked out with a dubbing needle
Rib & tag:	Silver tinsel
Thorax & wing pads:	Black seal's fur
Leg hackle:	Dark brown hen

Richard Walker has pointed out that the fly-dresser's objective when tying imitations is to pick out the salient features by which the fish might recognise the natural, and then to incorporate them in the artificial, and even exaggerate them. This applies to his Sepia Nymph where the body dubbing is picked out in generous tufts to simulate the gill filaments of the natural.

Hook:	12-14
Silk:	Black
Tails:	Very dark pheasant tail fibres left long and dyed sepia
Rib:	Black floss or black plastic strip
Body:	Natural black sheep's wool dubbed and picked out in generous tufts between the turns of ribbing and levelled
Thorax:	Black floss silk, fairly flat
Wing case & legs:	Very dark pheasant tail fibres

Richard Walker considered ostrich herl ideal for the body except that it had a tendency to fade, and so he has now replaced this with natural black sheep's wool.

Another good pattern which Peter Lapsley says will serve as either a sepia or claret nymph imitation is as follows:

Hook:	D/E 10-14
Silk:	Black
Tail:	Four to six black cock hackle fibres
Rib:	Fine silver tinsel (abdomen only)
Abdomen:	Dark brown seal's fur
Thorax:	Dark brown seal's fur
Wing case:	Any black quill slip
Hackle:	One turn of black hen hackle

Early in the season the nymph is best fished slowly along the bottom. Later on, when the adults begin to appear, it can be fished in shallower water especially near beds of reeds or weed with a sink and draw action.

A Sawyer Pheasant Tail Nymph will also serve as a representation of the sepia nymph.

Sepia Dun *(Leptophlebia marginata)*

Sepia Dun (Oliver Kite)

The sepia dun occurs in most parts of Britain. As far as I can see, J. R. Harris is the only authority to state that it is found in Ireland. Generally hatching around mid-day from early April to mid-May, it is the first of the upwinged flies to appear and provide the lake angler with an opportunity of fishing a dry fly. The hatches, however, are rarely profuse.

This attractive fly measuring up to half an inch (10 to 13mm) in length, and longer than the claret dun, has a sepia body-colour, though David Jacques notes some with a distinct maroon hue, hence his use of maroon or claret tying silk in his dressing.

Hook:	12-13
Silk:	Maroon or claret
Tails:	Furnace cock
Rib:	Fine gold wire
Body:	Pheasant tail fibres
Wings:	Brown game cock, speckled side out, two pairs
Hackle:	Furnace cock

Oliver Kite had a simple, straightforward pattern for the sepia dun which works well.

Hook:	14
Silk:	Dark brown
Tails:	Three dark brown or black cock hackle fibres widely spread
Rib:	Gold wire
Body:	Dark brown-dyed heron herls, doubled and redoubled at the thorax
Hackle:	Very dark brown cock

C. F. Walker omitted the tinsel ribbing from his Sepia Dun as he considered that the body was sombre and opaque. He stipulated that there should be a good bunch of whisks slightly longer than the body to keep the fly on an even keel.

Hook:	12-13
Tails:	Very dark grey or black fibres from a cock spade or saddle feather, splayed apart as in the nymph
Body:	Grey-brown condor herl without ribbing
Wings:	A bunch of fibres from a mallard scapular feather tied with a slight rake aft, as in the natural fly
Hackle:	Cock hackle dyed sepia

Cast to rising fish.

Sepia Spinner
(Leptophlebia marginata)

It is generally agreed that sepia spinners fall infrequently on the water in any significant numbers. If they do, C. F. Walker has a pattern.

Hook:	12-13
Tails:	Fibres from a dark grey or black cock spade or saddle hackle
Rib:	Gold tinsel
Body:	Dark brown seal's fur with a little yellow
Wings:	A ginger and grey grizzled cock hackle with the fibres divided laterally by two cross lashings of silk
Hackle:	Dark brown or honey dun cock, or none

Sepia Spinner (David Jacques)

David Jacques also had a dressing.

Hook:	12-13
Silk:	Maroon or claret colour
Tails:	Furnace cock fibres
Rib:	Fine gold wire
Body:	Dark pheasant tail fibres
Wings:	Tips of Rhode Island Red cock tied spent, rather large feather
Hackle:	Furnace cock

An angler without a specialist pattern can always use a dry Pheasant Tail.

Shadow Mayfly

Shadow Mayfly

Invented by Peter Deane to represent a mayfly but also a very effective sedge pattern. He always trims off the hackle flat below the hook which makes it an excellent floater.

Hook:	L/S 8-12
Silk:	Black
Tail:	Plymouth Rock cock hackle or grizzle cock
Body hackle:	Plymouth Rock cock hackle tied in at the bend by the tip and wound in touching turns to two thirds along the hook shank
Wings:	Two ginger cock hackles tied in back to back and the ends trimmed to a rounded shape
Front hackle:	Plymouth Rock cock hackle

Sharp's Favourite

Sharp's Favourite

This fly has been so christened by Bob Carnill whose articles on fly-tying are such an attractive feature of the monthly magazine, *Trout Fisherman*. Imitations of sedge pupae were not so common when he was asked to tie this pattern in the early 1960's by the late Jim Sharp of Nottingham. The dominating feature of the dressing was the brick-red seal's fur mix for the abdomen. It was only later that Bob learnt that this was a sedge pupa regularly used both by Jim Sharp and Cyril Inwood, revered by Midlands fly-fishers as one of the great stillwater anglers.

Hook:	10-12 wide gape standard shanks or Mustad 9578A or Partridge wide gape or Yorkshire Sedge hooks in sizes 10-14
Rib:	Gold wire (no.26) on smaller sizes and oval gold (14) on the larger
Abdomen:	Brick-red seal's fur
Thorax cover:	A slip of fibres taken from the grey/slate end of a mallard flight feather
Thorax:	Pale to medium insect green seal's fur
Hackle:	Six to eight long hot-orange cock hackle fibres tied as a beard

It is best fished as a single fly with a long leader to moving trout. The leader will be greased and the fly worked according to how high it is required to be fished in the water. It can also be fished as part of a team of sedges from a boat, especially when there is a fair ripple on the water.

This pattern should not be confused with the Sharpe's Favourite given in the *Sue Burgess Fly-Tying Library* which is as follows:

Hook:	D/E 12-14
Silk:	Black
Tag:	Fine flat silver mylar
Body:	Peacock quill stripped of its flue and wound leaving spaces for the black thread to show through in-between
Wing:	Waterhen (moorhen) wing quill
Hackle:	Furnace hen hackle

Sherry Spinner *(Ephemerella ignita)*

One of the classic imitations of the blue-winged olive spinner invented by William Lunn, the keeper of the famous Houghton Club, and, though devised for the chalk streams where the B.W.O. proliferates, there may be areas of stillwater where the natural appears.

The original dressing is as follows:

Hook:	14
Silk:	Amber or pale orange
Tail whisks:	Pale ginger hackle fibres
Rib:	Fine gold wire
Body:	Bright deep orange floss silk
Wings:	Buff cock hackle tips or two light blue dun hen tips tied in flat
Hackle:	Rhode Island Red cock hackle

Sherry Spinner (Richard Walker)

Skues' pattern is much used. He could tie flies without the use of a vice, and in *The Way of a Trout with a Fly* there is a delightful account of how he encountered a live sherry spinner in his railway carriage when travelling down to Winchester. By the time the train reached Farnborough he had dressed three imitations of it on one of which he took a two pounder the same evening.

Hook:	14
Silk:	Orange
Tail whisks:	Three fibres from a pale honey dun cock hackle
Rib:	Fine gold wire
Body:	Amber seal's fur. (Originally a mixture of orange, light orange and green seal's fur with a small amount of fur from a hare's poll added)
Hackle:	Palest honey dun, with a darkish centre if possible

Richard Walker gives a successful dressing using materials which he says, though readily available, are not required for other patterns and therefore not found in the stocks of professional fly dressers. This is where the angler who ties his own flies comes into his own.

Hook:	14
Silk:	Hot-orange
Tail whisks:	Ten or a dozen ginger cock tail whisks
Rib:	Three pound breaking strain clear nylon dyed hot-orange
Body:	Very pale pheasant tail fibres dyed hot-orange
Wings:	Grey squirrel tail, or any hair of similar texture, dyed in blue-dun (slate-grey) dye. Tied in a forward-facing bunch, and divided with figure-of-eight binding to set the fibres in two horizontal tufts
Hackle:	Ginger cock, three or four turns only

In all cases the hackle should be tied sparsely as the female, after laying her eggs, is to be found in the surface film rather than on it.

Cast in the path of rising fish taking the naturals and allow to lie motionless.

Shorthorns

A pupal imitation devised by Richard Walker to simulate the smaller sedges such as the grouse wing, brown or black silverhorns.

Hook:	12-14
Silk:	Brown
Rib:	Yellow tying silk
Abdomen:	Dark brown-olive feather fibre
Thorax:	Greeny-yellow fluorescent wool, ball-shaped (orange as alternative)
Wing case:	Black lurex
Hackles:	Brown partridge tied in two bunches at each side and sloping backwards

Shorthorns

Trout sometimes take these small sedges with gusto when there are a lot on the water, and if they are intercepting the pupae en route to the surface or as they hatch, then Richard Walker has found these small shorthorn patterns as effective as anything he has used. For him, the green has done better than the orange.

The Shredge

This is an all-purpose pattern invented by Tony Knight and designed to be taken for a sedge pupa, a hatching sedge or even a shrimp. It was accordingly named by John Wilshaw, the editor of *Trout and Salmon*, The Shredge. It is at its best in July and August, though it can be used throughout the season, and it is widely recognised to be one of the best taking flies at Rutland Water. The dressing is by Bob Carnill:

Hook:	10-12 Mustad 7780C
Silk:	Primrose or golden-olive (waxed)
Body:	Seal's fur blended from 70% cinnamon and 30% yellow to produce a light tobacco colour
Rib:	No. 26 gold wire
Wing:	Short mallard flight feather (grey)
Hackle:	Palest ginger hen

The hackled version without the wing is considered by Bob Carnill to be an equally good killer.

He fishes it in a team of three and finds that a variety of retrieves work according to the conditions. These vary from slow over shallows to very fast over open water. Sometimes it will be taken on the drop.

The pattern is also recommended by Steve Parton who gives dark sienna seal's fur taken well round the hook and thickened at the thorax for the body. For hackle he specifies ginger cock sparse and straggly and raked well back. He calls the pattern the Emergent Tobacco Sedge.

The Shredge

Shrimp

See under Freshwater Shrimp

Silver or Streaked Corixa

Taff Price, whose photographs and slides of natural insects are almost unrivalled, has had more opportunity than most to observe underwater life. He has studied corixa in his home aquarium and noted its sudden spurt to the surface and the silvery appearance it acquires on its way down after collecting its air bubble. His pattern called the Silver Corixa attempts to capture this impression.

Hook:	10-16
Silk:	Black
Body:	Flat silver lurex over a light silk
Rib, back & swimming legs:	Cock pheasant tail fibres. The fibres to be taken over the back, divided at the head and removed except for two for paddles. The back varnished for durability.

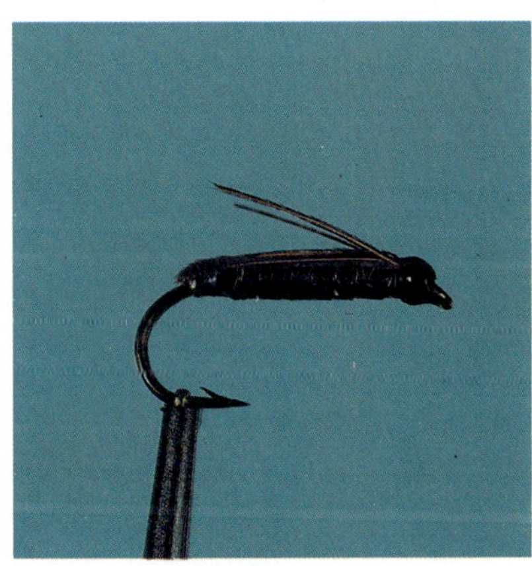

Silver Corixa

Taff Price found that Joscelyn Lane had already made similar observations and invented an equivalent pattern which he called the Streaked Corixa.

Hook:	12
Silk:	Golden olive
Body:	Strips of raffia over which is wound flat silver tinsel
Back:	Brown partridge
Paddles:	A small red cock hackle with the fibres clipped down

Sink and draw on a long leader is generally considered to be the best way of fishing corixa patterns.

Streaked Corixa

Silver Doctor

Originally a salmon fly, Peter Lapsley in his book *Trout from Stillwaters* records that it was used in smaller versions as a lure at Blagdon as early as 1917. It was reputed to be one of the best wet flies for big lake trout by Courtney Williams, and this legend seems to have been passed on by various authors without any justification or proof being offered.

Hook:	6-10
Tail:	Golden pheasant tippet
Rib:	Oval silver tinsel
Body:	Flat silver tinsel
Wings:	Strips of goose or white duck wing feathers, dyed red, yellow and green, covered on each side with a strip of a mallard's breast feather
Hackle:	Beard of bright blue cock

Silver Doctor

Sometimes a small golden pheasant crest feather is added to the tail, and in larger versions some speckled guinea fowl neck feathers are tied in front of the blue cock beard.

Silverhorns

See under Black Silverhorns and Brown Silverhorns

Silver March Brown

Silver March Brown

The offspring of the March Brown can often be more successful on stillwater than its parent.

Hook:	D/E 10-14
Silk:	Brown
Tail:	Two or three strands from a brown partridge hackle or tail
Rib:	Oval or fine silver tinsel
Body:	Flat silver tinsel
Wing:	Partridge tail or hen pheasant secondary wing feather
Hackle:	Mottled brown partridge

A good general pattern throughout the season with more than passing resemblance to a hatching sedge, it can be fished on the dropper from a boat. It can also be effective from the bank especially in the evening with the leader greased according to whether you want to retrieve it either just through or below the surface film.

If I fish it more slowly during the day as a nymph-suggesting pattern I omit the wing.

Silver Sedge *(Lepidostoma hirtum)*

Silver Sedge (Joscelyn Lane)

The small silver sedge which has light grey wings and a pale-coloured body was given its name by J. R. Harris. It hatches on stillwater in the evening in May and June, and possibly into July and August. Harris says that fish feed freely on both the pupa and the hatched fly, but that frequently other and more attractive flies are on the water at the same time.

The standard pattern is that of Halford's which is of *Odontocerum albicorne*, a large sedge with silver-grey wings commonly found on rivers. However, tied on a small hook, it serves well enough for the smaller stillwater sedge.

Hook:	12-15
Body:	White floss silk
Rib:	Fine silver wire
Hackle:	Pale sandy-ginger cock hackle, carried right down the body
Wings:	Landrail or substitute (coot)

I prefer Joscelyn Lane's method of winging sedges, and he has a pattern for the silver sedge. The only weakness of his patterns is that the clipped body hackle can come adrift after a trout has had its teeth in it. Varnishing the underbody first helps to overcome the problem.

Hook:	12-15
Silk:	Straw-coloured
Body:	Honey cock hackle wound with coils touching from bend to near the eye (all fibres clipped off close to the quill)
Wings:	Pale blue cock hackle fibres tied in a bunch and close to the body
Leg hackle:	Pale ginger cock (three or four turns of a small cock with fibres at right angles to the shank)

Cast to rising fish and allow to lie motionless or try skittering it back over the surface on a floating line and greased leader.

Sinfoil's Fry

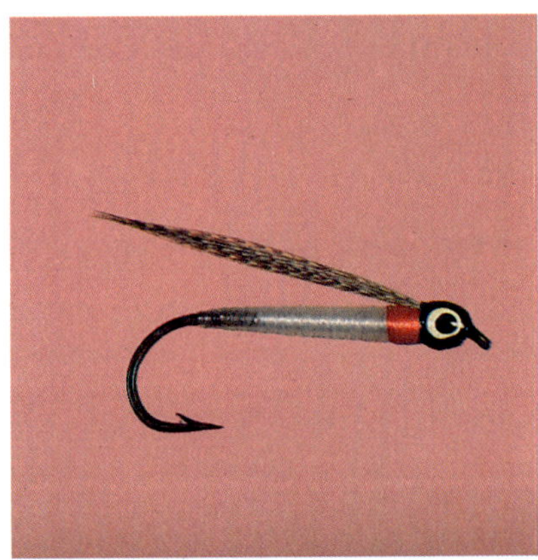

Sinfoil's Fry

Ken Sinfoil, formerly head bailiff of Weir Wood Reservoir, was the first person to appreciate the value of polythene in the construction of the bodies of flies. This pattern represents most effectively the almost translucent bodies of young coarse fish or fry.

Hook:	D/E L/S 8-12
Silk:	Black
Underbody:	Flat silver tinsel wound two thirds of the way down the hook shank from the eye and back
Overbody:	One eighth of an inch wide strip of 250 gauge polythene tied in at the eye, stretched and wound to build up a fish shape
Collar:	Scarlet floss silk
Back:	Strip of brown mallard feather
Head:	Black tying silk, built up and varnished, and white eyes painted

On the big reservoirs trout often attack fry shoals in the shallows from June onwards. The pin head or young fry represented by this pattern cannot move quickly at this stage, and so a slow retrieve with some variation in the vicinity of weed beds, especially if the glints of the fry themselves can be seen, will often produce the best results. From September onwards, larger imitations are required.

Small Buff Sedge

Small Buff Sedge

A pattern originated by Richard Walker to be used when small sedges such as the small red sedge are about.

Hook:	L/S 12
Silk:	Primrose
Body:	Pale buff ostrich or swan
Wing:	A bunch of buff cock hackle fibres
Hackles:	Buff (two)

To be fished dry.

Small Hatching Midge

Small Hatching Midge

John Goddard's unrivalled knowledge of underwater life and analytical and inventive approach to the design of imitative fly patterns have combined to make him Britain's foremost angler/entomologist. This pattern of his is best described as a specialist midge representation. It was designed originally for fishing at Hanningfield Reservoir in response to the prolific hatches of small midges he encountered in the afternoons from June until August in which the trout became totally absorbed. In so doing, they exhibited distinctive feeding patterns. In a ripple they fed in a straight line upwind rising every few feet, and in near calm circled or zigzagged as they rose.

Hook:	D/E 14-16
Silk:	Brown gossamer
Rib:	Narrow silver lurex
Body:	Two turns of silver lurex, followed by two strands of condor herl, dark red, green, orange, brown or black. A small amount of fluorescent silk of the same colour may be mixed with the body material if desired
Thorax:	One or two strands of dark brown turkey herl
Hackle:	Small honey cock tied sparsely

The pattern is intended to represent these black, orange, green or brown midges as they hatch and so must be fished in the surface film from a boat using a very long leader. John Goddard advises quick, accurate casting in front of the last rise.

Small Red Sedge

See under Little Red Sedge

Small Spurwing or Little Sky Blue *(Centroptilum luteolum)*

Small Spurwing (J. R. Harris)

This is a small fly, very similar to the small olives and pale wateries, which is common on rivers and may appear on some still-waters. J. R. Harris says it occurs in most of the large and many of the smaller Irish limestone lakes as well as in Windermere and several Scottish lochs. It appears throughout the season but is most common in May and June, and September and October.

Its other name, little sky blue or sky blue refers to the colour of its wings, although John Goddard believes that very pale grey is probably a better description. Its current name of small spurwing was given to it because it has a costal projection or spur on its hind wing. This can be seen only under a lens. Fortunately, no trout has a microscope and thus will happily accept a Little Marryatt or a Last Hope as a representation of the natural.

However, specific imitations of the natural exist. One comes from W. H. Aldam who published a book in 1875 with sunk mounts containing the most exquisitely tied flies.

Hook: 15
Silk: Sky blue
Body: Tying silk
Wings: Starling wing quill feather, the bluest part
Hackle: Fine black hen feather

Earlier, in 1836, Ronalds gave us a pattern which he called the Sky Blue.

Hook: 15
Tail: A whisk or two of the fibres used for the hackle
Body: Pale ginger mohair mixed with light blue fur
Wings: Very light blue dun hen
Hackle: Stained a pale yellow

Harris seems to have written more about the little sky blue as he called it than anyone, and his dressing is the most modern.

Hook: 15-16
Tail: Honey or pale blue dun cock
Body: Undyed raffia, palest yellow quill or very pale blue heron lightly dyed in picric acid
Wing: Fibres of pale blue dun hen breast feather tied in a bunch and inclined slightly forwards
Hackle: Honey dun or palest ginger cock

For the spinner, known as the little amber spinner, use a Cream Spinner, a Lunn's Particular or a Yellow Boy.

Snail *(Gastropoda)*

Floating Snail (Cliff Henry)

Pulmonate snails are those which mostly inhabit stillwaters, and can roughly be divided into either ramshorns or bladder snails. The former have coiled shells whilst the latter are rounder and more resemble garden snails in their appearance.

Molluscs undoubtedly play an important part in the trout's diet, and whilst an artificial can be fished slowly along the bottom to simulate the natural as it moves painstakingly among weeds and silt, the exciting occasions are those when the snails have ascended to the surface en masse, often on hot days from July to September, almost certainly in quest of oxygen. Such happenings are not always easy to discover as the shell of the snail is below the surface whilst its pad is clinging to the underside of the surface film.

One of the best dressings to simulate this phenomenon is considered to be Cliff Henry's Floating Snail.

Hook:	10-14
Silk:	Black
Body:	Pear-shaped piece of cork or plastazote, flattened at the end. The material is slit and tied onto the hook with the flat end facing the eye. It is then covered with stripped peacock quill except for the last two turns near the flattened top representing the pad of the snail for which bronzed peacock herl should be used

Taff Price's dressing is easy to make and utilises the splendid floating properties of deer hair.

Hook:	10-12
Silk:	Black
Body:	Deer hair clipped cone-shaped. They can be coloured by means of a felt-tipped pen olive, brown or green

Ann Douglas's Black Snail is rather in the mould of the Black and Peacock Spider which, incidentally, can be used as a snail imitation.

Hook:	Various sizes (can be leaded)
Silk:	Black
Body:	Black floss silk with stripped peacock herl over. Varnish is applied to make the fly more durable
Hackle:	Black hen

When the snails are in the surface film the feeding pattern of the trout is a head and tail rise, and then the fly should be cast out on a long leader in the vicinity of rises and left motionless.

Snipe and Purple

Snipe and Purple

Generally considered to represent the iron blue dun or nymph and a sure killer on northern rivers early in the season. It was a great favourite of mine on the River Wharfe, but I have had successes with it on southern stillwaters. I am not sure what the trout take it for. John Goddard suggests it can be used as a representation of the dusky yellowstreak. I am inclined to think that my early season pattern is taken for a dark chironomid pupa and, indeed, Arthur Cove has started using spider flies for that very purpose. I intend to experiment with them in the coming season.

Hook:	14
Body:	Purple floss silk
Hackle:	Small dark feather from the outside of a jack snipe's wing

Fish the pattern slowly to obtain the maximum movement from the delicate snipe wing.

The Snipe and Yellow is said to be highly effective on rough, cold days. It uses straw-coloured silk instead of purple.

Soldier Beetle *(Cantharis rustica)*

Soldier Beetle (Taff Price)

Soldier beetles have been imitated since the days of Charles Cotton when they were known as the fern fly. I am using the scientific name given by John Goddard. Alfred Ronalds described this slender half inch (13mm) beetle thus: "Two of the most common varieties of this genus are known by the appellations of the soldier and the sailor; one wears a red, the other a blue coat." A neat description of the soldier and the sailor beetles! His dressing is as follows:

Hook:	13
Body:	Orange floss silk
Wings:	Darkest part of a feather from the starling's wing
Legs:	A red cock hackle

Skues, incredibly, was out searching in the vicinity of the River Nadder for soldier beetles within a month of his eighty-ninth birthday. On close examination of the natural he felt that the body of his dressing was too red and should be nearer the colour of a ripe carrot!

Hook:	14
Silk:	Hot-orange
Body:	Bright red-orange seal's fur
Back:	Cock pheasant breast feather tied head and tail
Hackle:	Natural red cock, rather sparse

Taff Price describes a beetle called the black-tipped soldier beetle. Most of these insects have orange to red wings with black or bluish tips and are extremely common from June to August on the land and among the foliage. If they are blown onto the water the trout can be come interested in them. His dressing is:

Hook:	12-14
Silk:	Orange
Rib:	Black silk
Body:	Orange seal's fur
Back:	Brown raffene, marked black at the tip and varnished
Hackle:	Natural red or orange

The artificial should be fished dry and cast out to remain motionless and await a cruising trout.

The sailor beetle is less common and has matt blue wings.

Soldier Palmer

See under Red Palmer

The Sooty Olive

A traditional Irish fly and still one of the most popular. It probably gives a general impression of a hatching dark olive. Robert McHaffie, writing on Irish flies, says that the old Irish fly dressers often gave their wet flies fairly thick tippet tails possibly to imitate the nymphal shuck with the fly struggling to emerge.

Hook:	Partridge wide gape 8-12
Tail:	Fairly thick bunch of golden pheasant tippet fibres
Rib:	Silver or gold oval tinsel
Body:	Darkest olive seal's fur
Wing:	Mallard primary. Can be dyed olive though it was not in the original dressing
Hackle:	Black or alternatively Rhode Island dyed olive

The Sooty Olive

The dark olive is a river fly primarily, but the Sooty Olive is used with great success on many of the big Irish loughs like Conn, Corrib, Mask and Derravara from April to June.

Spiders *(Arachnida)*

Only the water spider *Argyroneta aquatica* spends all its life in the water. It spins a web which it attaches to plants and dwells there with the aid of air collected from the surface. The air, held on its fine body hairs, gives it a silver appearance. Other spiders found on water include the raft spider which uses floating leaves as rafts and pops overboard to grab its victims, the pirate spider which hunts on land and water, and the wolf spider which lives near water and can be blown onto it. There are many others.

Courtney Williams and Joscelyn Lane share the view that trout will take spiders if the opportunity presents itself and the latter has devised a representation of the wolf spider.

Wolf Spider

Hook:	12
Silk:	Pale olive
Body:	Cork-brown silko. One eighth of an inch thick in the middle and tapered at both ends, covering the rear half of the shank only
Thorax:	Brown ostrich herl, leaving a gap between body and thorax
Hackle:	Two turns of speckled brown partridge hackle between thorax and body

Wolf Spider

With his usual eye for detail, Taff Price suggests for his dressing the tying in of a human hair at the tail to suggest the gossamer thread that carries the spider onto the water.

The Windborne Spider

Hook:	14-16
Body:	A button of polypropylene (yellow, brown, red, grey, black, according to choice)
Hackle:	Cock hackle tied parachute style to match the body

Both patterns should be fished dry.

John Goddard considers that there is a lot of scope for the development of patterns to imitate spiders.

Squirrel and Silver

Squirrel and Silver

A combination of bright silver body, red tail and squirrel hair wing by John McLellan to produce that fishy flash most useful in September and October when, in the larger reservoirs, thousands of small roach, perch and bream are making their appearance, and trout are stacking up their larders for the winter.

Hook:	L/S 6-10
Silk:	Black
Tail:	Tuft of bright red wool
Body:	Flat silver tinsel
Wing:	Natural grey squirrel tail
Throat hackle:	Fibres from silver mallard breast feathers

Fish in the usual manner of fry imitators.

The S.S.

The S.S.

Frank Sawyer invented this nymph when he was fishing some lakes in Sweden high in the mountains. His host suggested it should be called the 'Sawyer Swedish'. It was an imitation of the nymph of a fly related to the large summer dun, and after Sawyer had agreed to name his artificial, which proved very killing, The S.S., he found that by an incredible coincidence the Latin name for the natural was *Siphlonurus spinosus*.

Hook:	13-14
Body:	Dark red wire tied in the manner of Sawyer's Pheasant Tail Nymph
Tails, body & thorax:	Darker shade of herls from the primary wing feathers of a farmyard grey goose

Back home, Frank Sawyer found that in the smaller sizes his pattern was taken very readily when claret duns and nymphs were on the water.

Standard Sedge (Terry Thomas)

See under Brown Sedge

Stick Fly

Stick Fly (Traditional)

The Stick Fly is one of the earliest and still one of the best methods of imitating the caddis larvae which are found on the lake bed. The traditional pattern is sometimes modified by the incorporation of a little DFM material in the thorax to distinguish the larva from its case.

Hook:	L/S 10-14
Silk:	Brown, black or yellow
Rib:	Fine gold wire
Underbody:	Fine lead wire
Body:	One strand of peacock herl and three of pheasant tail spun together
Collar:	Light buff floss silk
Legs:	One turn of furnace cock hackle

David Collyer's dressing, offering a number of options of body material and rib, reminds us that caddis make different kinds of cases, and so we should adapt our patterns according to the water we are fishing.

Hook:	L/S 8-10
Silk:	Black or dark olive
Ribs:	Copper, silver or gold wire or any combination of these
Body:	Cock pheasant centre tail fibres, dyed swan herl, peacock herl, various dubbings mixed to give the correct colours for the water to be fished
Thorax:	Yellow or grubby off-white floss silk
Hackle:	Pale ginger or dun cock or hen hackle, sparse
Head:	Bold in tying silk, varnished until glossy

Fished in a weighted version and on a long leader this is an excellent early season standby when it may be taken by trout as either a caddis larva or possibly an alder larva. Later on, as a point fly in combination with either sedge pupae and/or a big sedge pattern like the G. & H., it provides the fisherman with a team of flies representing the whole sedge life cycle.

Stonefly Creeper

The most popular method of fishing the larva or creeper of the stonefly in the North of England is to use the natural insect, and there are few imitations. It is very different in the United States and so for someone who would like to try it, here is a superb pattern by Al Troth. Though designed to simulate a stonefly not found in the British Isles it could well be taken for one of our larger stonefly nymphs. It is called Terrible Stone.

The dressing involves a bend of twenty-five to thirty degrees in the middle of the hook shank, but it is not as difficult to tie as it looks. The legs are put on early and the chenille and dubbing built up in and around them. The body is trimmed top and bottom to give a flattened effect. The joints in the leg are fixed by a drop of vinyl cement or other hard-setting adhesive. Full instructions can be found in Terry Hellekson's book, *Popular Fly Patterns*.

Hook:	Limerick L/S 6-10
Silk:	Black
Tail:	Natural grey goose quill fibres dyed dark brown and tied in a V
Rib:	Black and seal-brown synthetic fur mixed in equal parts
Body:	Dark brown chenille
Thorax:	Dark brown chenille
Legs:	Black hackle stems with barbles trimmed off
Feelers:	Natural grey goose quill fibres dyed dark brown and tied in a V

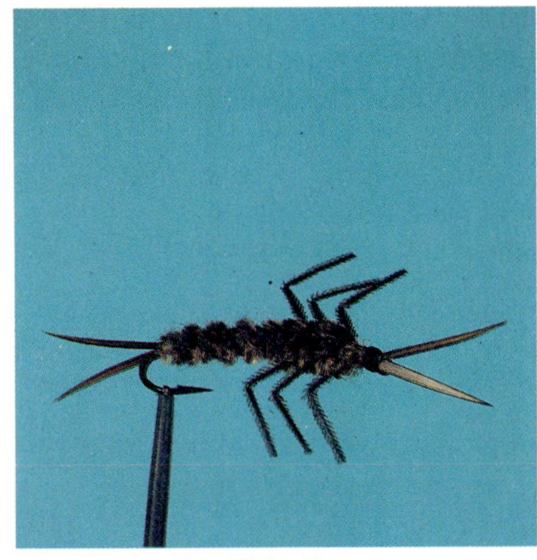

Terrible Stone

The pattern should be fished on a floating line and long leader slowly on the bottom. It might also be taken for a dragonfly larva.

See also under Dark Stonefly Creeper and Montana Nymph.

Stonefly *(Plecoptera)*

Stonefly (Roger Woolley)

There are many kinds of stonefly but the majority inhabit rivers. Of the eight or so to be found on stillwater the larger number are of particular interest to the angler in Wales, Scotland, Ireland, Northern England and Devon. They prefer water with a stony bottom and their larvae are often found under stones so their name is hardly surprising. The adults vary in size from three sixteenths to one and three sixteenths of an inch (5 to 30mm) and their wings, which are hard and glossy, lie straight and flat along the body when at rest. Most are long and narrow compared with many insects yet they give a greater impression of size when in flight.

The sluggish, creeping movement of the larvae when disturbed has earned them the angler's name of 'creeper'. They have two long tail appendages. There is no pupal stage but the wing buds go dark near the time for emergence. They crawl ashore where they are transformed into adults on rock, tree bark, etc.

Considering that the majority of angling writers have a low opinion of imitations as trout catchers, it is remarkable how many dressings have been evolved from the time of the first given in Dame Juliana Berners' original dozen. Most try to incorporate the yellow and brown of the natural's body according to the species, and use hackle tips to simulate the glossy wings which protrude beyond the body.

That of Alfred Ronalds, the pioneer angler/entomologist, is a good model. Ronalds seems to have been the first to perceive that although the stonefly adult does not feed it does drink.

Hook: L/S 10-11
Silk: Yellow
Tail: A strand or two of a brown mottled partridge feather
Rib: Yellow silk leaving most yellow at the tail
Body: Hare's ear fur mixed with yellow worsted or camlet
Wing: Quill feather from the hen pheasant's wing
Legs: A hackle stained greenish-brown or a natural dark grizzle

Roger Woolley's pattern is:

Hook: L/S 11
Rib: Yellow sewing silk
Body: A mixture of two thirds dark olive seal's fur and one third dirty-yellow seal's fur, or dark olive-brown raffia over a foundation of yellow wool
Wings: The tips of four dark grizzle cock hackles tied low and flat over the back of the fly, and projecting well beyond the hook
Hackle: Grizzled cock dyed brown-olive

The patterns are intended to be fished dry if the naturals are blown onto the water. Their only other contact is when the females lay their eggs there.

Other dressings of stonefly species can be found under Dark Spanish Needle, Medium Stonefly, Willow Fly and Yellow Sally.

Streaker

A lure from Syd Brock which uses a deadly black and orange combination rather like the Black and Orange Marabou but with different materials.

Hook: L/S 6-10
Silk: Black
Tail: Black squirrel
Rib: Silver or white stiff plastic tape
Body: Black plastic strip or black wool
Wing: Black squirrel tail
Overwing: Orange cock fibres, tied long
Throat: Orange cock hackle fibres, tied long

Streaker

Syd recommends that this pattern be fished just off the bottom with a fast sink line and long, almost continuous pulls. It is versatile, however, at all depths. In August and September it can be used with the other orange tempters like the Dunkeld, Whisky Fly and Jersey Herd.

There is another fly called the Streaker designed by the American, Darwin R. Atkins, which appears in his steelhead series called Mari-Boo Dressings.

Super Grizzly

Super Grizzly

So-called, I take it, because grizzle cock is used in the dressing. This pattern of John Goddard's represents a lake olive or a pond olive dun.

Hook:	U/E fine wire 14-16
Silk:	Orange
Tail:	A bunch of fibres from a pale red dun cock
Body:	Three natural grey heron herls
Hackle:	One each grizzle and red cock tied in together, both short in the fibre

To be cast to rising fish which may be taking the natural.

Suspender Midge

Suspender Midge

This makes use of the highly buoyant plastazote to suspend the artificial vertically in the water in a similar posture to the natural chironomid pupa. It can also be taken to represent the breathing filament. Another way to affix the plastazote is to cut it to the required shape and incise a small V to straddle the hook shank, using adhesive and securing with the tying silk.

Hook:	D/E 10-14
Silk:	According to body-colour
Tail:	White fluorescent wool
Rib:	Fine silver wire or lurex
Body:	Seal's fur of required colour
Thorax:	Brown-dyed turkey herl
Head:	Ball of plastazote wrapped in a small piece of nylon stocking mesh

This is another original idea from the fertile mind of John Goddard. It perfectly caters for trout taking midge pupae in the surface film, and should be cast into their path. An occasional nudge on the line, bringing the pupa parallel to the surface, which is the natural position as it hatches, can stimulate the trout's interest.

Suspender Nymph

This incorporates a novel method of holding an artificial nymph in the surface film evolved by Brian Clarke and John Goddard in conjunction with Neil Patterson.

The American angler, Charles E. Brookes, had the original notion of enclosing some floatable material in nylon mesh and attaching it to the hook shank. Clarke and his collaborators found ethafoam or plastazote extremely buoyant and enclosed it shaped to a small ball in nylon mesh from a lady's stocking. Mounted on top of the hook near the eye and coloured with a spirit-based felt-tipped pen it resembled the thorax of the natural and ensured that it would float more or less for ever.

Suspender Nymph

The dressing given in their thought-provoking book, *The Trout and the Fly — a New Approach*, is intended to represent an olive nymph and could be used to simulate both lake and pond olive nymphs in stillwater.

Hook:	D/E 14-16
Silk:	Brown
Tail:	Three olive-dyed golden pheasant tippets
Rib:	Silver wire
Body:	Olive seal's fur or sealex
Hackle:	Grizzle
Wing pad:	Ethafoam or plastazote ball enclosed in nylon mesh and coloured dark brown (Pantone shade 499M suggested)

Gordon Fraser, the professional fly dresser, extended the principle further with a Hare's Ear model, and then dressed black, red and olive patterns which he called Booby Nymphs. Tying is simplified by the use of uncrushed polystyrene balls. One or more can be employed.

Fished on a floating line, the Suspender or Booby Nymphs float high in the surface film, simulating a hatching nymph, and should be retrieved slowly. Gordon Fraser also fished them successfully with a lead impregnated line and short leader so that they lifted enticingly from just off the bottom by means of short, slow twitches.

Sweeny Todd

One of the great lures of the sixties and a 'must' in my fly box despite the competition from the likes of Black Chenille and Ace of Spades. The crimson throat hackle, I surmise, is a clue to its name, being an allusion to the 'demon barber of Fleet Street' and it has certainly accounted for more 'victims' than he ever did. Black and silver has been recognised since the earliest days as a deadly combination.

Hook:	Any size from 12 to two tandem size 6s; size 6 and 8 long-shank are perhaps the most useful sizes
Body:	Black floss, ribbed fine silver thread (oval tinsel). Just behind the wing roots two or three turns of magenta DRF wool
Throat hackle:	A false hackle of crimson-dyed cock hackle fibres
Wing:	Black squirrel tail hairs
Tail:	None

Sweeny Todd

It is a lure of great versatility which can be fished at any time of the season on big and small waters and in a variety of ways. It has taken fish for me pulled slowly near the bottom and retrieved quickly just below the surface.

All great flies tend to breed modifications, 'improvements' or just careless dressings, and the Sweeny Todd has suffered more than most. Richard Walker, who originated the pattern in conjunction with Peter Thomas, emphasises that the throat hackle is crimson and not magenta, the rib is oval and not flat tinsel, and there is no tail.

He also mentions that the Sweeny Todd often works very well with an extra long wing, long enough to extend to twice the length of the hook from eye to bend. Fish are sometimes choosy as to the size they want, and so it should be tied and fished in various sizes.

Tadpole *(Rana temporaria)*

Tadpoles are a familiar sight in the early months of the fishing season on many waters ranging from the smallest to the largest, yet few attempts have been made to imitate them, let alone fish them. Two of our foremost angler/entomologists have put this right.

Taff Price gives us two dressings. The first uses deer hair clipped to shape which takes a little time to dress but is a splendid floater.

Marabou Tadpole (Taff Price)

Tadpole Streamer

Hook:	8-10
Silk:	Black
Tail:	Two black hackles back-to-back, streamer fashion
Body:	Clipped deer hair dyed black; alternatively black chenille
Hackle:	Sparse black cock tied behind the body

The other one uses marabou to simulate the wiggle action of the tadpole.

Marabou Tadpole

Hook: 8-10
Silk: Black
Tail: A tuft of black marabou
Body: Black chenille tied a fat tadpole shape

These patterns should be fished as the sole fly at a steady pace on a slow or fast sink line.

John Goddard's pattern is:

Tadpolly

Hook: D/E 10-12
Silk: Black
Tail: Three black cock or hen hackles about the same length as the hook, tied in near the bend and projecting well beyond
Body: Black seal's fur
Head: Three or four green-bronze peacock herls

He suggests a fascinating alternative dressing incorporating ethafoam shaped tadpole-fashion for the body and coloured black with a felt-tipped pen. Its buoyancy will then lend itself to a fishing technique similar to that used with the Plastazote Corixa, namely a fast sink line which, when retrieved, will cause the fly to nose downwards in an attractive way to the trout.

I fished Rutland Water one day after weeks of hot sunshine when the trout would take nothing else but the black tadpole with a tuft of black marabou for its tail.

Teal Blue and Silver

One of the Teal series favoured by Scottish anglers since the beginning of the nineteenth century. The Teal Blue and Silver is a very popular sea-trout fly, and is often used for brown and rainbow trout as a flashy, general pattern. In this respect it is virtually a small lure. It is commonly employed in a team of flies for traditional boat fishing early in the season. Fished fast, just below the surface, it can be very effective when adult damselflies are about.

Hook: D/E 8-14
Silk: Black
Tail: Golden pheasant tippet fibres
Rib: Fine oval silver tinsel
Body: Wide flat silver tinsel or lurex
Wing: Teal breast or flank feathers
Hackle: Hen dyed bright blue

Teal Blue and Silver

The Teal and Green which uses green seal's fur for the body and either a natural light red hen hackle or a dyed-green hackle is popular with some anglers because it is one of only a few green flies. Bridgett thought it resembled a green midge pupa.

Hook:	D/E 8-14
Tail:	Two or three golden pheasant tippet fibres
Rib:	Oval silver tinsel, or fine flat silver tinsel on the smaller patterns
Body:	Green seal's fur
Wing:	Teal breast or flank feathers
Hackle:	Natural light red or dyed-green

Others in the Teal series are the Teal and Red from which developed the Peter Ross, Teal and Black, Teal and Mixed.

Terry's Terror

Terry's Terror

Donald Overfield in his additional section to Courtney Williams' *Dictionary of Trout Flies* says that this fly dressed small can be taken for an iron blue, somewhat larger it simulates all stages of the olives, and that larger still it makes a very good sedge pattern. In other words, a broad spectrum dry fly primarily for moving water but useful on stillwater too.

Hook:	10-16
Silk:	Brown (sherry spinner)
Tail/tag:	Orange and yellow goat's hair, clipped short and flared
Rib:	Fine flat copper tinsel or lurex
Body:	One strand of peacock tail herl
Hackle:	Four or five turns of two medium-red game cock hackles. The bottom half of the hackle can be trimmed according to taste

David Collyer considers the fly useful as a sedge imitation and fishes it on the big reservoirs cast out where calm meets ripple and allowed to lie motionless.

Tup's Indispensable

Invented by the professional fly-dresser from Tiverton, R. S. Austin, the specific dressing was a secret for many years between its originator, G. E. M. Skues and C. A. Hassam. Skues was ultimately given permission to publish it after the death of Austin's daughter who had carried on his fly-tying business.

The secret partly revolved around the use of ram's wool from the underparts of a ram or tup. For obvious reasons, substitutes are now often found for this part of the dressing. Even so, it is generally agreed that there have been many commercial dressings of the fly which have been atrocious.

Hook:	14-16
Tail:	Brassy or honey dun cock hackle fibres
Body:	Yellow silk or floss at the tail end, creamy-pink dubbing for the remainder which could be tup's wool
Hackle:	Brassy or honey dun cock hackle

For the wet or nymph imitation the dubbing is taken nearer the tail and the hackle should be a short-fibred blue dun hen hackle. The two or three turns of yellow silk at the tail create a yellow tip which Austin said was a desirable feature of the fly.

Tup's Indispensable

Austin's original recipe for the body was a mixture of ram's wool, cream-coloured seal's fur, lemon spaniel's fur and a few pinches of yellow mohair. Courtney Williams tells us that Skues suggested crimson seal's fur instead of the mohair which Austin adopted. Skues, in a letter written in 1939 in reply to a request for a correct dressing of the Tup's, said that he developed the nymph and pale watery variations by replacing the red (crimson?) seal's fur of the original with orange, yellow and olive seal's fur. The main point of this somewhat academic discussion is that the body shade can be varied according to the nymph or dun being imitated.

This is why I include it here although it is generally regarded as suggesting a pale watery, a river fly, because the wet pattern with a little variation of the body colour can be such a good general nymph imitation, especially an olive nymph. William B. Currie in his *The Guinness Guide to Game Fishing* talks about fishing a small loch in the Borders when hatches of very yellow olives were coming off the water, and taking fish on the Tup's. Tied in a small size it can also be used for tackling the infuriating angler's curse, the caenis.

See also David Collyer's Dark Tup, where the thorax has been darkened to good effect.

Twig or Debris Caddis

The larvae of the sedge or caddis use a variety of materials for their cases. This artificial by Taff Price is of the kind that use pieces of roots, leaves or reeds for their cases from the family *Phryganidae*.

Hook: L/S 8-14 (weight hook towards the head)
Silk: Green
Body: Green or yellow floss silk. Small cut portions of either green or natural raffia or both are stuck to the floss with adhesive. If desired, a small soft twig or root or two can be added
Hackle: Small to represent legs

Use on a long leader and trundle slowly along the bottom.

Twig or Debris Caddis

The Undertaker

The Undertaker

I suppose that this fly could be called the Baby Doll in mourning. The construction and materials are very similar to the Baby Doll except that they are black. A narrow silver rib is added. The following dressing is given in Richard Walker's *More Fly Dressing Innovations* from details submitted to him by D. T. Dale.

Hook:	R/B 8
Body:	Black wool
Rib:	Very narrow silver tinsel
Back & tail:	Black wool

It has, of course, no moving parts, but if it has anything like the success of its ethnic relative, it should do very well.

Viva

Viva

This is virtually a Black Chenille with a fluorescent green tag, but what a difference that tag can sometimes make!

Hook:	D/E L/S 6-10
Silk:	Black
Tag:	Green fluorescent wool
Rib:	Silver tinsel
Body:	Black chenille
Wing:	Four selected black cock hackles
Hackle:	Black cock

Victor Furse, the Viva's creator, called it after the Vauxhall car of that name. I have taken trout with it in red-hot August weather sunk deep in the morning and fished just below the surface in the evening on stillwaters as disparate as the little Holyfields Fishery at Waltham Abbey, the larger Siblyback Reservoir in Cornwall and Ladybower Reservoir in Derbyshire. The original dressing had a thick green fluorescent tail, three bands of wide metallic ribbing and a wing of mixed goat and marabou.

Vulture

Brian Harris originally designed this pattern for when trout were feeding on fry at Grafham in August and September. The vulturine guinea fowl feathers which have white centres merging to black and with electric-blue tips are rather expensive.

Hook: L/S 6-10
Silk: White
Tail: A bunch of hot-orange-dyed cock hackle fibres extending three eighths of an inch
Rib: Fine oval silver tinsel
Body: White chenille
Wings: Two vulturine guinea fowl hackle feathers to extend nearly the length of the hook behind the bend, back to back, and so that each butt is lying to one side of the hook shank
Beard hackle: A bunch of hot-orange-dyed cock hackle fibres extending underneath the hook and round the sides for about a quarter of an inch
Head: Bold and varnished red

Vulture

David Collyer suggested modifying this dressing to his favourite matuka style. Apart from anything else, it has the merit of securing and preserving the vulturine guinea fowl feathers!

Hook: L/S 4-8
Silk: Black or red
Tail: Hot-orange cock hackle fibres
Rib: Fine silver lurex or oval tinsel
Body: White chenille
Beard hackle: As for tail
Wings: Two vulturine guinea fowl hackles tied matuka style
Head: Red varnish

Either pattern should be fished as other fry-imitating lures.

Wainscott Moth *(Aphypirinae)*

Most anglers will be content to have one or two general moth patterns in their fly boxes according to size and colour, but some purists may prefer a more accurate representation of the natural. The wainscott group of moths are not aquatic, but their larvae are to be found in reeds and bullrushes, and the gingery-brown moths themselves are often in the vicinity of water. Here is Taff Price's version.

Hook: L/S 10
Silk: Brown
Body: Pale ginger fur or polypropylene dubbing
Wing: Two cinnamon hen body feathers tied across the back
Hackle: Ginger

Wainscott Moth

To be fished dry in the manner of moth imitations.

Wake Fly Sedges

Wake Fly Sedge — Brown

A well-known technique with dry sedge imitations is to retrieve or wake the fly across the surface so that it skims along creating a furrow like the natural. Richard Walker's Sedge is designed specifically to do this job, and so is this series of Wake Flies.

Brown

Hook:	L/S 10 or Mayfly hook 10
Silk:	Black (pre-waxed)
Body:	Palmered brown hackles
Wing:	Either set together streamer-fashion or tied in a V back to back
Front hackle:	Two brown cock hackles

Others in the series are the Black (black cock hackle), the Badger (badger cock hackle), Furnace (furnace or coch-y-bonddu hackle) and Grizzle (well-marked grizzle hackle).

Another method with these flies is to retrieve in short jerks with intervals between. A good soaking in Permaflote is essential so that they remain buoyant.

Taff Price suggests that the Grizzle and Badger also make good moth patterns as darkness approaches and moths skitter over the surface sometimes falling on the water.

Walker Mayfly

It is recognised that the incorporation of hot-orange into the imitations of some flies which have no similar natural colour sometimes makes them most effective. This is what Richard Walker has done with this pattern.

Hook:	L/S round bend 8-10
Tail:	Pheasant tail fibres
Body:	Very pale buff turkey tail fibres or suitable substitute, with two separate bands of pheasant tail fibre at rear end
Hackles:	One short-fibred hot-orange cock hackle wound directly behind the eye. Behind that, either one green-dyed cock hackle and one French partridge hackle; or one speckled duck feather, wound as a hackle, plus one green-dyed cock hackle; or one speckled duck feather, dyed greendrake colour, wound as a hackle, plus one ginger cock hackle

Walker Mayfly

The inventor says that it works best when the hatch is so heavy that trout can eat only a proportion of the naturals or when trout have become suspicious of other patterns. There are three variations all of which are equally effective.

Walker's Sedge

Walker's Sedge

There are probably more imitations of sedges than any other fly, but this is one that I would not be without. It is a specialist sedge pattern that can produce the most exciting fishing. There are times when sedges make a wake across the water, and especially is this so when the female may be dipping onto the surface to lay her eggs. Trout will sometimes make frenzied attempts to catch them.

Richard Walker, a graduate engineer, has given us a fly with aero-dynamic properties to simulate this movement. He advises us to use a long, fully greased leader and to retrieve very quickly by pulling the line with the left hand and raising the rod with the other. The fly then surfs along on its hackle points. It may be taken on the pull or during the pause. To achieve maximum effect, the fly should be soaked in Permaflote both after tying and before use. The hackles must be stiff.

Hook:	D/E L/S round bend 8-10
Silk:	Brown
Tag:	Arc chrome DF wool
Body:	Three strands of chestnut ostrich herl clipped close
Wing:	A bunch of natural red cock hackles tied sloping back and clipped square at the bend and level with it
Hackle:	Two stiff natural red cock hackles of good quality

Of course, the fly is also effective left motionless and twitched or on the dropper as part of a sedge team. Moreover, Richard Walker states that it also succeeds when fished below the surface.

In his *Fly Dressing Innovations* the author refers to the pattern as the Red Sedge, but such is its fame that it has become known as Walker's Sedge.

Water Boatman

See under Corixa

Water Cricket *(Velia caprai)*

Water Cricket (T. E. Pritt)

The water cricket belongs to that group of surface dwellers like the pond skater and the water measurer. Though only around a quarter of an inch (7mm) long, it looks larger because it has a stout body and six splayed legs. It has two orange lines running down the back, and both nymphs and adults have the undersides of their abdomens coloured orange. It can run skilfully over the water but can also dive below the surface. It looks ideal for imitating as a dry fly but, unfortunately, the trout take little or no interest in it.

Dressings, nevertheless have been devised. One of the first was by Alfred Ronalds who observed that the natural sucked the blood of small flies.

Hook:	14-15
Silk:	Black
Body:	Orange floss silk
Legs:	Two longest feathers of a peewit's topping or a black cock hackle. Wound all the way down the body and the fibres snipped off up to the shoulder

T. E. Pritt, whose book *Yorkshire Trout Flies* written in 1885 recorded many of the old favourite Dales flies, said his dressing of the water cricket was an imitation of the early stages of the insect when it was not a fly but an active little spider. He considered that when it ran on the surface it was taken greedily by fish. He was, of course, referring to rivers.

Hook:	14
Rib:	Black silk (optional)
Body:	Yellow or orange silk
Wings:	Hackled with a feather from the golden plover's breast, in its summer plumage, or the wing or back of a starling

Tom Stewart's pattern is a variation of Ronalds' and he stated that it was not taken for the natural water cricket but represented other forms of life on which fish feed. He fished his pattern on the tail of a team of three flies.

Hook:	14
Rib:	Black cotton thread
Body:	Orange or gold-coloured floss silk
Hackle:	Three turns of a sooty-black hen hackle

On a desperate day when nothing is taking, and these little surface dwellers are running about, it might be worth trying one of these patterns cast dry with an occasional tweak.

Waterhen Bloa

Waterhen Bloa

This is a traditional Yorkshire river pattern for the spring when dark olives or iron-blue duns are on the water. I have also used it successfully on stillwater. With the water rat's fur well teased out it may suggest a sepia nymph even though it has no tail, and if the water rat's fur is dubbed sparingly so that the yellow tying silk shows through as a rib, it may be taken for an olive nymph.

Hook:	14
Silk:	Yellow
Body:	Water rat's fur dubbed sparingly so that the silk shines through as a rib
Wings:	Hackled feather from the inside of a water hen wing

Fish the fly very slowly on a floating line and a long leader on small waters and on the middle dropper in a team of olive patterns.

Water Mite *(Arachnida hydracarina)*

The Multimite

These tiny creatures varying in size from one twenty-fifth to about one third of an inch (.5 to 8mm) were considered by C. F. Walker to be too small to imitate. Most are quite bright red in colour, are round in shape and have four pairs of legs. Some are brown, yellow, green or blue. Some swim quite actively or clamber about water plants whilst others are more sluggish and live in weed and debris on the bottom. The larvae are parasitic, adhering to other water creatures, but the adults lead an active independent life attacking and devouring insects smaller than themselves. They have been found in trout autopsies though whether trout take them purposefully is not known.

The larger ones have been considered worthy of imitation. This is a dressing by John Henderson.

The Large Red Mite

Hook:	14
Silk:	Brown
Body:	Weighted with lead or copper, then spun with red seal's fur or polymer
Hackle:	Two turns of black hen or starling

Richard Walker, who has given us a dressing, says that they appear to prefer the vicinity of dam walls.

The Red Mite

Hook:	16. The fly dressed short leaving a fair amount of shank free
Silk:	Vermilion
Body:	A feather fibre dyed vermilion, wound to a ball shape
Hackle:	One turn of a soft vermilion-dyed cock hackle. There may be some advantage in painting the hook red

Taff Price has devised a pattern in which more than one mite is tied on the same hook rather in the manner of Derek Bradbury's Green Aphis or the Knotted Midge.

The Multimite

Hook:	14
Body:	A button of red silk
Hackle:	Short red hen. Repeat the body and hackle

The water mites are most common during July and August, and an artificial can be tried on the bottom or near weed beds retrieved steadily, bearing in mind that some of the naturals are quite lively movers.

Water Tiger

See under Dytiscus Beetle Larva

Watson's Fancy

A traditional Scottish attractor fly fished on the tail of a wet fly cast, and still popular judging from the fact that it regularly figures in the winged wet fly lists of fly-selling firms. It is also used in Ireland on the big loughs like Corrib. Muriel Foster, in her delightful fishing diary, records a day in July, 1921 when she and two companions took eighteen trout from Loch Broom Glebe on Watson's Fancy. There are three exquisite drawings of the fly in the diary.

Watson's Fancy

Hook:	10-12
Tail:	Golden pheasant crest feather
Rib:	Fine gold wire or silver tinsel
Body:	Tail half of red, and the rest of black seal's fur, or floss
Wing:	From the tail of a black cock with a jungle cock feather or substitute on each side of the wing
Hackle:	Black cock

Wave Moth
(Cabaria pusaria or Deilinia pusaria)

Wave Moth

Another moth pattern for the purist by Joscelyn Lane. These white moths measure up to five eighths of an inch (14 to 16mm) and rest with their wings spread. They are not aquatic moths, but could be present near water if the vicinity is wooded.

I have decided to include Colonel Lane's pattern because, apart from the fact that it can represent any white moth, it may be taken for a sedge, and the originator says that on a larger hook and with a tail it may serve as a mayfly imitation.

Hook:	12
Silk:	Straw colour
Body:	Long honey cock hackle palmer-wise with coils close touching, trimmed close to the quill
Hackle:	Long yellow-badger cock hackle from halfway to the eye

Welshman's Button
(Sericostoma personatum)

Welshman's Button (W. J. Lunn)

The term, Welshman's Button, really belongs to a beetle not unlike the coch-y-bonddu, but for some reason that great exponent of the dry fly, F. M. Halford, gave it to this day-flying sedge which he said was usually on the water during the same period as the mayfly but earlier in the day. It is common to both rivers and stillwater from June to the middle of August. It is about half an inch (13mm) in length with a dark body and chestnut-brown wings.

The outstanding artificial pattern is considered to be that of W. J. Lunn who also called it the winged caperer.

Hook:	13-14
Silk:	Crimson
Body:	Four or five strands of turkey tail fibres, two strands of swan's feather, dyed yellow. The latter tied as a ring in the centre of the body
Wing:	Coot fibres, dyed chocolate-brown
Hackles:	Black cock in front of Rhode Island Red cock hackle

Roger Woolley's pattern for the male is:

Hook:	13
Rib:	Pale maroon horsehair
Body:	Quill dyed chocolate-brown
Wing:	Dark brown hen wing feather
Hackle:	Furnace cock

For the female the brown hen wing should be distinctly paler than for the male and three turns of a strand of cinnamon turkey tail feather are added to the tail end.

A more modern version is by John Henderson.

Hook:	12
Silk:	Nylusta, chestnut
Rib:	Fine gold tinsel
Body:	Four fibres from a cock pheasant's tail, tied in by the butts at the bend and wound up the body to the shoulder
Body hackle:	Dark rusty dun cock's, trimmed to taper from five eighths of an inch to one quarter of an inch. Tied in at the shoulder by the stem and wound down the body to the bend. Point of hackle fixed by a turn of the ribbing which is then wound up the body to the shoulder and tied in
Shoulder hackle:	Cock copper pheasant breast feather, fibres about three quarters of an inch long. Rhode Island Red breast feather or that of a cross between a Rhode Island and a Sussex will do just as well

This is one of the best sedge patterns and effective on all waters. David Collyer believes that it works best by casting out and allowing it to lie absolutely still, unlike a lot of sedge patterns which are retrieved quickly.

Welsh Partridge

Courtney Williams modestly said that he hesitated to pass on this pattern of his own devising as he had seen so many 'infallible' flies fade into oblivion. He used it mostly in April, May and September and considered it the equal of any dry fly he knew on lakes, going on to say that although it did not seem to represent any particular insect he thought it was nymph-suggesting. With its claret seal's fur body and double hackle of partridge and claret I feel that it comes as near as anything to a hatching claret dun in its smaller sizes.

Welsh Partridge

Hook:	12-16
Silk:	Black
Tail:	Two strands from a partridge tail
Rib:	Fine gold
Body:	Claret seal's fur
Hackle:	Snipe rump feather (or from the back of a partridge) with a short stiff claret hackle behind

Courtney Williams fished the pattern dry or semi-submerged. His devotees who, like me, take his *Dictionary of Trout Flies* to bed for late-night browsing will know that he has the endearing habit of endorsing certain flies as special attractors of big trout. This is one, but in this case he says that he can personally substantiate the claim.

Whisky Fly

Whisky Fly

This is the inspired creation of Albert Whillock, a casting coach of distinction. Since its Hanningfield early days it has proved a versatile killer and reached international renown. More than any other orange pattern it has provoked enquiry as to why rainbows sometimes go crazy for that colour. Bob Church particularly commends it for the big reservoirs on warm, windy days when algae is suspended high in the water.

The components of the original dressing are a little unusual, but John Goddard suggests that wide silver lurex can be used for the body and hot-orange bucktail for the wings.

Hook:	D/E L/S 6-10
Silk:	Orange
Tag or collar:	DRF scarlet nylon floss
Rib:	DRF scarlet nylon floss
Body:	One eighth of an inch wide strip of silver sellotape over the body and rib, varnished
Wing:	Hot-orange calf's tail
Throat hackle:	Hot-orange cock
Head:	DRF scarlet nylon floss

Here is a recent simplified version:

Hook:	L/S D/E 6-10
Silk:	Orange
Rib:	Red floss
Body:	Flat gold tinsel
Wing:	Orange bucktail or orange-dyed hackle fibres
Throat hackle:	Hot-orange

It works on a sinking line or a floater and at any time of the season although it is most favoured for the latter part. It will take fish at slower speeds but a fast or very fast retrieve is the most effective.

Cross-breeding of the Whisky Fly with a Muddler Minnow has produced a vigorous offspring called the Whisky Muddler. The dressing retains the essentials of the Whisky but leaves room at the eye for the incorporation of the oak turkey wing below the orange calf or bucktail plus, of course, the deer hair head.

White Lure

White Lure

A killing and popular lure which can be fished on either a floating line or a sinker. Like its counterpart, the Black Lure, it suffers from the disadvantage of the feathers at times tangling in the hook, and so has been supplanted to some extent in favour of bucktails, matukas and marabous.

Hooks:	6-10, two or more tied in tandem
Ribs:	Oval silver tinsel
Bodies:	White floss
Wing:	Four white saddle hackles tied back to back
Head:	White or black

A jungle cock cheek can be added if desired. The White Lure is at its best when simulating fish fry, and David Collyer recommends a somewhat slow and erratic retrieve from the bottom building up to a steady pace.

White Marabou Muddler

White Marabou Muddler

It was inevitable that someone would seek to combine the fish-taking properties of Marabou and Muddler, and the White Marabou Muddler is a typical result. The Americans also tie them in black, brown, grey, olive and yellow with appropriately coloured wing materials.

Hook:	L/S 6-8
Silk:	White
Tail:	Scarlet-red hackle fibres tied short
Body:	Silver tinsel chenille
Wings:	White marabou with a few strands of peacock sword feather over or a small bunch of grey squirrel tail hair and white marabou over
Topping:	Six strands of peacock herl or none
Head:	Natural deer hair

A White Marabou Tandem Muddler devised by Bob Church and Mick Nicholls described as "outrageously big" is used by them to boat fish very deeply at the big reservoirs, preferably with a lead core line.

Hook:	L/S 6-10 tied tandem
Silk:	Black
Body & tail:	White Sirdar brand baby wool
Wings:	Large plumes of white marabou (each hook separately)
Head:	Natural deer hair

White Moth

Various patterns have been designed to imitate white moths, and this dressing offers alternatives included in artificials since the middle of the nineteenth century.

Hook:	8-14
Rib:	Fine silver wire or oval silver tinsel
Body:	White wool or white floss silk or white ostrich herl
Wing:	White owl tied flat
Hackle:	White cock tied palmer-style

White Moth

Any moth landing on the water in the late evening struggles to take off again, and so this pattern should be frequently tweaked or even retrieved as a wake fly.

This pattern by Taff Price has a clipped deer hair body to give it good floating properties and white duck feathers for wings. It could be taken for the beautiful china mark moth or any other white moth. He calls it the No Hackle Moth.

Hook:	L/S 10
Silk:	Brown
Body:	Clipped deer hair
Wing:	Two white duck body feathers tied across the back

White Nymph

The White Nymph is one of those esoteric creations which represent no known creature but which at times can be extraordinarily effective. The first dressing is given by Donald Overfield in his *Fifty Favourite Nymphs* and was devised by James Nice. It incorporates fluorescent materials.

Hook:	12
Silk:	Any pale colour
Rib:	Thinnest silver tinsel and not lurex
Body:	Dubbed white DFM floss
Thorax:	White DFM floss
Wing case:	A pale mottled feather
Hackle:	Two turns only of a pale ginger cock pulled downwards and rearwards
Head:	Whip finish and clear varnish

White Nymph (W. S. Roger Fogg)

This next dressing was devised by Donald Downs, President of the Fly Dressers' Guild. What it represents I am not sure, but fished slowly on a floating line and long leader it works very well at Walthamstow Reservoir, the only fishery I know where you actually have to drive into London.

Hook:	12-14
Silk:	White
Tail:	White hackle fibres tied short
Body:	Grey horsehair or 3lb monofilament nylon to give segmented body
Thorax:	White fur
Wing case:	White raffene, the end left to act as a short tuft at the eye

The most telling feature of W. S. Roger Fogg's nymph is the translucent effect which is achieved by applying the dubbing loosely over the silver underbody. An impressionist pattern, it should be fished very slowly on a floating line and long leader greased to within a foot of the nymph.

Hook:	10-14
Silk:	White
Underbody:	Silver mylar or flat tinsel
Tail:	A few white rabbit guard hairs
Rib:	Fine oval silver
Tag:	Silver mylar or tinsel
Body:	A loose dubbing of white rabbit or white wolf fur
Hackle:	Two turns of a small white hen feather tied to incline backwards

Wickham's Fancy

This has been an enormously successful fly on both rivers and lakes. At my own club, the Amwell Magna, which has fished the River Lea continuously since 1831, it figures consistently as a taker of trout. Ernest Philips in his *Trout in Lakes and Reservoirs*, one of the earliest books on reservoir fishing written in 1914, states that Wickham's Fancy is his favourite fly along with Greenwell's Glory.

Wickham's Fancy (Traditional)

Dr. T. C. Wickham, a well-known angler in the Winchester area in the early part of this century, is generally credited with the design of the fly. However, Francis Francis gave a dressing as early as 1867 in his *A Book on Angling* and another version was given about 1880 by H. S. Hall who perfected the design of the eyed hook.

I give first the traditional version which uses medium starling wings dressed split:

Hook: D/E 12-16
Silk: Yellow or brown (sherry spinner)
Tail: Gallina dyed brown-red or red game cock
Rib: Fine gold wire
Body: Wide flat gold tinsel or lurex
Body hackle: Ginger-red or red game cock tied palmer-fashion
Wings: Medium starling dressed split or grey duck wing quill for larger sizes
Front hackle: Ginger-red or red game cock — two for dry pattern

A modern dressing given by David Collyer in his *Fly Dressing II* has its wing sloping back over the body wet fly style so that the fly can be fished wet or dry.

Hook: 12-16
Silk: Brown (sherry spinner)
Tail: Ginger cock hackle fibres
Rib: Gold wire
Body: Flat gold tinsel or lurex
Wing: Starling primary feathers
Hackle(s): Ginger cock tied palmer-fashion

This fly has moved effortlessly into the new stillwater era. Its rich reddy-brown colour combined with flash makes it a valuable early season pattern for the boat fisher, usually on the top dropper, and it is equally useful to the bank fisher on the lookout for the odd riser when it can be fished singly and may be taken for a sedge.

Wickham's Fancy (David Collyer)

Francis Francis invented a modified version called the Pink Wickham which incorporated a landrail wing. Pink floss silk is now often used for the body although this does not appear to have been given by Francis himself. It certainly makes it easier to wind the hackle over the body.

Williams' Favourite

One of Courtney Williams' favourite flies and one of mine. It was first tied by his father, Alfred. Father and son must have fished the fly for nigh on a hundred years. It has, of course, strong affinities with the Black Pennell.

Hook: 12-16
Silk: Black
Body: Black silk
Tail: Two or three black cock fibres
Rib: Silver tinsel
Hackle: Black hen for wet and black cock for dry

Williams' Favourite

I find it most useful on stillwater fished dry when black gnats are on the water and fish will look at nothing else. I then use it without the tail. Although I have often taken fish with it on rivers fished wet early season, I can recall only one occasion when it worked for me on stillwater. Late one morning in June it brought me a bag limit in an hour for reasons unknown. It is often considered a useful imitation of a black chironomid.

Incidentally, Courtney Williams always spelled it Williams's Favourite, a splendid example of English syntax!

Willow Fly *(Leuctra geniculata)*

This is a member of the stonefly family, about three eighths of an inch (8 to 11mm) long, with a darkish olive-yellow body and brown slate wings. It is a September, October fly although a near relative is on the water in April.

Alfred Ronalds, whose pattern I give, said it was a killing fly on the Derwent until November.

Hook: 14
Silk: Yellow
Body: Dubbed mole's fur
Wings: Dark part of a starling quill feather
Hackle: Dark dun hen hackle

Willow Fly (Alfred Ronalds)

J. R. Harris found the species on Blagdon and John Henderson said that it was numerous on some upland reservoirs, giving the following dressing:

Hook: 13-14
Rib: Fine gold wire
Body: Seal's fur shading from golden yellow at tail to dark olive at shoulder
Body hackle: Medium dun cock trimmed a little if necessary, tied in by the stem at the shoulder and wound down the body to the bend, where the tip of the hackle is bound on top of the shank by the ribbing which is then wound up the body to the shoulder
Shoulder hackle: Medium dun cock. The hackle point left at the tail can be shortened and rounded so as to represent the folded wings of the natural which extend beyond the body

It is one of those gregarious flies which will settle on any part of the angler and certainly has been known to him for hundreds of years. Eric Taverner says that trout will feed on it when it has fallen on the water spent after dropping its eggs, in some cases from as much as twelve feet above the surface. He gives this dressing for the spent fly.

Hook: 12-14
Body: Peacock quill dyed red-orange
Wings: Medium grizzled blue cock longer in the fibre than that used for the hackle, and tied spent
Hackle: Medium grizzled blue cock

All patterns should be fished dry, hopefully to rising fish.

Wobble-Worm

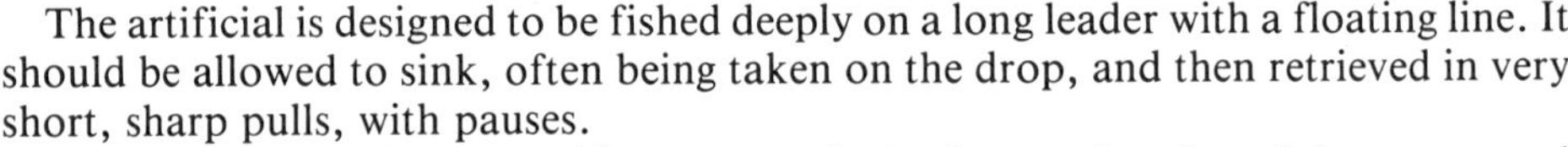

Wobble-Worm (Green)

Several dressings have been devised for the chironomid larva, and the big problem has been how to simulate the movement of the natural. Peter Lapsley's pattern meets all the requirements of colour, shape and translucency, and suggests the movement of a midge larva — that is a distinctive lashing motion — by the use of a small shot crimped onto the shank just behind the eye of the hook.

Hook:	Partridge sedge hook (K2B) 12-14
Head:	Number 3 or 5 split shot, crimped onto the shank just behind the eye of the hook and painted (enamel) red, buff or green, as appropriate
Tail:	Six strands of red, buff or green marabou as appropriate, half an inch to one inch long
Underbody:	Silver lurex for the red version, gold lurex for the buff and green
Body:	*Very* lightly dubbed red, buff or green seal's fur ribbed with fine silver for the red version and gold wire for the buff and green

The artificial is designed to be fished deeply on a long leader with a floating line. It should be allowed to sink, often being taken on the drop, and then retrieved in very short, sharp pulls, with pauses.

I had an opportunity to try this pattern only on the very last day of the season and took two fish in fifteen minutes. I look forward to giving it a more extended trial next season.

Wolf Spider

See under Spiders

Woodcock Series

These traditional lake flies have retained a certain popularity in a more scientific era because their success is almost certainly due to their resemblance to sedge pupae or flies. They are commonly used as part of a team of wet flies especially in Scotland.

One of the best-known in the series is:

Woodcock and Hare's Ear or Hare's Lug

Hook:	10-14
Tail:	Two fibres of brown mallard
Tag:	Flat gold tinsel
Body:	Dark fur from the hare's ear
Wing:	Woodcock wing feather
Hackle:	Long fibres of hare's flax picked out to form a hackle

One which was fished extensively by R. C. Bridgett, author of *Loch Fishing in Theory and Practice* was:

Woodcock and Yellow

Woodcock and Yellow

Hook:	10-14
Tail:	A few fibres of golden pheasant tippet
Rib:	Oval silver
Body:	Yellow seal's fur
Wing:	From the wing feather of a woodcock
Hackle:	Natural medium red or yellow the same colour as the body

A favourite fly of Arthur Cove, one of this country's premier stillwater anglers, when sedges are about is:

Woodcock and Orange

Hook:	10-14
Tail:	A few fibres of golden pheasant tippet
Rib:	Oval tinsel
Body:	Orange seal's fur
Wing:	From the wing feather of a woodcock
Hackle:	Natural medium red or the same orange colour as the body

Other flies in the series using appropriately coloured seal's fur and hackles are Woodcock and Green, Woodcock and Red and Woodcock and Mixed.

Woolly Worm

Woolly Worm

A pattern suggestive of a number of underwater creatures, but it probably comes closest to representing a caddis larva or a damselfly nymph. It can be tied in a variety of colours including brown, green and yellow, and the tying silk and body chenille should match whichever is chosen.

Hook:	Standard or L/S 8-14
Silk:	To match body colour
Body:	Appropriately coloured chenille
Tail:	A tuft of red wool
Hackle:	Grizzle cock wound palmer-style

Robin Lemon, writing in Ann Voss Bark's book, *West Country Fly Fishing*, says that it has taken more fish for him from

West Country stillwaters than any other fly. The hackle gives it a sparkle of life whilst the chenille helps it to sink in the water. It can be fished slowly at all depths.

Tied in a large size, the black Woolly Worm has the reputation of taking what the Americans call 'trophy fish' on the alkaline western lakes. Thom Green, the American angler, says that trout take them for leeches.

Worm Fly

Worm Fly

Tom Stewart believed that the inventor of this fly was Donald Watson, originator of Watson's Fancy, and not his close friend, William Black, to whom it is commonly attributed.

It is an old pattern which has come back into its own with the vast increase in stillwater fishing. The fly was first used for loch fishing in the Inverness area. It does not look like a worm, and is basically two Red Tags tied in tandem. William B. Currie in *The Guinness Guide to Game Fishing* states that 'worming' is an old word for copulating, and a worm fly is a representation of flies coupling on and in the water. It has been variously stated to suggest an alder larva, two beetles coming up for air, a caddis imitation and an early season small lure. With that specification it can be taken to be God's gift to the desperate fisherman not knowing what to fish next!

Hooks:	8-12, two or more tied in tandem
Tag:	Red floss silk or wool
Bodies:	Bronze peacock herl
Hackles:	Red cock

General tactics are to fish the pattern deeply and slowly. John Ketley, however, has used it successfully as a dry fly, well greased, and dragged across the noses of cruising trout when they have been feeding selectively on midge pupa and ignoring most offerings.

Yellow Boy

Although designed by the famous Houghton Club river keeper, W. J. Lunn, to represent the spent pale wateries, I include it here because it will equally serve both as the spinner of the small spurwing called the little amber spinner and, tied in a larger size, the yellow may spinner.

J. R. Harris says that the spinners of the latter have a slow and deliberate flight, swarming in the late afternoon or evening. The lightish yellow of the females contrasts with the dark colouring of the males. They frequently hover over the edge of a lake sometimes as high as twenty or thirty feet.

If they fall and trout take them, cast out on a floating line and leader, allowing the fly to lie quite inert.

Hook:	U/E 13-16
Silk:	Light orange
Body:	White hackle stalk dyed medium yellow
Tail:	Pale buff cock hackle fibres
Wings:	Two light buff cock hackle tips tied spent
Hackle:	Light buff cock

Yellow Boy

Yellow Corixa

This is a very simple tying devised by Richard Walker in 1973 to simulate small corixa with bright yellow beneath and olive-green backs which he encountered at Damerham and Latimer Park Lakes.

Hook:	14
Silk:	Yellow
Body:	Primrose floss silk wound over two strips of lead foil on top of the hook shank
Back:	Olive-green feather fibre

Yellow Corixa

The lead foil on top of the hook shank not only takes the fly down quickly but brings it to rest point up, thus avoiding the annoying habit of catching on the bottom. Richard Walker fishes it on a floating line, pulling it up when he sees a trout in its path, but it can be fished speculatively with a sink and draw action.

Soaking the fly in clear varnish makes it harder wearing.

Yellow Fellow

Yellow Fellow

A gaudy streamer designed by David Collyer for murky or pea soup conditions when visibility of the fly can be important.

Hook:	L/S 10
Silk:	Yellow
Tail:	White baby wool
Body:	Silver lurex or tinsel
Wing:	Four slim, bright yellow cock hackles
Hackles:	Rear, well-marked badger cock; front, short-fibred yellow cock

Pull this one smartly through the water just below the surface. Black tying silk can be used and eyes painted on if desired.

Yellow May Dun
(Heptagenia sulphurea)

Yellow May Dun (Taff Price)

A fly which appears in Dame Juliana Berners' original dozen, yet seemingly a singularly unprepossessing candidate for inclusion in a list of stillwater flies. Skues said it was such a beautiful fly it should be attractive to trout but it was practically boycotted by them. He was referring to its vivid yellow colour which makes it the most conspicuous of all the ephemeropterans. Possibly because of its sparse hatches it seems to have the reputation of evoking little response from the trout when it is on the water in May.

J. R. Harris agreed that it did not appear to attract trout when in small numbers, but said there were occasions on hot bright days after sunset when they hatched in large quantities whereupon trout fed on them keenly. It is, indeed, quite a common fly on the Irish limestone lakes where it is called the yellow hawk, and it may hatch on some English and Scottish stillwaters particularly if they are stony. Harris's dressing is of the yellow evening dun, but the natural resembles the yellow may so closely that it serves very well as a representation of the latter.

Hook:	14
Tail:	Ginger cock
Rib:	Gold wire
Body:	Bright orange floss silk or yellow-orange quill
Wing:	A bunch of fibres of a pale yellow cock hackle tied so as to incline slightly forwards
Hackle:	Ginger cock

Taff Price says that he has seen a few on his local lake though they may come in on the chalk stream feeder, but in other areas very large numbers are known to hatch out. He therefore gives us a dressing which he says looks like a small canary!

Hook:	12-14
Tail:	Yellow hackle fibres
Rib:	Pale green terylene
Body:	Yellow-dyed swan or goose
Wing:	Two swan or goose slips, or partridge dyed yellow
Hackle:	Yellow

Both patterns are intended to be fished dry.

For the yellow may spinner a Yellow Boy can be used in a larger size.

Yellow Sally *(Isoperla grammatica)*

Yellow Sally (Taff Price)

The most easily recognisable of the stonefly species because of the brilliant yellow colouring of its wings, legs and body. This has attracted many imitations since the middle of the eighteenth century although there is some doubt as to how freely the natural is taken. As far as stillwater is concerned the yellow sally is confined mainly to the northern parts of the country and is most prevalent during June and July.

The early tying by Henry Wade ('Halcyon') in 1861 still seems as good as any.

Hook:	Limerick 13
Silk:	Fawn
Rib:	Fawn-coloured silk
Body:	Pale yellow (seal's) fur or mohair
Wing:	White feather dyed yellow and tied flat
Legs:	Ginger hackle

Taff Price's dressing uses more modern materials and, tied on a 14 or 16 hook, will also serve for the small yellow sally which is only around one quarter of an inch long (7mm).

Hook:	12-14
Silk:	Yellow
Tail:	Two swan or goose fibres dyed yellow, or hackle fibres
Rib:	Brown silk or terylene
Body:	Yellow polypropylene
Wing:	Yellow partridge varnished and tied flat
Hackle:	Yellow

Both patterns are intended to be fished dry.

Eric Taverner warns us not to confuse the yellow sally with the yellow may dun. He contends that the fish are not confused as they dislike the latter and eagerly greet the former.

Zero

This hairwing pattern devised by Steve Parton, writer of many articles for *Trout Fisherman*, and an expert on boat fishing, was originally included by Richard Walker in his book, *More Fly Dressing Innovations*. He stated that it was a lure designed to fish deeply with regular but not quick pulls and was intended to simulate bream fry.

Zero

Hook:	4/0 silvered flounder hook
Tail:	Hot-orange calf tail hair
Rib:	Wide embossed silver tinsel
Body:	Heavy white daylight-fluorescent chenille
Wing:	Composite: white goat hair with silver baboon hair above and three white cock saddle hackles on each side. The wing cocked up so that its top makes an angle of about forty-five degrees to the body
Throat hackle:	White goat hair, tied false
Head:	Black, with eye painted on

Richard Walker suggested that with the tail and throat hackles of crimson it could be used to represent roach fry. Since then the dressing has been somewhat simplified and appears to have taken into account this suggestion. The modified dressing given by Steve Parton in his book, *Boatfishing for Trout*, is as follows:

Hook:	2/0 L/S, 4/0 L/S silver Aberdeen
Tail:	Long scarlet-dyed cock hackle fibres
Rib:	Silver oval
Body:	Heavy white chenille
Wing:	Skunk tail three inches long
Hackle:	Scarlet and white cock wound together and raked back

Zulu

Probably descended from a Dove pattern given by Charles Cotton which he called the Black Fly, and certainly it has much in common with the likes of the Black Palmer and the Black Pennell.

It has been fished for many years in Scotland and Ireland, and continues to be used extensively in both its Black and Blue versions on hill lochs in the North of Scotland and in the Orkneys. Those who have browsed through Muriel Foster's fascinating fishing diary will note that she took more fish from Scottish lochs on the Black and Blue Zulus than any other fly. It is most commonly used as a bob fly in a team of flies.

Used in a similar manner, its success has embraced the big English reservoirs. As it dribbles along the surface it often brings fish up from a long way down. It can also be used as a dapping fly. Eric Taverner in his classic work *Trout Fishing from all Angles* said he knew of it used on a large hook as a single tail fly cast close to reeds at the margin of the loch to invariably deadly effect.

Hook:	10-14
Silk:	Black
Tail:	Scarlet ibis or scarlet or red wool
Rib:	Fine flat silver tinsel or lurex
Body:	Black wool or seal's fur
Hackle:	Black cock palmer-fashion

Zulu

The Blue Zulu has a dyed-blue hackle instead of the black one. The Gold Zulu which is not as effective as the other two has bronze peacock herl for its body, a gold tinsel rib and a palmered coch-y-bonddu hackle.

A Glossary of Terms referring to Flies, Fly-Dressing and Fishing

Abdomen
Posterior part of an insect's body behind the thorax.
Acid Water
Water with a pH value of less than seven. Less conducive to the growth of animal life than alkaline water.
Alkaline Water
Water with a pH value of more than seven.
Algae
Minute plants possessing chlorophyl. Their immense numbers make them of great importance as primary food producers. Blue-green algae is the most common.
Annulation
Marked with rings, usually in reference to the tails of insects.
Antennae
Mobile appendages on the heads of insects.
Anterior Wing
The fore-wings of an insect.
Aquatic
Found or living in water.
Arachnida
An order which includes spiders.
Arc Chrome
Luminous pigment used in dyed wools, etc.
Autopsy
Investigation of the stomach contents of a trout usually with the aid of a marrow scoop, valuable in discovering what the fish is feeding on.

Badger Hackle
Black centred feather with white or cream points, and sometimes with black tips.
Beard
Usually a bunch of fibres tied in below the hook shank at the eye. Sometimes referred to as a 'false hackle'.
Blue Dun Hackle
Slate grey feather.
Bob Fly
The top dropper of a team of flies designed to 'bob' or skate on or in the surface.
Bouquet
Refers to a bunch of fibres.
Bucktail
Hair from deer tails used for the wings of lures.
Bumble
Virtually another name for a fly where the hackle is palmered from tail to shoulder.
Butt
Thicker end of the quill which carries the feather fibre.
Buzz
Refers to a hackled fly, generally if the hackle is bushy or palmered.

Chenille
A thick, soft, tufty silk used for fly bodies, especially lures, which saturates rapidly, thus aiding sinking.

Cilia
Short threads projecting from the body of aquatic creatures which create movement.
Chrysalis
The pupa of a moth or butterfly in a case or cocoon.
Coch-y-Bonddu Hackle
Black centre with red outer fibres tipped with black.
Coleoptera
An order of insects which includes beetles.
Condor
The wing and tail quills make durable herls for bodies of flies.
Cree Hackle
Alternating bars of red and black occasionally with touches of white.
Crest
A topping or tuft of feathers from the top of the heads of some birds like the golden pheasant.
Crewel
Loosely twined worsted yarn used for bodies.
Crustacea
Members of the order *Amphipoda* of which the freshwater shrimps and louse are the most common.

Daphnia
Types of water flea with rounded bodies enclosed in a transparent shell. They are very sensitive to light and vary their depth accordingly. A major form of food for trout on big reservoirs like Grafham.
Dapping
A form of fishing using a floss blow line and long rod. The wind holds the line above the water surface so that the fly touches or skitters the surface. Real insects like mayflies, daddies and grasshoppers can be used or artificial flies. Pre-eminently an Irish technique.
Deer Hair
An important addition to the fly dresser's materials since the 1960's. Used for heads, wings and bodies. Has an outstanding floating capability.
Detached Body
The body of an artificial fly built up separately from the hook shank but attached to it, especially in some mayfly and crane fly imitations.
Diptera
The order of insects referred to as flat-winged flies to which belong midges, crane flies and terrestrial flies.
DF Material
Daylight-fluorescent material which reflects its own colour when exposed to ultra-violet and other forms of light. Can be incorporated into silk, wool or chenille or used to dye furs and hackles. It works only with the pastel shades of primary colours.
Dry Fly
A fly designed to float on or in the water surface.
Droppers
The flies used in a team in wet fly fishing which are above the point or tail fly.
Dubbing
Various materials such as furs or wool spun onto the tying silk and wound round the body of the fly.
Dun
The first winged state or sub-imago of an insect of the *Ephemeroptera* order like the mayfly or lake olive. Looks duller than the spinner.

Ecdysis
The shedding of the cuticle or skin prior to the emergence of the adult insect.
Ephemeroptera
The order of upwinged flies of which on stillwater the lake and pond olives are the most common.

False Hackle
Bunches of fibres tied below the hook shank at the eye in wet flies and lures.
Floss Silk
Two-strand silk or thicker. The strands are easily separated and used for bodies and underbodies of flies.
Flue
The short points on each fibre of a feather or herl.
Forewings
Either wing of the anterior pair of an insect's two pairs of wings.
Fry
The young of fish.
Furnace Hackle
Black centre with reddish brown points.

Gallina
Guinea fowl.
Gill Plate
Gills of nymphs, plate-like in appearance, on the abdominal segments, which by vibrating keep a flow of water moving over the body, respiration taking place through their thin skin.
Goat Hair
A longish, soft hair useful for winging lures like Mrs Palmer.
Goldfingering
An acrylic wool into which is woven lurex, used for fly bodies and producing a glitter effect.
Goose
Shoulder feathers used in wings and also for herl in bodies. Egyptian goose breast feathers which are lightly barred are used in some mayfly patterns for wings and hackles.
Grizzle Hackle
Alternate bars of black and white from a Plymouth Rock fowl. Also known as cuckoo.
Grouse
Various feathers from the grouse are used for hackles and wings, notably for the Grouse series of flies.
Guard Hairs
The coarser hairs of animals like the rabbit or hare used for tails.
Guinea Fowl
Neck feathers used for hackles and tails particularly of nymphs.

Hackle
Tapered feather from the neck of a fowl taken round the hook shank as a collar to represent legs or wings of a natural fly.
Hackle-point Wings
A pair, usually of glossy, stiff cock hackle tips employed commonly for wings of 'spent' flies or spinners.

Hair Wing
Commonly used for bucktail lures and may be bucktail, calf's tail, goat, skunk or other animal hairs.
Hare
Traditional fur material usually taken from the hare's ear and used for dubbing bodies.
Hemiptera
The order of insects to which corixa and water bugs belong.
Herl
Fibres which, taken from complete feathers, are taken round the hook shank whereupon the flue or short points stand out to form a body. Pheasant, ostrich, peacock, heron and condor are commonly used.
Heron
Breast and wing feathers are utilised for herls of fly bodies.
Hind Wing
Smaller pair of posterior wings behind the anterior wings and springing from the third thoracic segment of duns and spinners.
Honey Dun Hackle
Centre of dun or blue dun but with honey tips.

Ibis
The breast feather of the ibis was used to provide bright red tails for flies like the Butcher. The ibis is now a protected species, and dyed feathers of other birds like the goose are used.
Imago
The complete, ultimate stage of an insect like the mayfly after it has gone through its various transitions. Also known as the spinner.
Impressionist Pattern
An artificial designed to give the general impression of an insect without being a specific imitation. The Gold-Ribbed Hare's Ear is a good example.
Induced Take
The raising in the water by a lifting of the rod tip of the artificial to simulate the ascending movement of the natural nymph intended to trigger off a reaction from the trout.

Jackdaw
Neck and shoulders provide feathers for hackles whilst the wing feathers can be used for wings.
Jay
Smaller blue feathers for throat hackles as in the Invicta.
Jungle Cock
Used pre-eminently for cheeks of lures. The bird is now on the protected list, but some Sonnerati Jungle Fowl are now reared in this country and their feathers can be purchased.

Landrail
Its primary and secondary feathers were used for winging, and a number of older patterns include it in the dressing. Now that it is rare, Mavis Thrush or Lapwing are used as substitutes.
Larva
The young stages of certain insects not resembling their adults and in which the developing wings are not visible.
Lateral Gills
Refers to the gills on the sides of various nymphs and larvae.

Latex
A rubber derivative sometimes known as dental dam supplied in sheet form, and particularly useful for creating a segmented effect on bodies of creeper and larval patterns.
Lead Core Line
Imported originally from America and designed to sink very quickly either as a shooting head or a complete line for trolling deep, if permitted.
Lepidoptera
That order of insects which includes moths.
List
A name for the centre of a feather.
Lurex
The trade name of a plastic substitute for tinsel which will not tarnish. It is not as durable as tinsel.

Mallard
Still one of the most popular sources of feathers for wings of all kinds and for tails.
Mandibles
Mouthparts of insects such as dragonfly and alder larvae which bite and crush their victims.
Marabou
Long, fluffy and mobile feather obtained originally from a large black and white African stork, and now from the turkey. Used increasingly as a winging material and in other ways.
Magpie
Tail feather used for the wing cases of beetles.
Married Fibres
Fibres coming from different feathers which are joined together to form the wing of an artificial fly or lure.
Midge
The common angler's name for the chironomids which are part of the *Diptera* order of insects.
Mohair
Hair of the Angora goat, softer than seal's fur, and used for dubbing bodies.
Mole
Used as a body material, in particular for thoraces of some nymphs. It provides a dark-blue effect.
Mylar
A synthetic tinsel finer and thinner than lurex. The plaited tubular form gives a scaled effect and is used for the bodies of lures, especially those which imitate little fishes.

Nocturnal
Night-flying.
Nymph
The young stages of certain insects which resemble their adults, and in the case of winged insects develop wing cases after several moults.

Odonata
An order of insects to which belong damselflies and dragonflies.
Ostrich
The large plumes have quite long flues and are commonly used for herls for bodies, particularly for imitating the gills of nymphs and larvae.
Ovipost
The act of laying its eggs by the female insect or spinner.

Owl
Wing feathers used for winging especially of moth patterns.

Palmer Fly
One with the hackle wound from shoulder to tail.

Parachute Hackle
A hackle wound horizontally instead of as a collar and acting as a parachute in the artificial fly's descent.

Peacock
Provides both green and bronze herls from the long 'eye' and 'sword' tails. The latter is used in the wing of the Alexandra.

Pheasant
One of the most versatile of all birds for providing from its various parts feathers for wings, hackles, tails and herls.

Plastazote
An expanded polyethylene material, easy to cut and shape, and extremely light and buoyant. Flies such as the Plastazote Corixa and Suspender Nymph used with a sinking line can have an attractive diving action imparted.

Plecoptera
The order of insects with hard wings lying flat along and a little over the body such as stoneflies.

Plover (Lapwing)
Occasionally used for hackles and as a winging substitute for landrail.

Point Fly
The fly on the end of the cast and thus fishing deepest.

Polypropylene
A very light man-made fibre used for dubbing and a good substitute for seal's fur. Available in many colours.

Polythene
A thermoplastic material made from ethylene in common household use, employed to make translucent bodies for flies like the Polystickle and Sinfoil's Fry.

Primary Feather
The chief long feather of the first joint of a bird's wing.

PVC
Short for polyvinyl chloride, a man-made thermoplastic material made by polymerising vinyl chloride. Similar properties to polythene and used notably for the body of the PVC Nymph.

Pupa
The point between the larval and adult stage of an insect. Pupae are often active as in the case of the midges and caddis or sedge pupae.

Pupal Shuck
The thin skin or membrane containing the pupa, and which splits to allow the emergence of the adult.

Quill
Fibres from which the flue has been scraped off. The 'eye' of the peacock feather is a good medium when stripped giving an alternate brown and grey effect used to simulate the rib markings of various insects.

Rabbit
Fur used for the dubbing of flies like the Grey Duster. The face whiskers are employed for tails.

Raffene
A plastic form of raffia used for the backs of patterns like the Chompers and Polystickle.
Rhode Island Red
A fowl of dark reddish-brown plumage, American in origin, the cape of which is much valued for red-brown feathers for fly hackles.
Rib
Generally an imitation of the body segments of insects, using wire, tinsel, silk or herl. Sometimes used to increase the durability of the fly body against the trout's teeth.
Rusty Dun Hackle
Blue-grey with rusty tipped fibres.

Scapular Feathers
The small feathers of a bird which lie along the shoulder.
Seal's Fur
Probably the best and most commonly used of all dubbing furs for its radiance and translucence.
Secondary Feathers
Those growing on the second joint of a bird's wing.
Skunk
Hair used for the wing or tail of a few lures like the Concorde.
Snipe
The back feathers are used for the hackles of spider flies like the Snipe and Purple.
Species
A group of insects sharing the same characteristics. All insects are divided into Orders which are further divided into Families, then into Genera, and ultimately into the Species.
Spent Adult
The name given to the males and females after they have mated.
Spent Gnat
A term commonly used in describing the mayfly spinner.
Spent Wings
Wings tied so that they lie flat on the water on each side of the body and extending outwards to imitate those of the spent fly. Hackle points from a cock hackle or fibres are frequently used.
Spinner
Another name for the imago or final form of an upwinged fly like the mayfly or pond olive when it is transformed from the rather drab dun to the fragile beauty of the spinner.
Split Wings
A common way of winging dry flies where the points are separated in the form of a V.
Squirrel
The tails of squirrels such as the grey, black and red/brown are used mainly for hair wings as in the Squirrel and Silver lure.
Starling
The primary and secondary feathers are used in many dry flies for wings whilst for hackles the under and marginal coverts are used.
Summer Duck
An American bird, its flank feathers which are brown and barred are used for mayfly hackles.
Swan
Makes a good herling material, and the soft white shoulder feathers can be dyed many colours.

Tandem
Two, but possibly more, hooks connected the one behind the other for lures.
Tag
A short tail in a trout fly usually of wool or ibis.
Teal
Breast and flank feathers employed in wings of wet flies like the Peter Ross and the Teal series.
Terrestrial
A term describing insects whose existence is wholly bound up with the land as opposed to the water.
Tinsel
Either metal or metal-covered silk usually in gold or silver used for ribbing or whole bodies.
Thorax
The part of the insect's body between the head and the abdomen which usually carries the wings and legs.
Tippet
The barred orange and black feather of a golden pheasant used as a tail in countless traditional wet flies.
Trichoptera
The order of insects with roof-shaped wings of which the sedge or caddis flies are the most common.
Topping
The long golden crest feather of a golden pheasant used as a tail in flies like the Invicta.
Tracheal Gills
Gills on the abdominal segments of nymphs and larvae imitated in various artificials by herls and furs.
Turkey
The tail feathers are used for herls, wing feathers for the Muddler Minnow wing and others.

Vycoat
The trade name for a hard-setting varnish derived from polyurethane.

Waterhen
Breast and under-wing feathers used for wings and hackles, notably in the Waterhen Bloa.
Wet Fly
One designed to sink and fish below the water surface.
Whisks
Feather or hair fibres used for the setae or tails of artificials.
Wing Case
The incipient wings in nymphs which become larger and darker as they develop.
Woodcock
Wing feathers used mostly for wings of traditional wet flies as in the Woodcock series.

Bibliography

Andrews, Ted, *Basic Fly Tying in Pictures*, Stanley Paul, 1983.

Boyle, Robert H. & Whitlock, Dave, *The Fly Tyer's Almanac*, Crown Publishers Inc., New York, 1975.

Bridgett, R. C., *Loch Fishing in Theory and Practice*, Herbert Jenkins, 1924.

Brooks, Joe, *Trout Fishing*, Harper & Row, New York, 1972.

Brown, E. S., *Life in Fresh Water*, O.U.P., 1955.

Bucknall, Geoffrey, *Modern Techniques of Stillwater Fly-Fishing*, Frederick Muller, 1980.

Burgess, Sue, *Fly-Tying Library* (five booklets, one each containing 100 dressings of dry flies, wet flies, nymphs, lures, hair and fur dressings).

Church, Bob, *Reservoir Trout Fishing*, A. & C. Black, 2nd edition, 1983.

Clarke, Brian, *The Pursuit of Stillwater Trout*, A. & C. Black, 1975.

Clarke, Brian & Goddard, John, *The Trout and the Fly*, Ernest Benn, 1980.

Clegg, John, *Freshwater Life of the British Isles*, Frederick Warne, 1952.

Collyer, David, *Fly Dressing*, David & Charles, 1975.

Collyer, David, *Fly Dressing II*, David & Charles, 1981.

Currie, William B., *The Guinness Guide to Game Fishing*, Guinness Superlatives Ltd., 1980.

Dunne, J. W., *Sunshine and The Dry Fly*, A. & C. Black, 1924.

Edmonds, H. H. & Lee, N. N., *Brook and River Trouting*, published by the authors, 1916.

Flick, Art, *New Streamside Guide to Naturals and their Imitation*, Crown Publishers, New York, 1969.

Fogg, S. W. Roger, *The Art of the Wet Fly*, A. & C. Black, 1979.

Foster, Muriel, *Fishing Diary*, Viking Press, New York, 1980.

Goddard, John, *Stillwater Flies — how and when to fish them*, Ernest Benn Ltd., 1982.

Goddard, John, *The Superflies of Still Water*, Ernest Benn, 1977.

Goddard, John, *Trout Flies of Stillwater*, A. & C. Black, 1969.

Halford, F. M., *Dry Fly Entomology*, Vinton & Co., 1902.

Halford, F. M., *Floating Flies & How to Dress Them*, Barry Shurlock, 1974, (reprinted from first edition of 1886).

Harris, Brian, *The Art of Fly Fishing*, Ward Lock, 1980.

Harris, Brian, *Stillwater Trout*, Osprey Publishing Co., 1974.

Harris, J. R., *An Angler's Entomology*, Collins, 1952.

Hellekson, Terry, *Popular Fly Patterns*, Peregrine Smith Inc., 1977.

Henzell, H. P., *The Art & Craft of Loch Fishing*, Philip Allan & Co. Ltd., 1937

Hickin, Norman E., *Caddis Larvae*, Hutchinson, 1967.

Hills, J. W., *A History of Fly Fishing for Trout*, Barry Shurlock, 1921.

Hi-Regan, *How & Where to Fish in Ireland*, Sampson Low, Marston, Searle & Rivington, 1886.

Ivens, T. C., *Stillwater Fly Fishing*, Pan Anglers Library, 1973.

Jacques, David, *The Development of Modern Stillwater Fishing*, A. & C. Black, 1974.

Jacques, David, *Fisherman's Fly*, A. & C. Black, 1965.

Jorgensen, Poul, *Modern Fly Dressings for the Modern Angler*, Winchester Press, New York, 1977.

Jorgensen, Poul, *Modern Trout Flies and How to Tie Them*, Ernest Benn, 1979.

Keen, Joseph, *Fluorescent Flies*, Herbert Jenkins, 1964.

Kite, Oliver, *Nymph Fishing in Practice*, Herbert Jenkins, 1963.

Lapsley, Peter, *The Bankside Book of Stillwater Trout Flies*, A. & C. Black, 1978.

Lapsley, Peter, *Trout from Stillwaters*, A. & C. Black, 1981.

Lane, Joscelyn, *Lake and Loch Fishing for Trout*, Seeley Service & Co.

Lawrie, W. H., *Modern Trout Flies*, Macdonald, 1972.
Lawrie, W. H., *A Reference Book of English Trout Flies*, Pelham Books, 1967.
Macan, T. T., *A Key to the Nymphs of British Ephemeroptera*, Freshwater Biological Association, 3rd edition, 1979.
Macan, T. T. & Worthington, E. B., *Life in Lakes and Rivers*, Collins, 1968.
Mellanby, Helen, *Animal Life in Fresh Water*, Chapman & Hall, 1938.
Moore, T.C. Kingsmill, *A Man May Fish*, Herbert Jenkins, 1960.
Mosely, Martin E., *Insect Life and the Management of a Trout Fishery*, George Routledge & Sons, 1926.
Mottram, J. C., *Fly Fishing: Some New Arts and Mysteries*, The Field & Queen, (Horace Cox) Ltd.
Overfield, T. Donald, *Famous Flies and their Originators*, A. & C. Black, 1972.
Overfield, T. Donald, *Fifty Favourite Dry Flies*, Ernest Benn, 1980.
Overfield, T. Donald, *Fifty Favourite Nymphs*, Ernest Benn, 1978.
Parton, Steve, *Boat Fishing for Trout*, George Allen & Unwin, 1983.
Pearson, Alan, *Catching Big Trout*, Stanley Paul, 1979.
Phillips, Ernest, *Trout in Lakes and Reservoirs*, Longmans, Green & Co., 1914.
Price, S. D. (Taff), *Lures for Game, Coarse and Sea Fishing*, A. & C. Black, 1972.
Price, S. D. (Taff), *Stillwater Flies*, Bks 1, 2 and 3, Ernest Benn, 1979.
Ransome, Arthur, *Rod and Line*, O.U.P., 1982.
Reynolds, Christopher, *The Pond on my Window Sill — the story of a freshwater aquarium*, Andre Deutsch, 1969.
Rice, Freddie, *Fly Tying Illustrated for Nymphs and Lures*, David & Charles, 1976.
Ronalds, Alfred, *The Fly-Fisher's Entomology*, Herbert Jenkins, 1921.
Sawyer, F. E., *Nymphs and the Trout*, A. & C. Black, 1958.
Skues, G. E. M. (V.C.), *Silk, Fur and Feather*, The Fishing Gazette, Ltd., 1950.
Skues, G. E. M., *The Way of a Trout with a Fly*, A. & C. Black, 1921.
Spencer, Sidney, *The Art of Lake Fishing*, H. F. & G. Witherby, 1934.
Stewart, Tom, *Two Hundred Popular Flies and How to Tie Them*, Ernest Benn, 1979.
Ed. Sutherland, Douglas and Chance, Jack, *Trout and Salmon Flies*, Pelham Books, 1982.
Swisher, Doug. and Richards, Carl, *Selective Trout*, Crown Publishers, New York, 1971.
Taverner, Eric, *Trout Fishing from all Angles*, Seeley, Service & Co.
Veniard, John, *Fly Dressing Materials*, A. & C. Black, 1977.
Veniard, John, *Further Guide to Fly Dressing*, A. & C. Black, 1972.
Veniard, John, *Reservoir and Lake Flies*, A. & C. Black, 1970.
Ed. Voss Bark, Ann, *West Country Fly Fishing*, B. T. Batsford, 1983.
Voss Bark, Conrad, *Fishing for Lake Trout*, H. F. & G. Witherby, 1972.
Ed. Walker, C. F., *Angling Letters of G. E. M. Skues*, A. & C. Black, 1956.
Walker, C. F., *Brown Trout and Dry Fly*, Seeley, Service & Co.
Walker, C. F., *Fly-Tying as an Art*, Herbert Jenkins, 1957.
Walker, C. F., *Lake Flies and their Imitation*, Herbert Jenkins, 1960.
Walker, Richard, *Dick Walker's Trout Fishing*, David & Charles, 1982.
Walker, Richard, *Fly Dressing Innovations*, Ernest Benn, 1974.
Walker, Richard, *More Fly Dressing Innovations*, Ernest Benn, 1980.
West, Leonard, *The Natural Trout Fly and its Imitation*, William Potter, 1921.
Williams, A. Courtney, *A Dictionary of Trout Flies and of Flies for Sea-trout and Grayling*, A. & C. Black, 1973.
Woolley, Roger, *Modern Trout Fly Dressing*, The Fishing Gazette 1932.
Journals:
Trout and Salmon
Trout Fisherman

INDEX

Artificial Flies

Natural Flies

Stillwaters

People